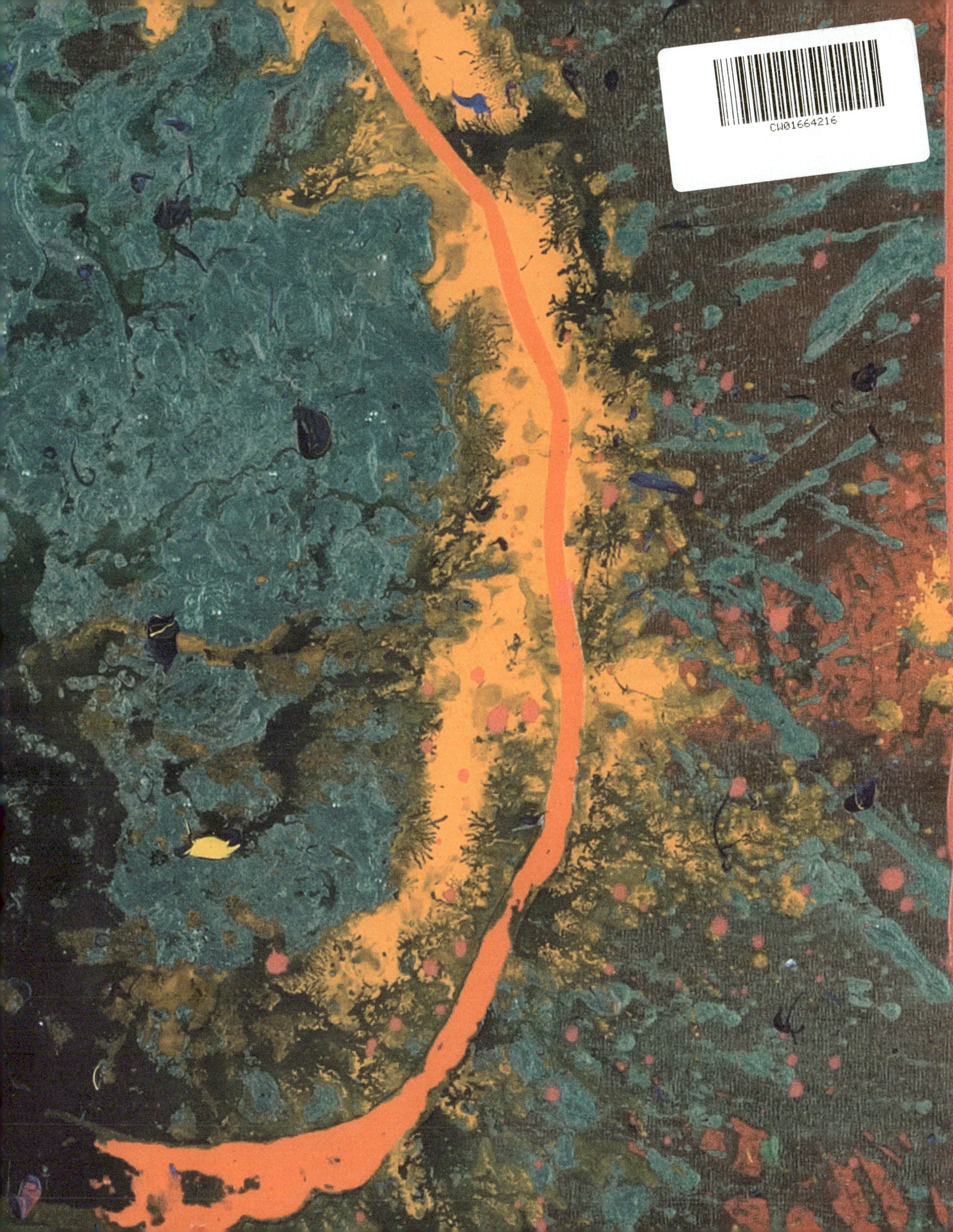

CW01664216

John Hoyland
SCATTER THE DEVILS

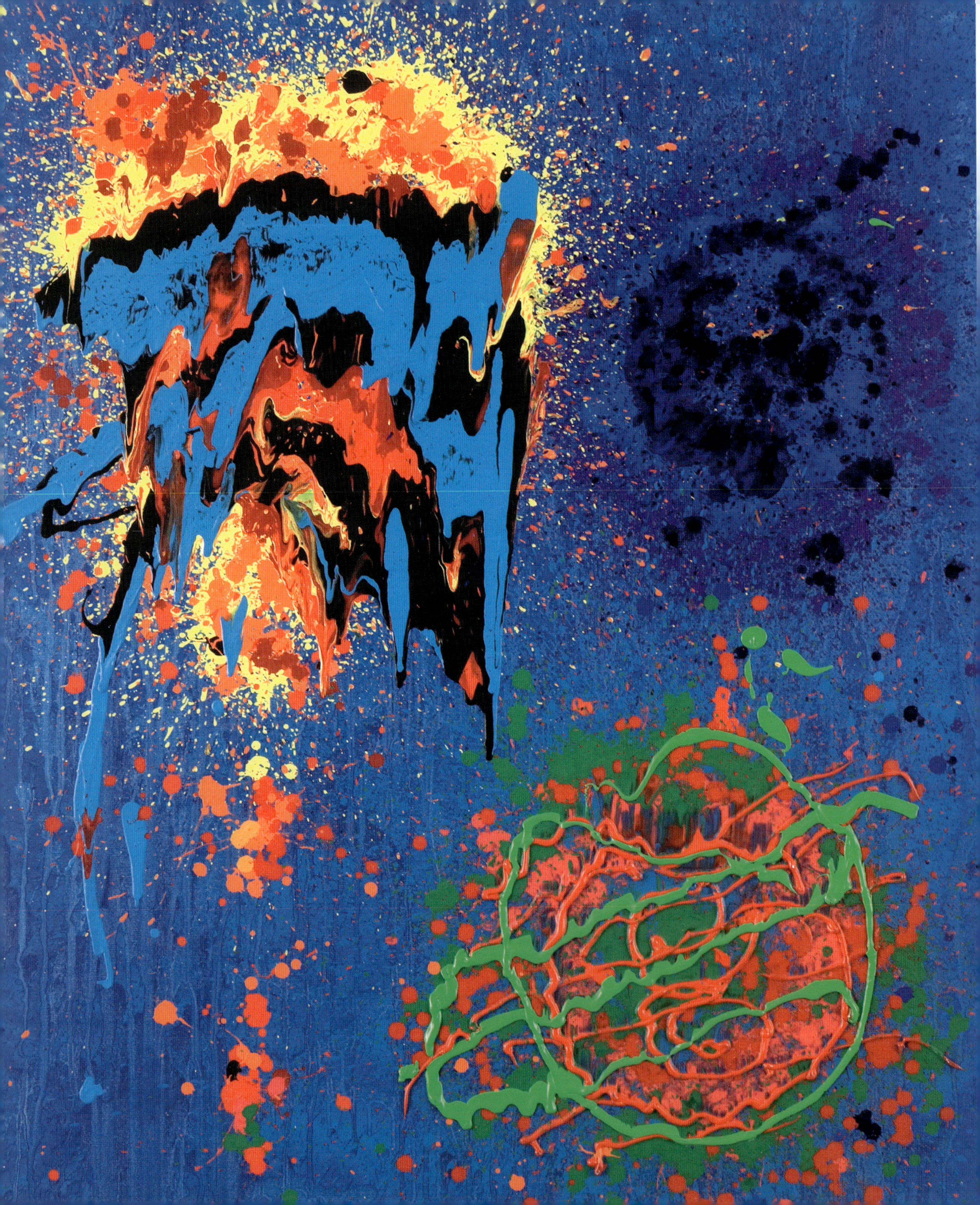

John Hoyland
SCATTER THE DEVILS

Andrew Lambirth

Unicorn Press

FRONTISPIECE
Scatter the Devils, 30.4.03
Acrylic on cotton duck
127 × 102 cm (50 × 40 inches)

Text Copyright © 2009 Andrew Lambirth
Images Copyright © 2009 John Hoyland

All rights reserved. No part of the content of this book may be reproduced, stored in or introduced into a retrieval system, or transmitted, in any form or by any means (electronic, mechanical, photocopying, recording or otherwise), without the prior written permission of the copyright holders and the publisher of this book.

First published 2009 by
Unicorn Press
47 Earlham Road
Norwich
NR2 3AD

www.unicornpress.org

ISBN 978 1 906509 07 1

Designed by Nick Newton
Printed in Slovenia for Latitude Press

ENDPAPERS
Restless Heart, 3.8.08 (detail)

Contents

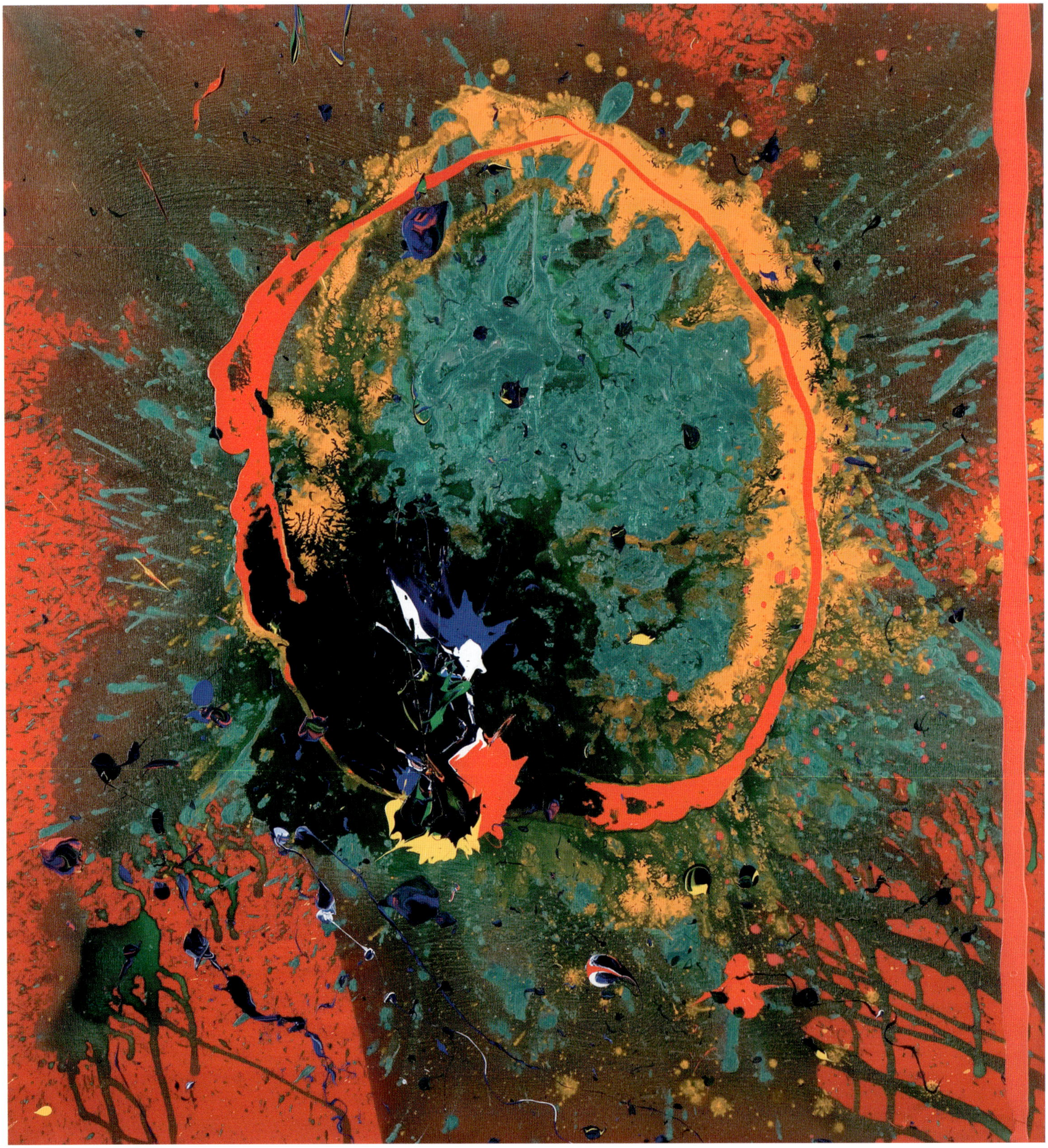

1

Introduction

Artists are society's eyes, they do its looking. By this I do not mean that they should simply mirror the surroundings that we are too lazy or too busy to look at, but that they have the ability to look beyond the appearance of the visible world. The artist connects, making visual links between things which resonate in the viewer's feelings. Artists give form and coherence to states of mind. They enunciate and bear witness. They encompass emotions not easily described. Through art we attempt to reconcile the contradictions of human life and contemplate its wholeness.

John Hoyland paints pictures which inspire the spirit, which liberate and fire the imagination. He describes imaginary worlds, offers interpretations of this world which are not of this world, and encourages us by the beauty and effervescence of his colours to respond to them and contemplate their meaning. We don't have to arrive at any conclusions: the act of contemplation is enough. We are encouraged to wander in the domain of the imagination. Here is true freedom.

These effects are not achieved by chance. The artist controls his subject matter with all the skill and cunning acquired over a long career in order to ensure that our response is as he wishes it to be. Despite the stillness of the final, resolved image, nothing is at rest, all is becoming, and content is inseparable from form and style. The artist's ordering of sensation prompts us to search for deeper significance, and once more art seems to guide us to the truth of the human condition.

It is not an order based on the everyday world, but on the universe. Hence the difficulties some have in recognizing its contours and declivities. With Hoyland, think wider, and then wider still. He stretches our imaginations to capacity. His work is structurally assertive – as declarative as a good sentence by Hemingway – but Hoyland has never been programmatic about how his paintings should be looked at, or what they mean.

His aim is to quicken the public pulse, to challenge the national sang-froid, to shift the phlegm of the traditional English head cold. Both metaphorically and

Restless Heart, 3.8.08
Acrylic on cotton duck
152.5 × 140 cm (60 × 55 inches)

literally, he wants us to breathe deep and experience the smell and tastes of life, as well as noticing its startling and sometimes incandescent colours. He wants to make us see and feel, not hedge ourselves about with protective layers.

Hoyland is no formalist, though he has the gift of form. 'The structure of form is meant to be a container for colour, a container of feeling. Structure or colour alone could never be an answer in itself,' he says.

The poetry in Hoyland's work summons forth poetic parallels. Again and again I found myself thinking of 'a noose of light' when looking at his recent paintings, the whipping linearity summoning up the notion of a lasso. Eventually I tracked the idea back to *The Rubaiyat of Omar Khayyám*, in Edward FitzGerald's immortal translation (1859). Here it is in the first quatrain:

Awake! for Morning in the Bowl of Night,
Has flung the Stone that puts the Stars to Flight.
And lo! the Hunter of the East has caught
The Sultan's Turret in a Noose of Light

The whole ethos of the *Rubaiyat*, with its emphasis on wine and roses ('Ah, fill the cup ...'), is sympathetic to Hoyland, though he has never read the book. 'The Bird of Time has but a little way / To fly – and lo! the Bird is on the Wing.' The philosophy is one of *carpe diem* – seize the day. 'Ah, make the most of what we yet may spend, / Before we too into the Dust descend; / Dust into Dust, and under Dust, to lie, / Sans Wine, sans Song, sans Singer, and – sans End!' Hoyland's Epicureanism finds an echo here.

The Persian poet Omar Khayyám (1048–1131) was also a resourceful mathematician and a leading astronomer. (A parallel with Hoyland's galactic paintscapes.) FitzGerald's translation has been criticized by some, including Robert Graves, for its lack of literalness. This is something also that would appeal to Hoyland. FitzGerald's justification was that he preferred 'a live sparrow' to 'a stuffed eagle'. TS Eliot and Ezra Pound both admired his *Rubaiyat*, Eliot writing (on first reading it) that 'the world appeared painted anew, in bright, delicious, and painful colours.' Rather like the effect of looking at John Hoyland's pictures.

On the bookshelves in his living room is a book entitled *Banter*. Hoyland claims not to have read it. He certainly doesn't need to: his gift for repartee is well-established, even notorious. He is also a superb raconteur, who likes nothing better than a good lunch with plenty of wine after a morning in the studio. Over the lunch table he will regale guests with hilarious anecdotes of the famous and the unknown, and tell jokes against himself as well as mercilessly lampooning the pretensions of today's fashionable figureheads. He says that somewhere he has another volume, of classic insults down the centuries. Again, it's a reference book he doesn't need. When it comes to invective, his imagination knows no bounds. This is just another

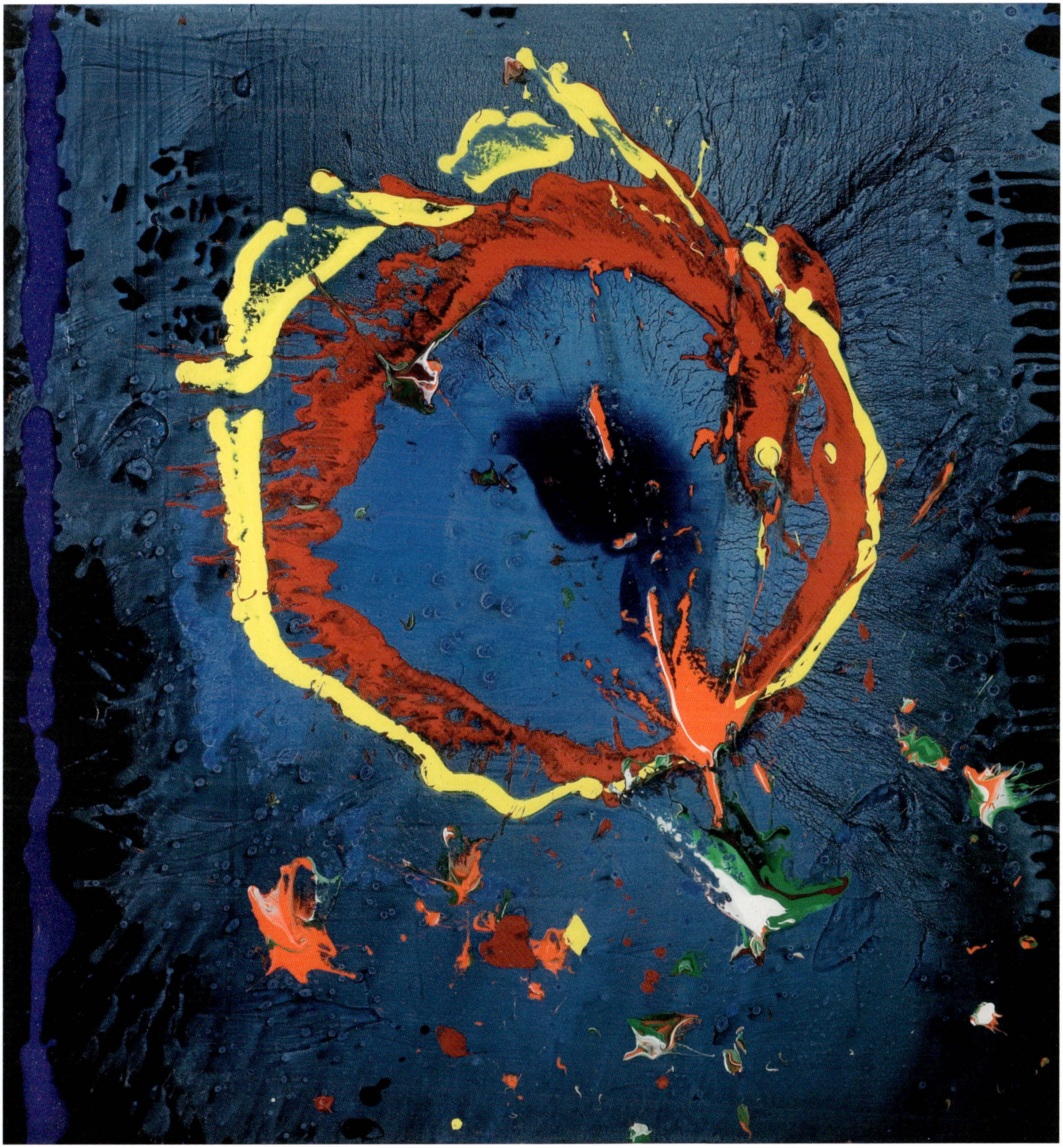

Star Thrower, 7.4.09
Acrylic on cotton duck
152.5 × 140 cm (60 × 55 inches)

aspect of the inventive and fertile mind which has dazzled the art world with 50 years of intensely original painting.

Hoyland is a trouble-maker. Not just in his outspoken jousting with the accepted values of the current Establishment, but in his art. He makes trouble for himself. He doesn't carry on making beautiful paintings in a recognizable Hoyland style of 20 or 30 years ago, he challenges himself, breaks his latest mould, and pushes himself beyond all expectation to come up with something new that interests him. The only thing that remains constant is his lifelong commitment to paint. His extensive knowledge of paint comes from decades of using it experimentally. Always he has to deepen the game, raise the stakes, risk all. Besides exploring new forms of beauty, he takes up the challenge of ugliness, kitsch, vulgarity, and uses these negative qualities as ways of launching a new sensory attack on himself and his public.

Hoyland refuses to be typecast. He constantly reinvents his art, pushing it to new limits, pursuing new lines of thought and formal invention. Partly this is a result of huge ambition: his determination to paint the whole world into a picture. Partly it is the self-doubt and modesty which lie on the other side of that ambition, the feeling that he hasn't quite succeeded yet and must try something else. He is a man who lives very much in the present, enjoying life to the full, feasting and fighting, longing for the next adventure. These days, in his mid-70s, the adventures are mostly foreign travel and the next painting, but Hoyland does not let up the pace. Like an Elizabethan buccaneer he is out to win new territory and cover himself once more in glory. For him, it's very much do or die. And in this age of sensation-overload, he still manages to shock the eye.

The American poet Donald Justice wrote: 'There is a mysterious and hidden consciousness within the artist of being other; there is an awareness of some reality-beyond-the-reality that lures and charges the spirit; it charges and gives power to one's very life.' Hoyland's pursuit of that reality is supported by a hard-won freedom, steadily and forcefully maintained, and dedicated to disrupting complacency and disturbing preconceptions. All this is to do with what might be called an intelligence of feeling, but there is another component to the story. Mystics and visionaries have rarely been artists, though there are notable exceptions such as William Blake. Hoyland is a visionary without a manifesto, an artist of great imaginative and intuitive powers who can paint the essence and feel of a place he has never visited, only to find his paintings confirmed by the experience of going there. (This has happened many times: before going to Australia, as is the case with *Jinel*, opposite, and particularly before visiting Bali.) That projection is a rare gift, an essential part of Hoyland's capacity for energizing the spirit.

Some people have called Hoyland Europe's answer to Mark Rothko, but that is perhaps to ignore the parallel with Jackson Pollock, which has recently emerged all the more strongly in the inspired linearity that has become an essential component

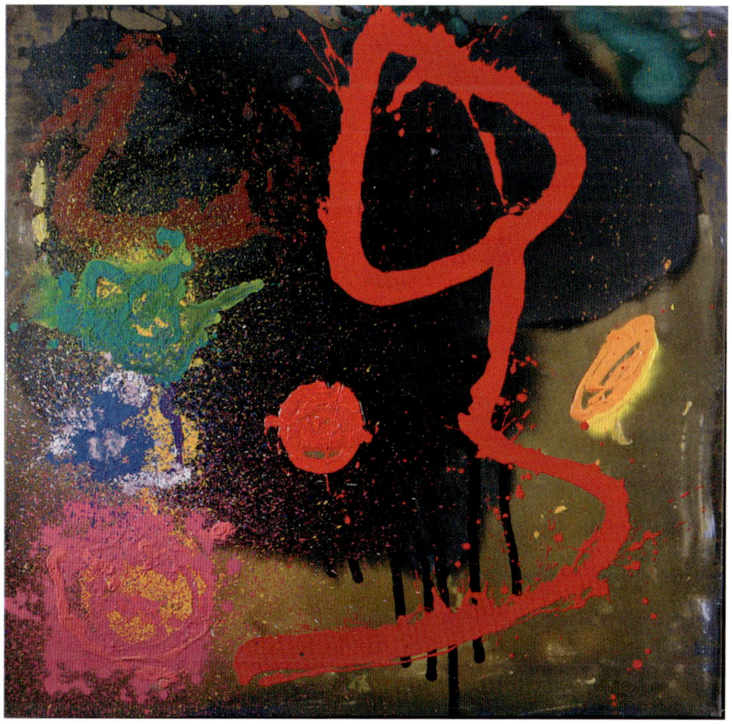

Jinel, 26.2.89
Acrylic on cotton duck
152.5 × 152.5 cm (60 × 60 inches)

of Hoyland's late paintings. Comparison with either artist is of limited use, however, for Hoyland is a one-off, an original, and one of the finest painters we have. In an age of drastically qualified imagination and spurious hype, Hoyland is still being heroic, still entering the lists to do battle for his creativity. He is uncompromising, working with the fixed intent of producing masterpieces which will give back to us some of the glory of the world. This is not just painting about painting – it is an enquiry into the limits of human perception.

This is a book about John Hoyland's recent paintings (late 1990s–2009). Hoyland has been a consistently interesting and inventive printmaker, working with a number of master printers in a variety of media, but that aspect of his work deserves separate treatment, and encompasses a substantial enough achievement to merit a book of its own. Hoyland's very first paintings were mostly titled portraits and landscapes, but around 1960, when his work turned entirely abstract, he stopped using titles, simply distinguishing his paintings by dates which refer to the day on which a canvas was completed. They thus give no indication of how long a work might have been in gestation, or even how long it took to execute. Then, in the mid-1970s, verbal titles began to re-appear. Hoyland says that this was at the suggestion of his New York dealer, André Emmerich, who pointed out that 'people like them'. For Hoyland, the titles are intended not so much as a signpost to the picture's meaning as a counterpoint. 'If they are too descriptive I think they're no good. I like them to be very open to interpretation. An oblique resonance, if there can be such a thing.'

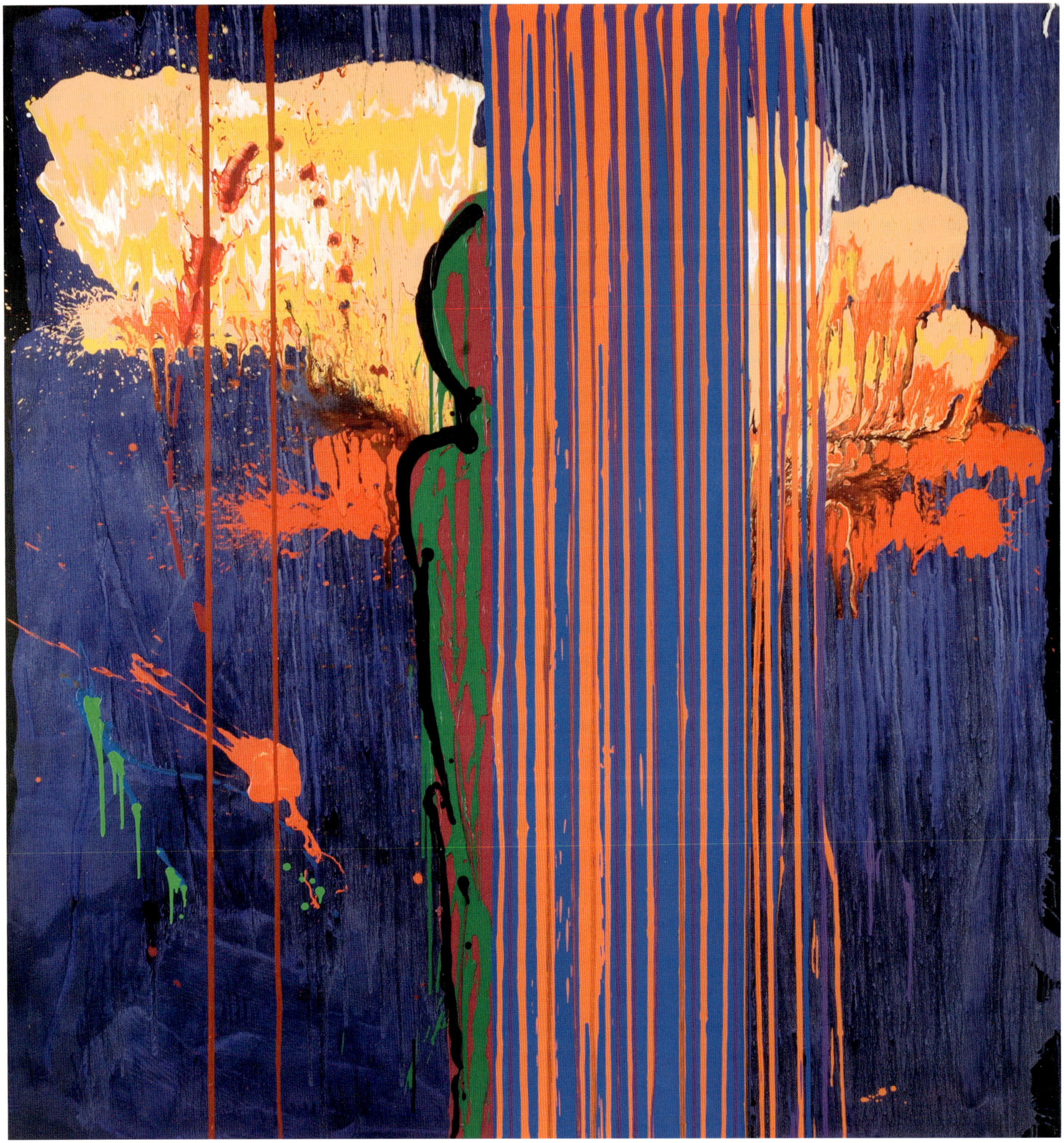

Traveller, 20.7.99
Acrylic on cotton duck
254 × 236 cm (100 × 93 inches)

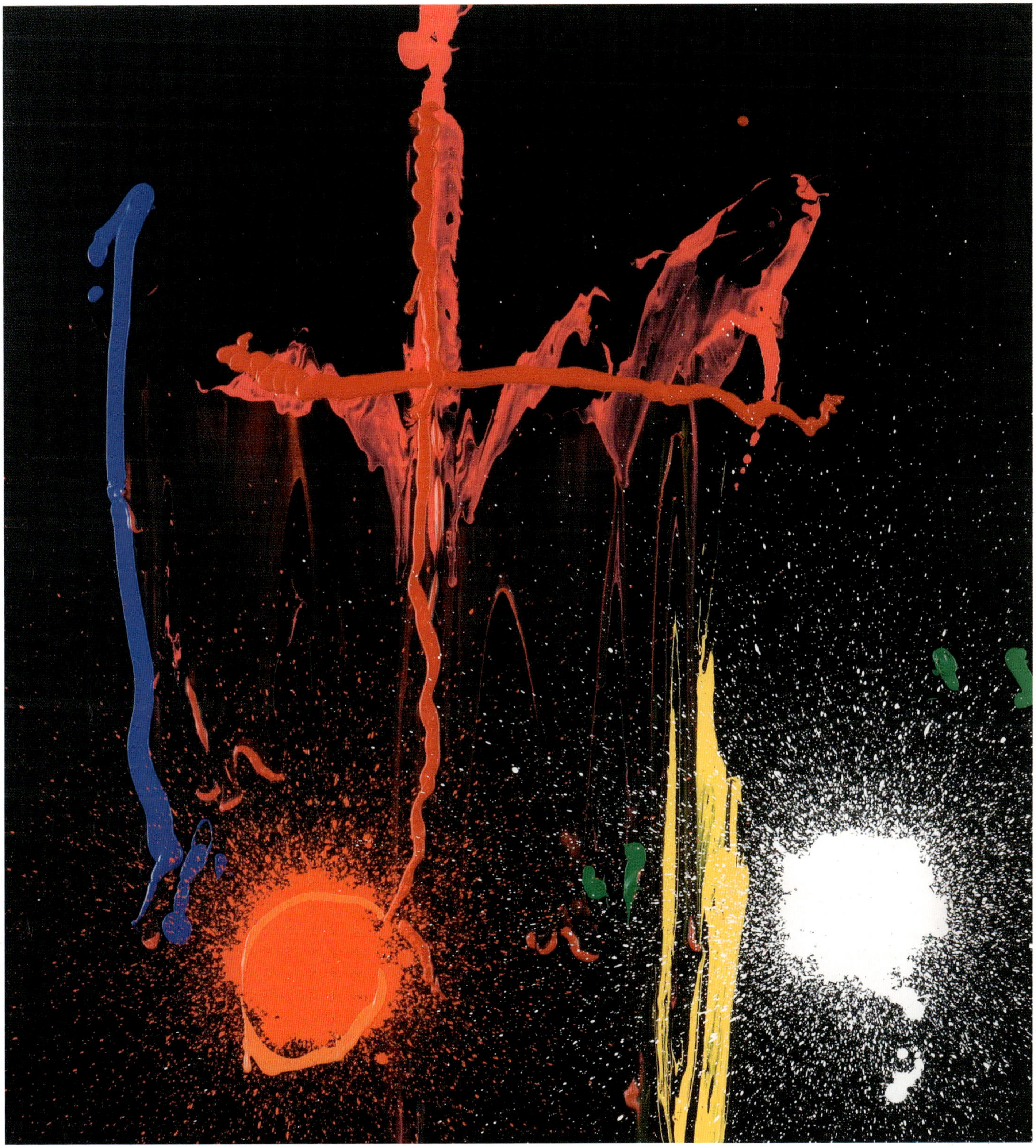

Song, 5.4.09
Acrylic on cotton duck
127 × 114 cm (50 × 45 inches)

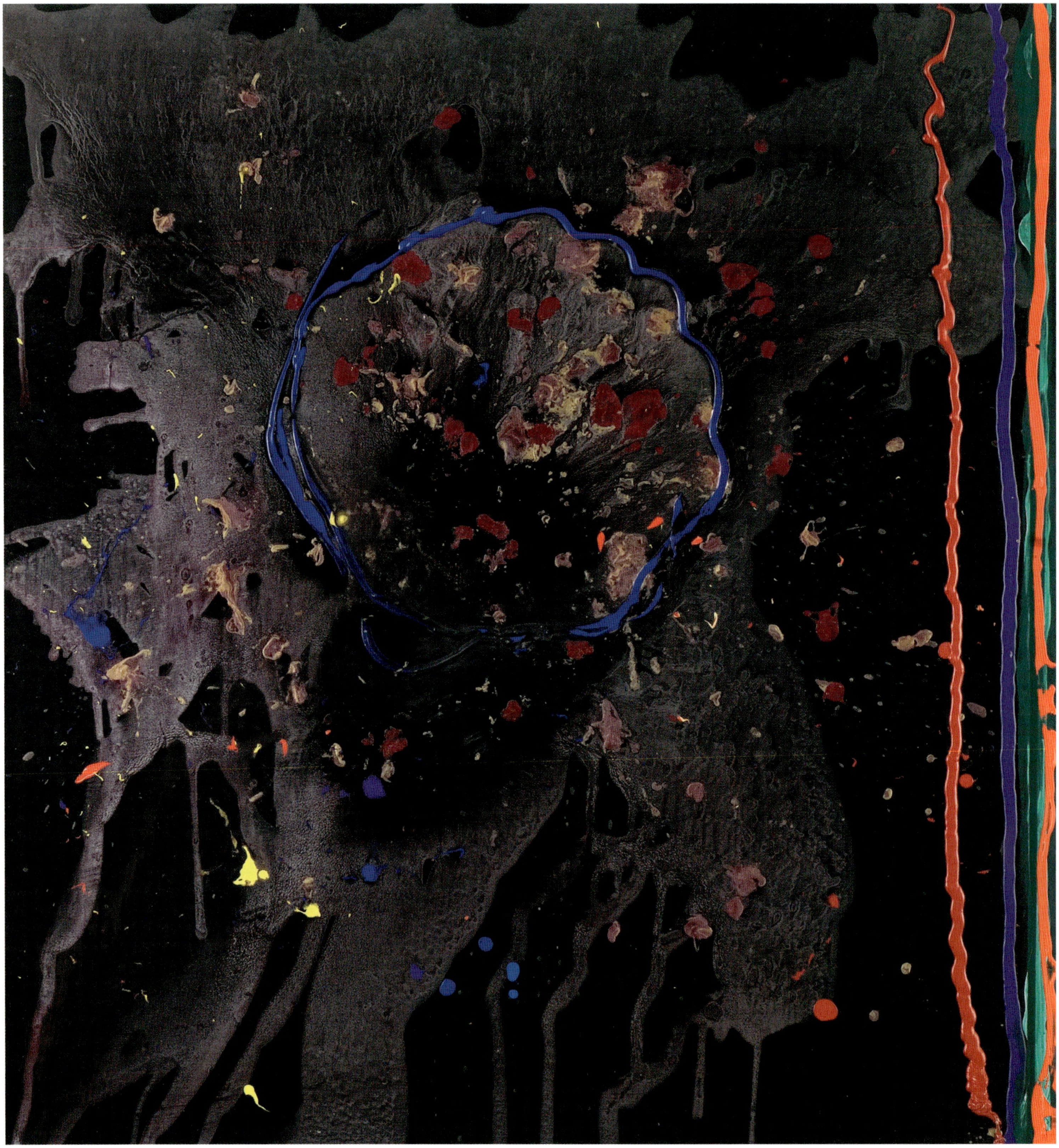

2

Collaborating with Chaos

I interviewed John Hoyland for The Spectator *in May 2008. I re-print the greater part of the ensuing article here as it makes an appropriate introduction to the man and his work. When it first appeared, various of Hoyland's artist friends and contemporaries remarked on the article's true-to-life directness and humour, its unapologetic bravado. This was typical, but also poignant. Although I didn't know it then, Hoyland was about to go into hospital for major heart surgery. Part of his post-op recuperation was spent painting, and he has subsequently returned to the fray with unabated energy. Since his illness, he has produced more than 70 new paintings.*

John Hoyland dislikes being called 'one of Britain's leading abstract painters'. He thinks it's lazy thinking, and an over-reliance on labelling. 'They don't say: "Lucian Freud, leading figurative painter" – he's just a painter. Or "Francis Bacon, leading melodramatist".' Mention of Bacon sends him off on a tangent, one of the digressions that make Hoyland's conversation – along with his forthright opinions – so rewarding and enjoyable. 'I look at Bacon's paintings and instead of being moved by them they make me want to laugh. They're supposed to be horrible and moving and frightening, but they're so shrill and so theatrical. I like drama in music or painting, but not melodrama.' And having dismissed one of the most expensive and sought-after of modern British artists, he leans back and grins. Hoyland is not too keen on auction rooms and the prices they generate. His own 1960s' work is currently a focus of buyers' attention, generating auction records, and he finds it rather annoying. A true artist, he is really only interested in his latest work or what he is about to do, not the achievements of 40 years ago.

'I think the vultures are circling a bit,' he says with a chuckle. 'I suppose artists' early work always fetches more money. It can be irritating when people forget whole swathes of work, like the paintings I did in the 1970s and 1980s.' Of course, what is needed is a full-scale Hoyland retrospective, and the Tate is the place for such a show, though under the current regime such an exhibition is unlikely. Has England so many artists of international stature that it can afford to ignore such a

Black Sunday, 24.4.08
Acrylic on cotton duck
152.5 × 140 cm (60 × 55 inches)

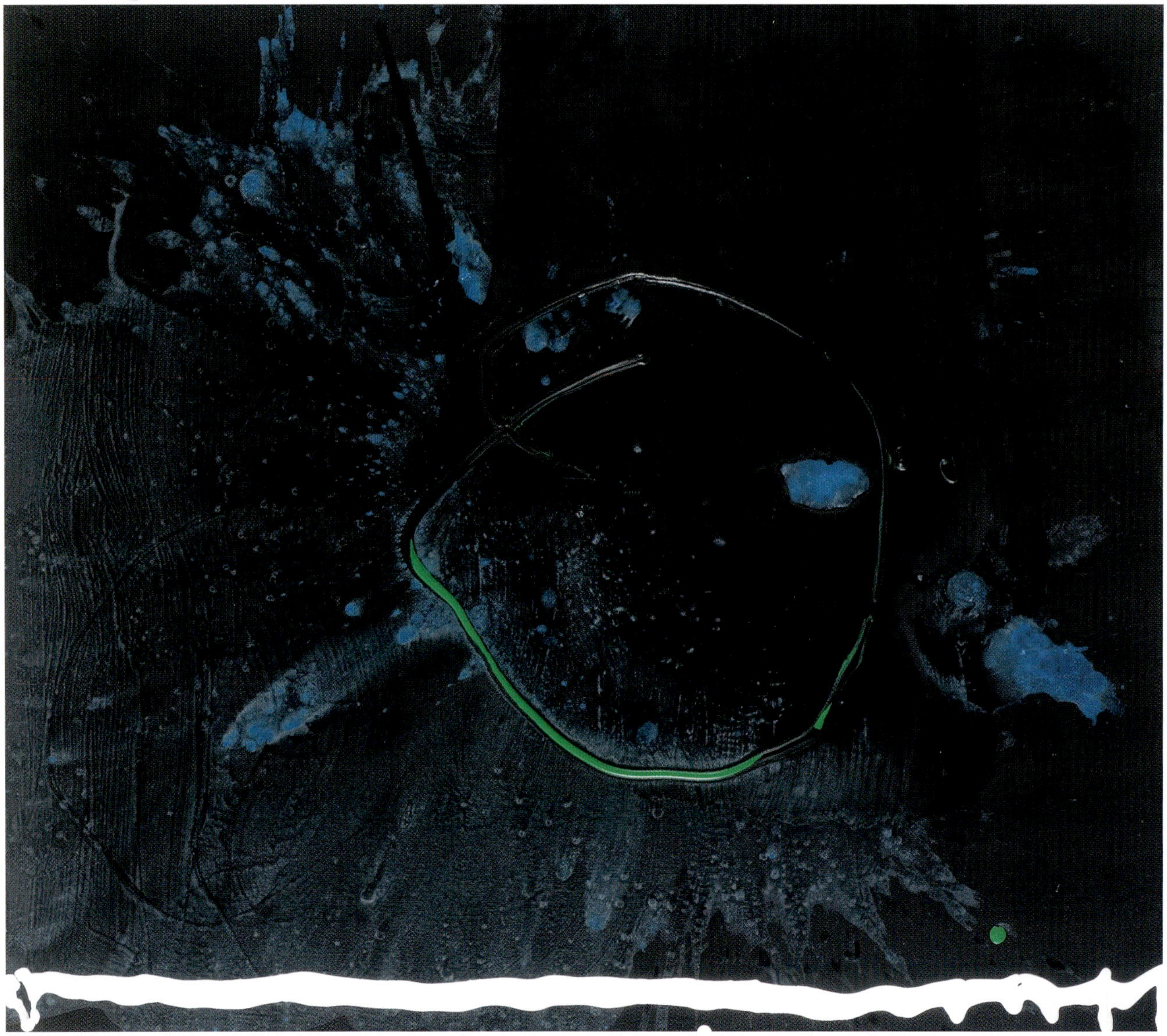

Goodbye, 23.3.08
Acrylic on cotton duck
114 × 127 cm (45 × 50 inches)

figure as Hoyland? Of course not, yet it seems that our museums are more interested in showing foreign artists than the home-grown variety. Meanwhile, Hoyland continues to paint in his London studio just north of Smithfield Market, and to have shows up and down the country of vibrant new work.

Although Hoyland's latest work with its effervescent colour combinations and its wild paint-trails seems to some like an arsonist's night out in a firework factory, it's not all madcap celebration. A very recent painting, a dark beauty we look at in the studio, is called *Goodbye*; not exactly exuberant. In fact, he can't stand art that is perpetually euphoric. He himself is more often than not in elegiac mood these days. 'I've been doing these paintings called "Letters" to people I admire. There's one to Chaim Soutine and a couple to van Gogh [see pages 66, 69 and 71]. I've been re-reading his letters. I've done a number of paintings in the last couple of years

Bryan Robertson

Bryan Robertson (1925–2002) was a key figure in Hoyland's life. His revolutionary exhibition programme at the Whitechapel made a wide range of artists available to the startled eyes of post-war England. Among those accorded solo shows at the Whitechapel who were to be particularly important for Hoyland were Nicolas de Staël (1956), Jackson Pollock (1958), Mark Rothko (1961), Philip Guston and Serge Poliakoff (both 1963), as well as Caro in that year, Morris Louis (1965) and Robert Motherwell (1966). Robertson's list of exhibitions was remarkable. In his own words, the Pollock exhibition created 'an absolute furore', and police were summoned to control the crowds queuing to get in. The same happened with Rauschenberg in 1964.

Robertson showed not only leading American contemporary artists but also the best painters and sculptors working in Britain. (Not just the likes of Hoyland himself and Caro, but Prunella Clough, John Craxton, Cecil Collins, Keith Vaughan.) Nor did he neglect the historical context. Robertson was well aware of the importance of the English tradition, showing Turner, Gillray, Rowlandson, John Martin and Stubbs during the 1950s. His Turner show in 1953 was (unbelievably) the first major museum show of this artist since 1851, and it proved a revelation to contemporary painters.

Robertson has said: 'What I look for in art of any period is imaginative energy, radiance, equilibrium, composure, colour,

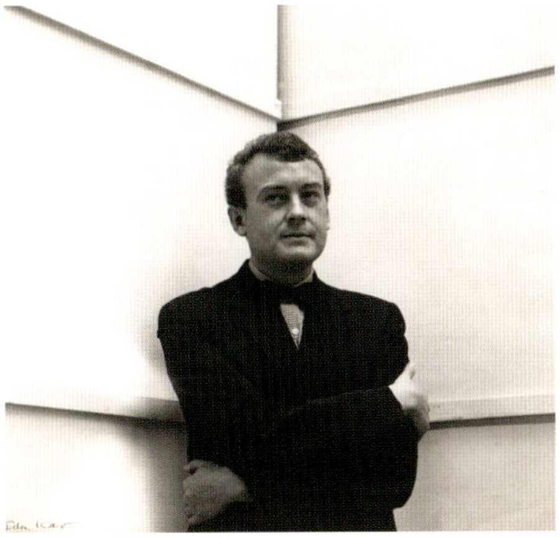

Bryan Robertson, 1958

light, vitality, poise, buoyancy, a transcendent ability to soar above life and not be subjugated by it, the avoidance of rhetoric, a resolved formal tension.' He was a lifelong supporter of Hoyland's work, and wrote in a letter of 1995: 'As an artist, without the shadow of a doubt, you've provided for me the greatest and most acute – and often, very often, the most astonished, really surprised – pleasures. The sheer imaginative force of invention, its rigour, always, and its intelligence – pictorial intelligence – never ceases to delight me. I see very clearly – that you're doing your best work, the finest and most complex, freest paintings of your life so far.' Quite a valediction.

This praise is especially valuable when one considers that Robertson was also a dedicated opponent of expressionism 'or any extreme form of visual, theatrical or literary self-indulgence … I am more comfortable with formality than informality.' At first glance that might seem to rebound fatefully against the wilder manifestations of the Hoyland output – at least it might seem to if you are taken in only by the surface pyrotechnics of Hoyland's late work. Of course what Robertson recognized is the essential formality of Hoyland's paintings, however delirious they might seem; the underlying emphasis on structure that informs all his work.

Robertson understood the quality of Hoyland's imagination and formal gifts from an early point, and offered him crucial encouragement and support. He selected him for the Whitechapel's prestigious *New Generation* show in 1964, and was instrumental in locating for him the Peter Stuyvesant travel bursary which enabled Hoyland first to visit America. And it was Robertson who offered Hoyland his first museum exhibition in 1967. Robertson's series of shows for living artists was a great innovation, as were the accompanying catalogues. As he himself commented: 'Contemporary artists had never before – until they were in their 70s, or dead – enjoyed presentation on this scale in England.' The level of seriousness accorded contemporary art was unprecedented, and it paid huge dividends – not only in terms of public interest but also in boosting the self-confidence of the artists so honoured. Hoyland made great use of this sustained evidence of belief in his work.

that just came over me from the death of friends. Patrick Caulfield, Bryan Robertson, Terry Frost, Piero Dorazio.' Robertson was the inspired critic and director of the Whitechapel Art Gallery who gave Hoyland his first museum show in 1967, Dorazio was a famous Italian painter, all were close friends that Hoyland misses. The Grim Reaper has been busy.

'I think painting should express all kinds of different things, not be limited. I can't think of anything worse than just taking painting towards refinement, if you don't allow yourself to change. I don't force change on myself, it just happens. I'd probably get bored if I did the same thing all the time. Not so long ago I said I'd like to be able to paint anything in a painting. I think I'm getting there slowly. Robert Motherwell gave me a book on Miró. He's supposed to be the great Surrealist with a fantastic imagination but he went on the beach every day picking stuff up – a bit of string, a shell, a bit of wood. If Miró needed outside stimulation then who am I to think that I can keep on developing through a kind of formalist grid? That opened me up to plundering nature.' Hoyland's work now is as likely to take its impulse from something seen on his travels as it is to be formed from one colour working with or against another. After half a century of endeavour, he has won through to a hard-earned freedom of expression.

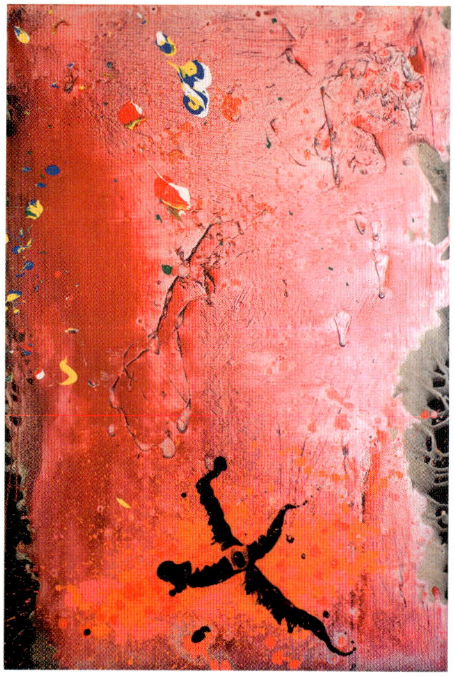

Free, 6.4.04
Acrylic on cotton duck
152.5 × 102 cm (60 × 40 inches)

John Hoyland was born in Sheffield in 1934 and went to art school there before gaining a place at the Royal Academy Schools and coming to London. He first made his name in the 1960s for bold abstract works which entirely rejected the observable world and dealt exclusively in shape and colour. From 1967 he spent increasing amounts of time in America, associating with such artists as Rothko, Newman and Motherwell, but in the 1970s he returned to settle in England.

'I've managed to make a living out of painting – a precarious one. When I came back from New York in 1972, the big announcement had been made – it hadn't hit America – that the death of painting had already occurred. I'd had a posh job here, principal lecturer at Chelsea [1965–69]. When I gave that up, William Scott said to me: "You're mad, that's the best job in London: three days a week and seven months' holiday a year with pay". But I'd heard this David Sylvester interview with de Kooning. De Kooning said that he thought it was important psychologically to put "Artist" in your passport, not "Artist/Teacher". So I decided I was going to do that and get out of teaching. Looking back on it, it was a smart thing to do.'

Why did he come back? 'It was partly private. My girlfriend at the time was a singer. I learnt a lot from her and really enjoyed being around that music scene and meeting all those guys – Thelonious Monk, people like that. But the trouble was that she wanted me to travel with her. The thing is, if you're an artist, you've got to stay in a room on your own and work. You can't be always hanging around late at night for the second show. I'm an early riser. And I missed the richness of Europe and my friends. So it was a combination of things. Also I wasn't a great success in America. Art has to come from inside you. What I really didn't like was that in America, it was all coming at you. Like [and he switches to the famous Hoyland send-up of a transatlantic drawl]: "Are you in this show? D'you know what he's just sold for? You'd better get on the ball, kid, you'd better get in there." Pressure all the

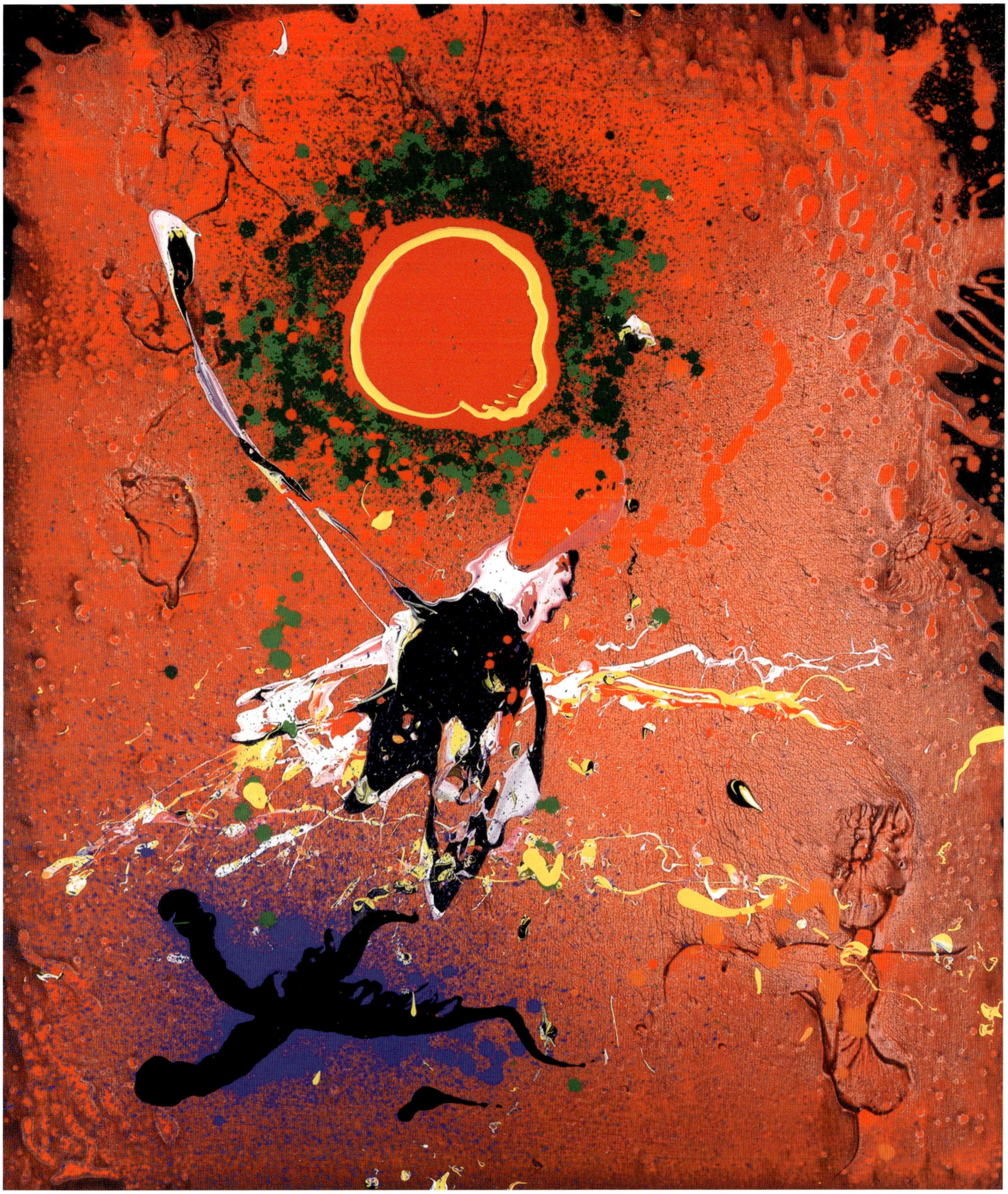

Mystical Anarchy, 12.2.04
Acrylic on cotton duck
152.5 × 127 cm (60 × 50 inches)

time. I came back and decided I wouldn't paint a lot of pictures, I'd just keep on one until I'd completely resolved it. So I switched working methods.'

Instead of the staining of colour he was known for, he began to use a palette-knife and polyfilla along with the paint. It was a very different approach and typical of his ability to change tack, whatever the cost to his reputation. Since then, he has altered course whenever he had to. He lives and works in London, travels regularly to Spain and the Caribbean, making little diagrams of possible forms for his paintings in sketchbooks. In the studio he tends to put down a dark ground on a canvas with a paintbrush and then add glazes of iridescent paint. On top of that he works mostly with spilled or poured paint, with the canvas on the floor. 'And of course I throw paint which gives it a kind of energy. I can throw four colours in one clump. It's like the blind Zen archer – you gradually get more accurate.

'Pollock used to draw with paint through holes in cans to get the extended line you can't get with a brush. I'm doing something very similar.' Hoyland squeezes liquid acrylic paint from bottles, exploiting the unpredictability of its behaviour, though long years of experimenting have taught him how his materials will react. 'I'll often do a test on the floor, to see how the paint is going to come out.' (Hoyland's studio floor is famous and much-photographed, rather like his paint-spattered working boots. People have even wanted to buy sections of it.) 'But when it comes to the actual act on the painting you just have to grab your balls and charge.

'I've spent a lot of the last 10 years looking for visual structures that I find satisfying, though at the moment there is less and less structure in my work. Suddenly I find that my paintings seem not to require it. I'm painting oxygen or something. Air. I've always thought that paintings needed to be structured, otherwise all you've got is chaos.' But now he is collaborating with chaos and still somehow managing to ride the wave. 'I like to try and make these pictures paint themselves', he says. 'The less you impose, the fresher it is. Painting is a kind of alchemy. When you're young, you want to show everybody what a tough guy you are, how strong you can paint and how you can knock everybody around. As you get older you want to show how intelligent you are, how you know the game and how subtle and penetrating you can be. Then when you get old, you're just compelled to paint what you don't know. That's what's happened to me.'

Hoyland's working boots

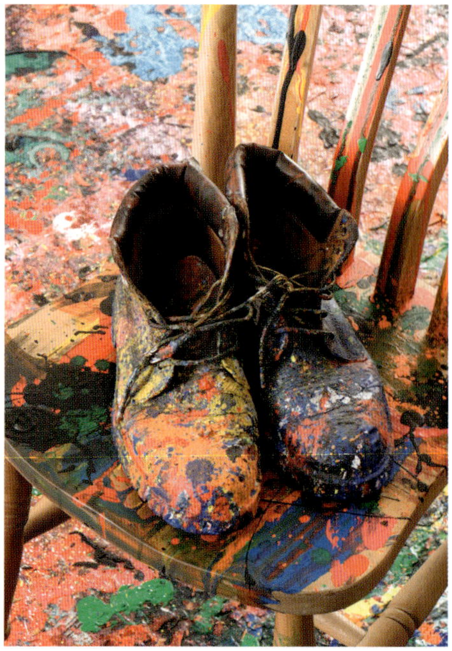

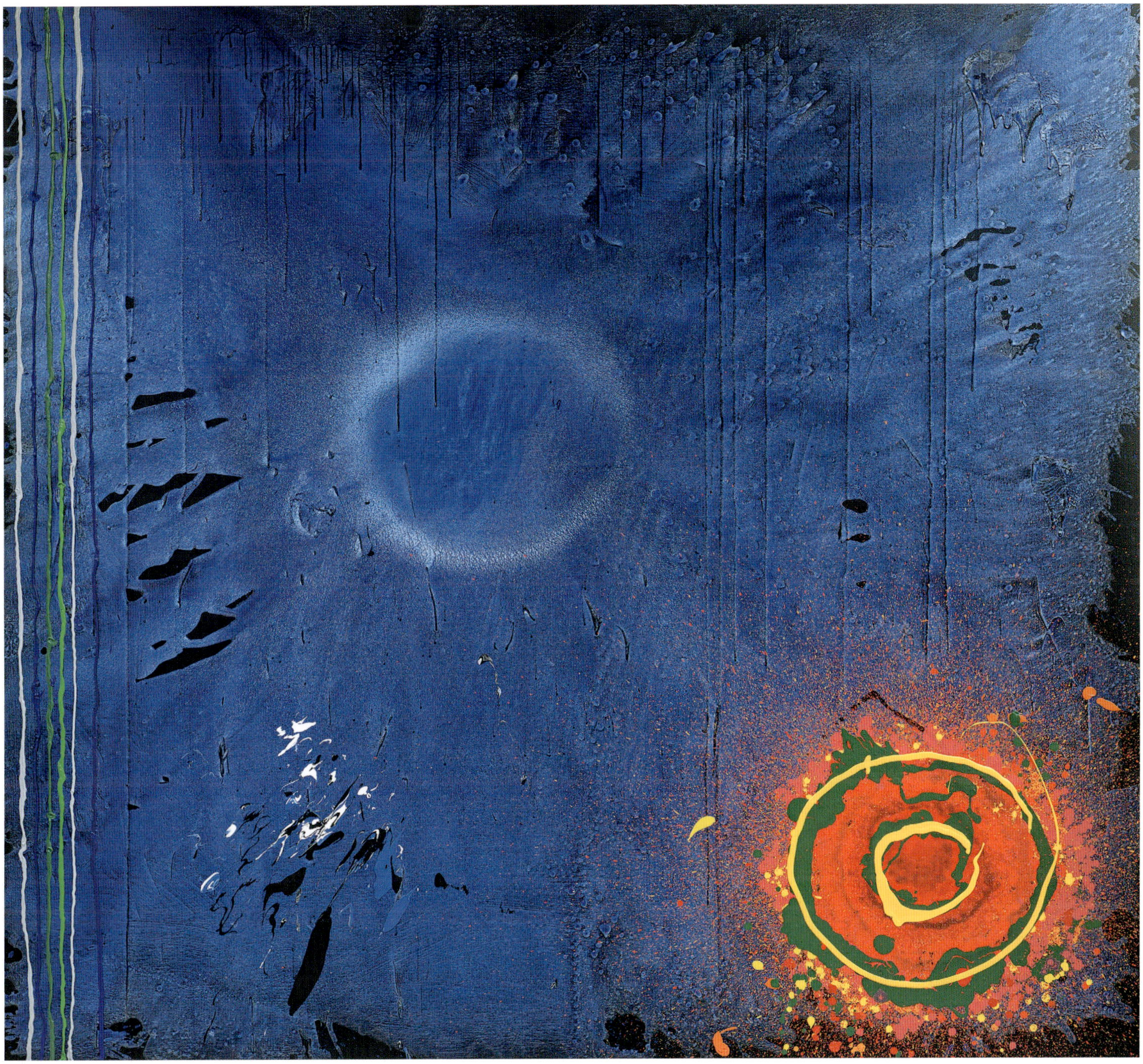

Forever, 8.6.04
Acrylic on cotton duck
236 × 254 cm (93 × 100 inches)

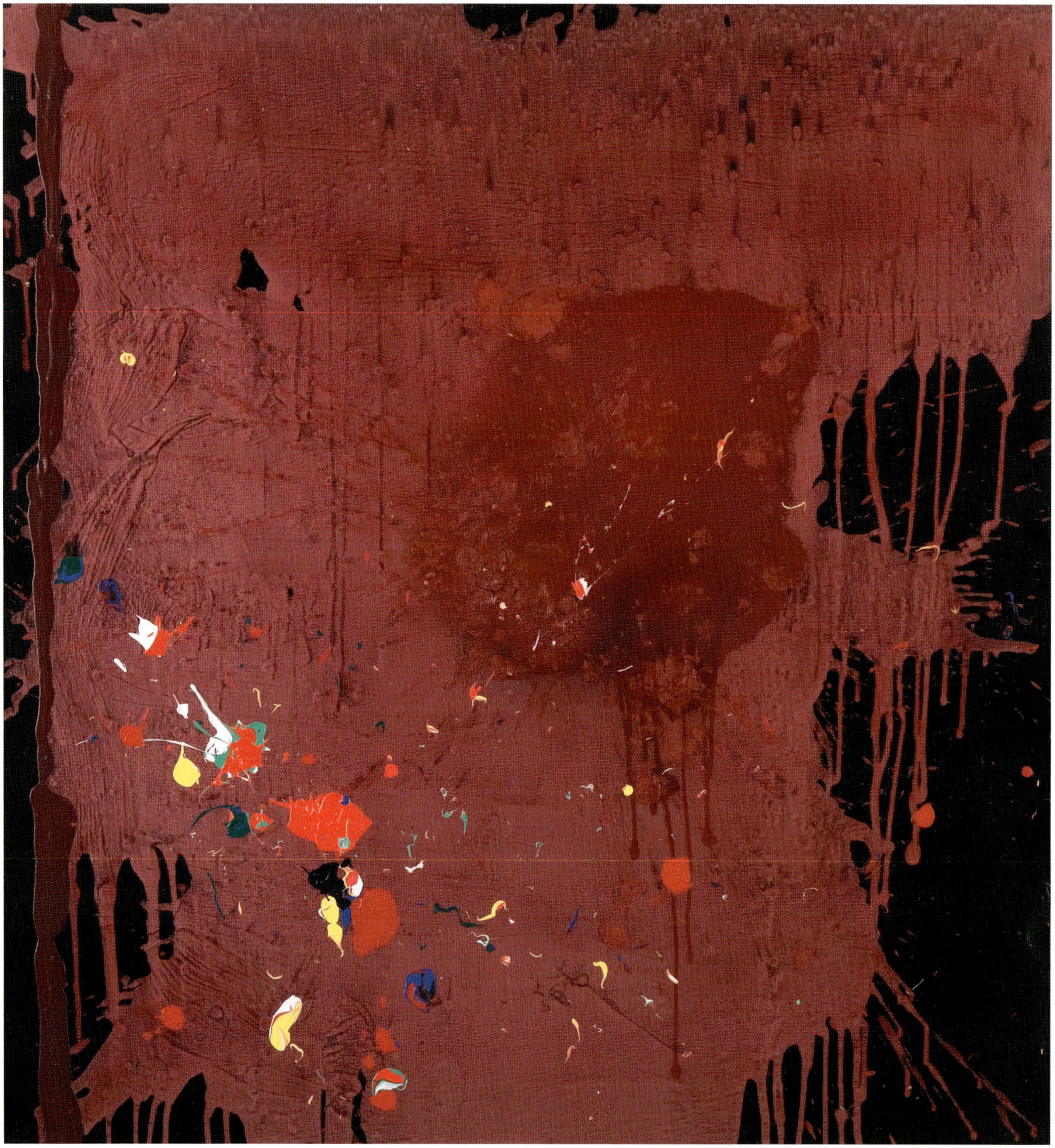

The Bleeding Heart, 13.11.08
Acrylic on cotton duck
152.5 × 140 cm (60 × 55 inches)

3

Background: Resolving the Nose

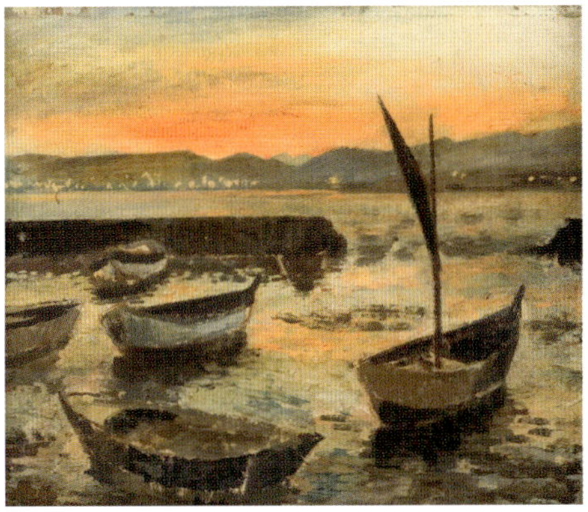

Sunset 'La Madrague', 1953–4
Oil on canvas
30.5 × 36 cm (12 × 14 inches)

John Hoyland grew up in an artistic context very different from today's. By comparison with the contemporary glut and bombardment of images, it was visually starved. There were few art books, no slide libraries, art magazines were rare and mostly illustrated in black and white. In some ways that was a blessing, but there were other drawbacks. The well-known critic Eric Newton, writing in 1945, deliberated on the typical joylessness (with honourable exceptions, such as Matthew Smith) of English art. He wrote: 'Few British artists have painted as though they loved the very act of painting, the flow of the pigment over the surface of the canvas, the contact of the brush with that surface. Hogarth is an exception, so is Gainsborough, but for the most part there is a dryness, even a harshness, that contrasts strangely with the vibrant shimmer of Watteau or the easy fluency of Matisse. And with that dryness of surface goes an aridity of colour, as though the rich harmonies that sing in the pictures of Chardin or Braque and become ecstatic in van Gogh were beyond the normal range of British vision.'

This absence of painterliness, though to be regretted, is counterbalanced (says Newton) by the talents of the British artist as a draughtsman: 'He rejoices in arabesque and is often carried away by it.' That and 'a romanticism that concentrates on mood rather than on appearance' are, for Newton, what give British art its distinctive flavour. Hoyland had to fight against that lack of painterliness and for a long time he distrusted the linear and Romantic heritage, but in his recent work he has triumphantly united colour, varied paint-surface, line and his own particular interpretation of Romanticism. But the journey to reach that point has been a long and arduous one, though it has resulted in a whole sequence of fine paintings along the way.

One of Hoyland's favourite dismissals of the English figurative tradition is enshrined in the phrase 'I don't think you've quite resolved the nose.' He uses it in all manner of contexts and situations, with a sly and apposite humour. It's quite evident that he first heard it at art school, where it was directed at him (no doubt said of a student exercise – a self-portrait or study of a friend), and he has never forgotten it. The phrase's original mild censure has been turned, in typical Hoyland fashion, into a stick to belabour all unimaginative rule-followers ever since. But the history of the phrase and his reaction to it is not so simple. Each time he says it, whether consciously or not, he relishes his triumph over it, his subsequent development into an abstract painter of international renown; yet he also remembers – with an endearing degree of self-mockery – his own early insufficiencies, and his continuing doubts and hesitancies.

In a 2005 interview, Hoyland recalled his student days at the Royal Academy: 'Nobody knew anything I wanted to know; the Academicians couldn't tell me anything. William Scott taught at the RA but never talked about art, all he talked about was money and property but he (an Irish Scot) once said to me: "Don't fiddle with a painting – this is an English disease. Matisse, Derain or Vlaminck, they didn't fiddle. They did it and left it. The English would say, 'I don't think I have completely resolved the nose.'" I have to hold myself back from fiddling, even now.'

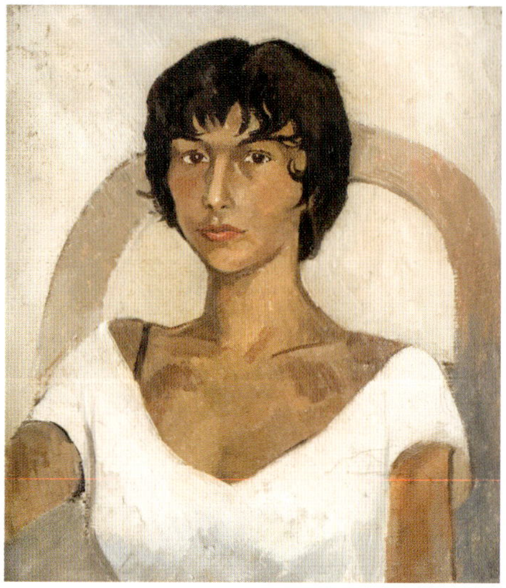

Portrait of Janine, 1953–4
Oil on canvas
36 × 30.5 cm (14 × 12 inches)

This book is not intended as a biography or a study of Hoyland's whole career, that double task having been most ably undertaken by Mel Gooding in his two books on the artist. It is instead a monograph on Hoyland's recent work, focusing on the paintings he has produced over the last ten years. Of course, it is not usually helpful to study an artist's late work completely in isolation, without paying some attention to the context of the earlier achievement. So it is that the beginning of Hoyland's journey plays its part in this narrative. The 1960s were a crucial decade for Hoyland, a time of change in all quarters of his life. In these years he first made his reputation in England, and then began to establish an international profile as well. His work developed dramatically as he found his voice as an artist. And the early dialogue with American art which was so important for his breakthrough to original work began to take on a more personal aspect in the 1960s.

After the chaos and destruction of World War II, there was a general desire and need for a clean slate in art, at least amongst those capable of new directions. The old world had ended with the death camps and Hiroshima, and Europe reluctantly began to look to the New World for leadership and renewal. In America there was a powerful post-apocalyptic feeling, which manifested itself in art as an urge towards reconstruction that entailed a search for a basic primordial language. In the yearning for a new beginning, a making good, Abstract Expressionism with its huge canvases and cosmic sense of scale – reflecting the vastness of the American continent – seemed to offer a way forward. It demanded a total human involvement, a sense of commitment that was very attractive to those disillusioned by war. Those big Abstract Expressionist paintings not only filled the whole field of the spectator's vision but were emotionally compelling also. They embraced the body and the spirit as well. Their heroic statements engaged solely with the present: the past was not just a foreign country, it was a ridiculed one. Look what nightmares the old world had brought down upon itself; it was time to leave them far behind.

Between 1960 and 1963, Hoyland was making large, 'hard-edge' and very abstract geometric paintings. They are about space and movement, rendered in optical effects that in other hands would become the eye-games of Op Art. He didn't feel at ease with this kind of work, it was too cold and cerebral for his rambunctious nature. He wanted an art of greater expressiveness and sensuality, and this became his long-term aim. In the short term, he determined to shake off the constrictions of geometry and explore further his interest in space and light. This move from hard-edge to a more sculptural approach to colour can best be understood as Hoyland's maturation as an artist, reflected in his new ability to pick and choose among the key issues of the day, absorbing and translating what he required for his own purposes.

Hoyland's was an intensely subjective approach, not the illustration of a theoretical position. Even from those early days he was more interested in the subtle differences of stained colour which play on emotional nuances and promote unexpected changes of mood, than in debating the future of painting. And already he was complicating matters. He refused to leave the picture to its formal or programmatic devices, insisting on introducing a fine drizzle of atmosphere, a bat-squeak of disquiet to layer and qualify the response of the attentive viewer.

17.5.63
Acrylic on cotton duck
175 × 175 cm (69 × 69 inches)

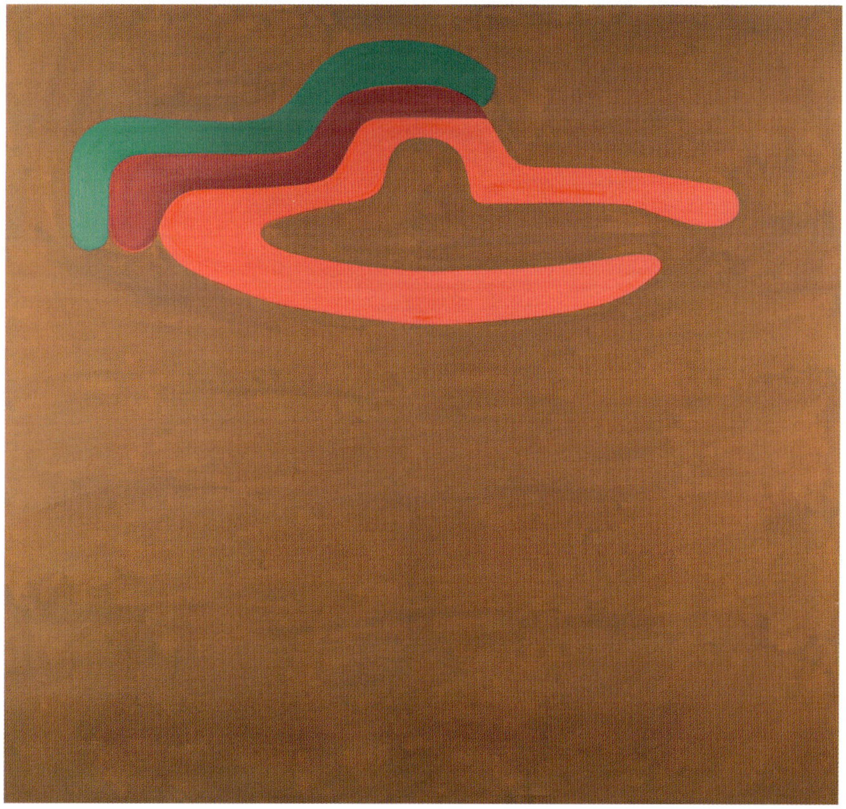

Frankenthaler and Hoyland

Helen Frankenthaler (born 1928) has said: 'I think that a really good picture looks as if it happened all at once, an immediate image.' And she continues: 'It might take years of laboured efforts and discards to produce a really beautiful motion that is synchronized with your head and heart, and therefore it can look as if it were suddenly born.'

Hoyland comments: 'She's a marvellous artist, a beautiful artist. When she came to London and she came to my studio, I had so many paintings in that front room in Oppidans Road, you had to go in through the window. You couldn't open the door because of the paintings. She said, "God, you're painting real pictures!" I think she was rather surprised that anyone in England would be painting real pictures.'

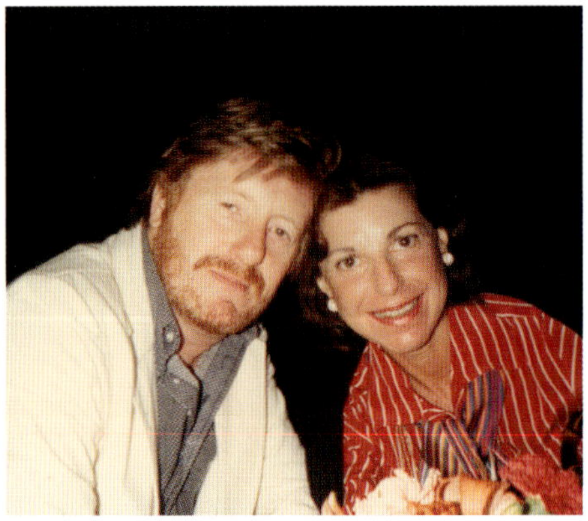

Hoyland with Helen Frankenthaler at Langan's Brasserie in the late 1970s

It's that spirit of devilment, the pure feeling of risk and the wild enjoyment of his own remarkable skills that signifies mature Hoyland. He does it because he can do it, and then he pushes it a bit further. That intrepidity is as much a characteristic of his best 1960s' paintings as it is of his work today.

There was more variation to his early work than is often thought. Hoyland soon ditched hard-edge optical painting and began to pursue a kind of curly biomorphic imagery that owes something to the distinctive shapes of Arp. The forms are playful and even liquid, schematized and themed, the colours deliberately brash and unappealing, a response to Pop Art which was then in its first hot flush of success. These works relate also to the radical sculpture of the 1960s – the kind of thing Phillip King and the *New Generation* sculptors were doing in plastics and metal. In 1963 Anthony Caro held a one-man show at the Whitechapel Art Gallery which was to be hugely influential on Hoyland. It enabled him to believe it was possible to be a great artist working in England. And he discovered similarities of outlook in Caro's work. For instance, both artists exploit the process of making art as a means to discovering the form. Their work has evolved in fascinating parallel ever since.

Also in 1963 Hoyland had met the American Abstract Expressionist painter Helen Frankenthaler, who was visiting England and wanted to see the work of the young sculptors who were beginning to make a name for themselves. Bryan Robertson, then the trail-blazing director of the Whitechapel, asked Hoyland to take her round the studios and she issued him with an invitation to visit her in New York. He took up the offer the following year when he was awarded a Peter Stuyvesant Foundation travelling bursary to America. There he met Robert Motherwell, Rothko and Barnett Newman for the first time, and visited their studios. Temperamentally Hoyland was much in sympathy with these artists, though very aware that he had to find his own path through the thickets of fashion and theory.

The full disclosure of American art was a slow process in England. Key events were the two Tate exhibitions in 1956 and 1959, *Modern Art in the United States* and *The New American Painting*. But Robertson's Whitechapel shows played an important and underrated role in acclimatizing the British to current American achievements. Hoyland's dialogue with American art was to be at the heart of his own work for at least the next decade. On that 1964 visit, he also met the intimidating critic Clement Greenberg, who was the first to alert him to the work of Hans Hofmann. (Hofmann's use of colour was to be an inspiration for Hoyland's later 1960s' paintings.) Hoyland enjoyed a prickly relationship with Greenberg, but it was the Greenbergian watchwords of 'clarity and openness' that he now took to heart.

Hoyland's artist's statement in the catalogue for *The New Generation: 1964* exhibition (which included *7.11.63*, below), at the Whitechapel Art Gallery, reads thus: 'The shapes and colours I paint and the significance I attach to them I cannot explain in any coherent way. The exploration of colour, mass, shape, is, I believe, a self-exploration constantly varied and changing in nature: a reality made tangible on the painted surface.' Here is confirmation of his belief that painting must come from within, a creed that was to moderate significantly over the years. In 1963,

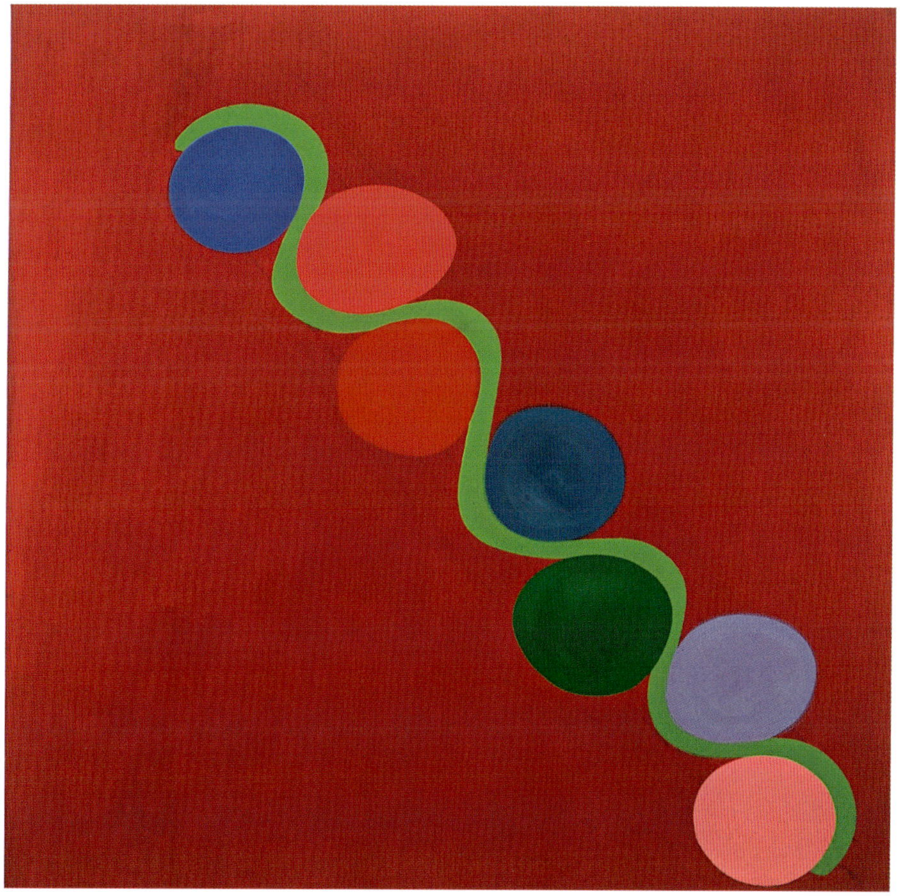

7.11.63
Acrylic on cotton duck
213 × 213 cm (84 × 84 inches)

The Art Czar of New York

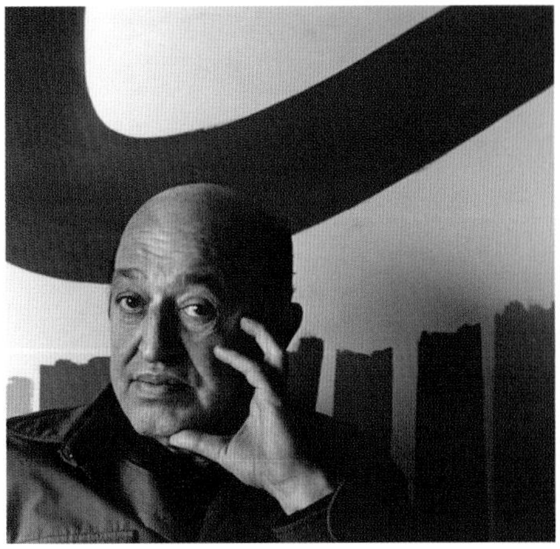

Clement Greenberg (1909–94) was an immensely powerful American art critic. When Hoyland lived in the city, Greenberg would invite him up for drinks at 5.30pm to meet people. It was a chance to look at the latest paintings, because Greenberg always hung half-a-dozen new pictures in his sitting room and asked his guests which was the best painting. If they judged differently from Greenberg himself, he'd say, 'You're wrong – look again.' Hoyland's grand riposte to this was: 'I will look again, but I don't need to. I'm an artist.' Greenberg paid no attention to celebrity status and hung all sorts of work together, by the known and the unknown. He wished to cultivate an innocent eye in his guests, albeit he was also pushing his own theories of flatness and the 'truthfulness of the canvas'.

Although Hoyland's relationship with Greenberg was somewhat abrasive, with the mighty critic always trying to keep the rebellious young artist in his place, Greenberg did say things that stayed in Hoyland's mind and were sometimes useful. For instance, when Hoyland was in the midst of his stain paintings, Greenberg said simply, 'Don't you ever think about texture?' It was a question that was to bear fruit in the 1970s, when Hoyland began to explore different ways of handling his paint surface.

On another occasion, Greenberg said to Hoyland, 'Why do you paint more than one image?' (Hoyland always sees this as typical of the American approach to picture-making: basically you paint one work in endless variations.) Hoyland retorted, 'Because I've got more than one idea.' This did not go down well with the great man, who pontificated, 'Painting more than one image betrays a psychological weakness.' Given Hoyland's prolific and wonderfully varied output since then, one can only speculate on the extreme of psychological debility he must now be reduced to, at least according to the Greenberg rules …

Op artists were always talking about the precedence of the eye above all else. Frank Stella famously said, 'What you see is what you see.' Others did not agree. Philip Guston maintained that painting was an illusion, a piece of magic; it was definitely not just what you see. Hoyland remembers a dinner party, at which Motherwell disputed the dominance of the eye. He said that it was a combined effort: 'the eye, the hand and the heart'. (Interestingly, for such an intellectual artist, he did not mention the mind.) Hoyland has always remembered this.

Clement Greenberg in a 1958 essay on Hofmann wrote: 'The variety of manners and even of styles in which he works would conspire to deprive even the most sympathetic public of a clear idea of his achievement. At the same time, such a diversity of manners makes one suspect an undue absorption in problems and challenges for their own sake; or else that this artist too implicitly follows wherever his inventive fertility leads him instead of bending that fertility to his vision.'

Greenberg went on to say: 'The notion of experiment has been much abused in connection with modernist art, but Hofmann's painting would seem to justify its use. He is perhaps the most difficult artist alive – difficult to grasp and to appreciate. But by the same token he is an immensely interesting, original and rewarding one, whose troubles in clarifying his art stem in large part from the fact that he has so much to say.' The same could be said for Hoyland.

Hoyland had discovered acrylic paint, brand-new to the market, and this revolutionized his practice. He'd always been impatient with the drying time of oils, and the speed and versatility of water-based acrylic – together with the interesting range of colours developed over the years – proved a huge attraction. As the art critic John McEwen has memorably observed: 'Acrylic was to painting what the electric guitar was to music.'

With his next group of paintings, Hoyland made a quantum leap forward. He noted what his sculptor friends (taking their lead from Anthony Caro) were doing in terms of space and the de-materializing of metal. In their sculptures, brightly painted steel elements seemed to float weightlessly. In response, Hoyland's painting became more structural, but in an intuitive way, deploying flat and ambiguous planes of colour. He used changing light effects (by varying the colour of his backgrounds) to situate his elements in space – the steps and squares, columns and trapezia that populate his canvases. More specifically, Hoyland acknowledges that the idea of hanging rectangles from the top of a canvas was one of the things he got from sculpture.

In 1964, on his return from New York, Hoyland built a new studio in Kingston-upon-Thames where he was now living that would be large enough for the big pictures he wanted to paint. Even so, these were so big that he rarely had the chance to look at more than one at a time, so the activity of making small studies in watercolour and gouache on paper (with the occasional admixture of acrylic) became a valued way of seeing ideas for colour and space juxtaposed together, albeit on a small scale. The gouaches were private works, not made for exhibition but for the artist's own satisfaction, and for the exploration of ideas. They filled the role that is today taken by his sketchbooks.

If Hoyland had grown up in an age of austerity, he was beginning his professional life in quite another milieu. As David Thompson wrote of the artists in *The New Generation: 1964*: 'They are starting their careers in a boom-period for modern art. British art in particular has suddenly woken up out of a long provincial doze, is seriously entering the international lists and winning prestige for itself. The atmosphere is one of self-confidence, but also of competition.'

The acrylic paintings Hoyland made in the mid-1960s have a grandeur and startling economy of means. The great expanses of canvas are stained with paint of different intensities. The surfaces, mostly fields of a single colour, are animated by

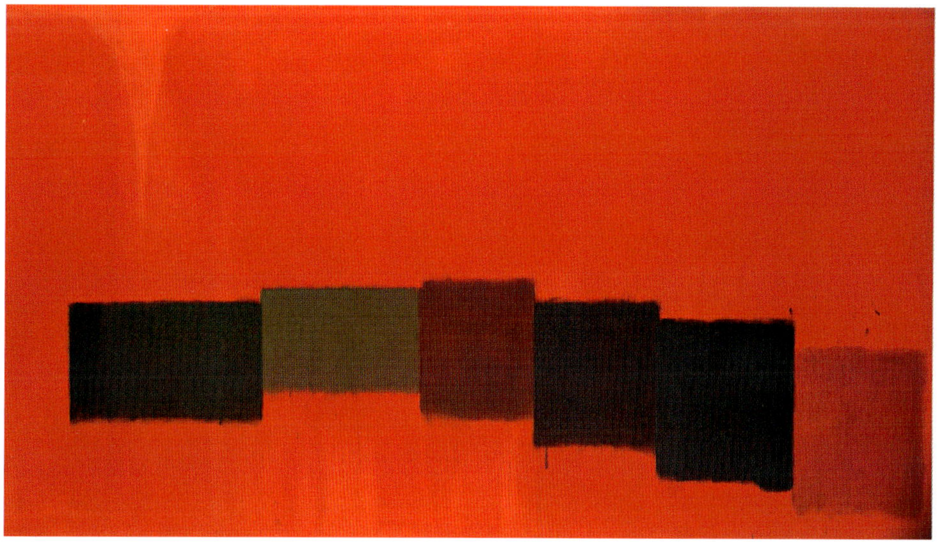

11.9.65
Acrylic on cotton duck
198 × 353 cm (78 × 139 inches)

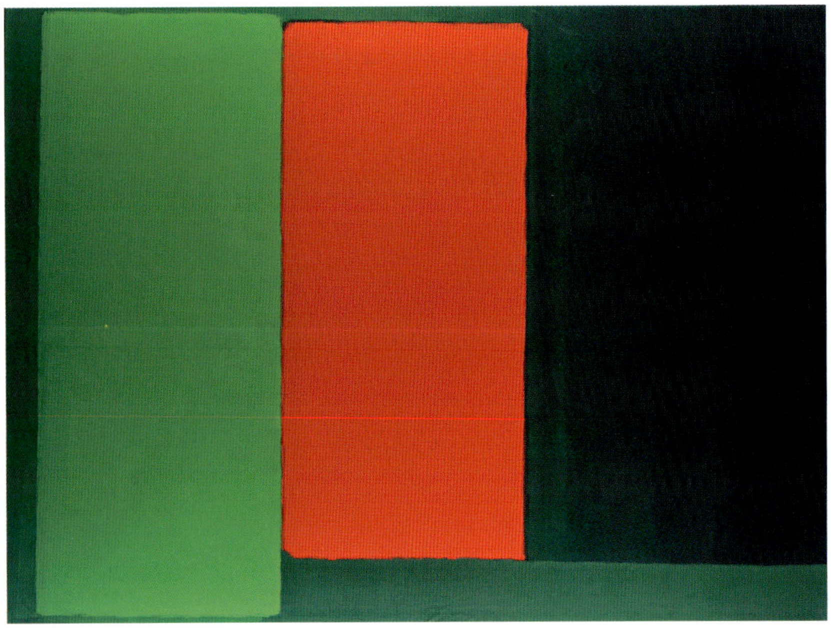

20.4.66
Acrylic on cotton duck
198 × 297 cm (90 × 117 inches)

Hoyland's vigorous brushwork, his ability to articulate space. The thin acrylic paint is applied in long brushy gestures, worked vertically or diagonally into the weave of the cotton duck. This activity is accompanied or qualified by an area of horizontal incident generally confined to the lower part of the picture. Hoyland did not attempt to paint immaculate fields of colour, rather the reverse. He didn't try to hide the history of an image, and in the variegated expanse of (for instance) green can be seen shadowy events in the paint which may signify previous ideas or simply an interest in texture. Hoyland is not precious about his paintings, and the effect is tremendously fresh and revitalising.

Colour was used instinctively in the process of composition, and Hoyland aimed for maximum visual impact through strong contrast. (This is a habit he has managed to develop and extend over the years.) His reds, oranges and greens in those 1960s' paintings are full, saturated, often brilliant, but it isn't so much the colour itself that concerned him, as where to place it. That remained the crucial problem – the orchestration of shapes. Edges, no longer clear-cut, were another consideration: how colours impinge on one another. Hoyland solved this by judicious shimmer and blur, a tactic he developed from his watercolour studies.

He celebrates unequivocally the autonomy of the modern artist. He paints with the whole man: for him painting is a complete and enveloping activity of body, mind and heart. He is both tough guy and sensitive soul – at once uniting and confounding stereotypes. He is also impatient, wilful, restless. For him there was too much purity in Greenbergian formalism, and he resolved to go his own way. His paintings are abstracts but they are not about absolutes. They are about contingencies and specifics: very particular emotions, thoughts and feelings

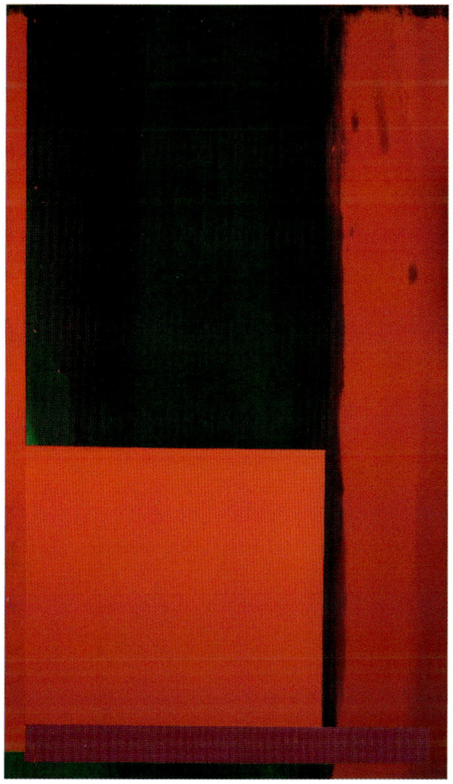

12.6.67
Acrylic on cotton duck
300 × 168 cm (118 × 66 inches)

dependent upon the act of looking. In the paintings of the 1960s we see developing the grand impetuosity which characterizes Hoyland's mature work: the daring deployment of shape, interval and mass, the vibrancy of his architecture of light and, over all, the sacramental presence of colour. It is the passion with which these are conveyed that is so compelling.

As Charles Harrison pointed out in his essay on Hoyland in the catalogue for the 1969 São Paulo Biennale, in which Hoyland and Anthony Caro represented Great Britain. Hoyland was not only one of those English artists to be decisively affected by American postwar painting, he was also 'one of the very few members of this generation whose work is not made to look provincial by the achievements of the Americans.' Hoyland, like Caro, is an international figure. This has been recognized ever since the 1960s, which makes his current relative neglect even more extraordinary. The problem is that Hoyland doesn't abide by the rules, he keeps changing and developing, and he's highly critical of current orthodoxies. In fact, as has been noted on more than one occasion before, he's a fully paid-up member of the Awkward Squad, and does his own cause no good by his intemperate railing against the darlings of the art establishment.

As Harrison went on to say in his 1969 essay: 'The example of Rothko has been particularly important in suggesting the possibility of emotionally-charged paintings in which the process, as we can reconstruct it, and the image, as we perceive it, are inseparable as means of embodying human sensation on a literal

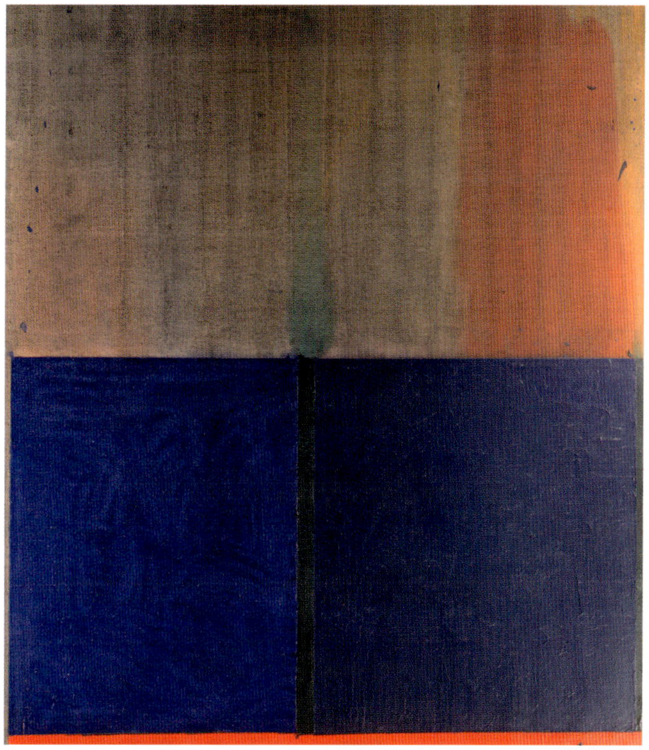

12.12.68
Acrylic on cotton duck
213.5 × 183 cm (84 × 72 inches)

human scale.' Harrison emphasized the centrality of colour for Hoyland. 'He has kept his colour, and thus his means of expression, free, somewhere between calculation and accident, by keeping it physical and real.

'This ability to make us sense colour as something physical and emotive in itself, neither the representation of a physical object nor the record of an emotive gesture, is a part of the new dimension of abstraction gained for painting since 1950. Hoyland is one of the few painters anywhere who can move within this dimension with confidence and with authority.' It's a judgement that still applies to Hoyland's work. He is a master colourist who continues to invent the most audacious combinations.

1970s & 1980s

Hoyland's work of the 1970s gave voice to an entirely different attitude, of insistent materiality, as opposed to the dematerialised floating wedges and bars of the 1960s. The surfaces of his paintings were repeatedly built up and scraped back, as texture became an overriding key to their identity. This period of his work has received comparatively little exposure, and a proper museum assessment is called for. In default of that, here are a few comments and lines of enquiry. Hoyland's new-found interest in surface texture owed something to looking at Hofmann, but also to the example of the heaped paint of Jean Fautrier and the other Europeans he admired: de Staël, Tàpies, Poliakoff.

Hoyland's new palette was also influenced by the experience of driving to Las Vegas with his girlfriend the black American jazz singer Eloise Laws (she was singing there), and experiencing a whole lot of different colours in the desert, from rock and scrub to the more silvery effects of plant life. And as John McEwen has perceptively noted: 'The change to unusual colour combinations, pinks and tans, instead of the primaries, notably red and green, used by the artists he first admired – van Gogh, Matisse and the Fauves – in particular owed something to his New York-based painter friend Jules Olitski.'

Hoyland himself has remarked of his 1970s' work: 'I liked the idea of doing paintings with a meaningful dumb centre, that just kind of blanked you, gave nothing away. I liked the blankness, the stillness and yet assertiveness in Morandi's still-lifes.' As a result, he concentrated on opaque rectangles and superimposed edges. He started to use a palette knife much more, after the rollers and brushes favoured in the 1960s. The 1970s' work may be said to be dominated more by the diagonal, after the colour blocks and walls of light of the 1960s. A guide to the way he was thinking about his art can be found in Hoyland's statement for the catalogue of his

5.9.70
Acrylic on cotton duck
274 × 152.5 cm (108 × 60 inches)

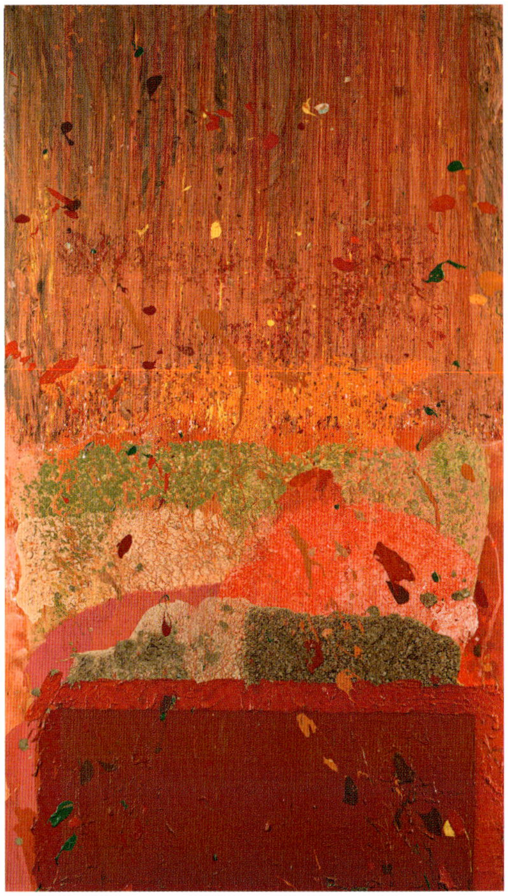

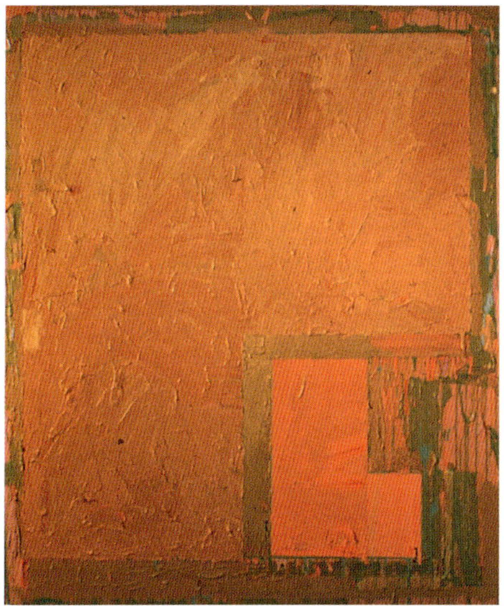

27.4.73
Acrylic on cotton duck
183 × 152 cm (72 × 60 inches)

Serpentine retrospective (1979–80). It reads as follows:

> 'Paintings are there to be experienced, they are events. They are also to be meditated on and to be enjoyed by the senses; to be felt through the eye.
>
> 'The way that they are perceived, as with nature, will be conditioned by the individual onlooker's feelings, background and temperament. Paintings are not intellectual, they don't describe events, don't tell a story, they are not concerned with history, literature, science, theatre, mathematics, or movement; they are still.
>
> 'One discovers a painting as one might discover a forest with snow falling, and then suddenly, unexpectedly, come upon an open glade with sunlight penetrating the falling snow, simultaneously.
>
> 'Paintings are not to be reasoned with, they are not to be understood, they are to be recognized. They are an equivalent to nature, not an illustration of it; their test is in the depth of the artist's imagination.'

Hoyland was painting with huge ambition, energy and authority as he entered the 1980s, composing repeatedly around the triangle and the lozenge. In 1982, he won first prize in the John Moores Liverpool Exhibition with *Broken Bride* (13.6.82), a magnificent arrangement of triangles and wedges, made spatially complex by adventurous juxtapositions of colour. It was that year that Hoyland painted *Hoochy Coochy* (10.2.82), a darker rhomboidal intrigue, in quasi-homage to his old friend Barnett Newman who famously remarked that painting could not be achieved by the gyrations of a hoochy-coochy dancer. In fact, the structure of Hoyland's painting owes more to the overlapping spiral of Matisse's *L'escargot* in the Tate.

As early as 1980 he acknowledged that 'nature is the source of all inspiration', but that he was painting an equivalent of it, not a description or an illustration of appearances. Interestingly, the shape that dominates the 1980s is the circle, a natural form, unlike the straight line, which is man-made – as in the diagonal of the 1970s, or the blocks and walls of the 1960s. In 1983, he embarked on the circle motif, evoked so lyrically by Mel Gooding: 'These paintings are like the reports from deep space of a solitary astronaut concerning his encounters with strange and unanticipated worlds, improbable planets … . They are beautiful and monstrous; they spin in our sight from the banal to the metaphysical, from the comic to the cosmic.'

Broken Bride, 13.6.82
Acrylic on cotton duck
254 × 229 cm (100 × 90 inches)

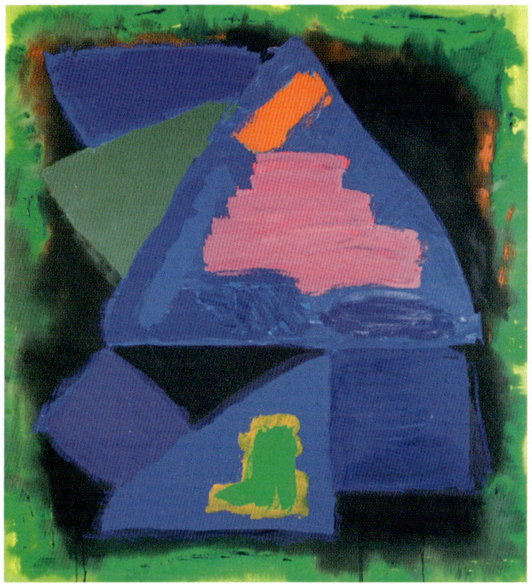

Perhaps it was recognition of this comic aspect which encouraged *Private Eye* to think Hoyland was fair game for satire. Like most artists, he doesn't welcome being attacked in print, but he cherishes the spoof which appeared in February 1987 when he won the Athena Art Award. The *Eye* reproduced his winning painting, claiming it was by 'Mr Howard Zoomin, a freelance artist from Neasden' and that it was called 'Intercity Sizzler', being a depiction of a railway breakfast, complete with bacon, fried tomatoes, mushrooms and chipolatas.

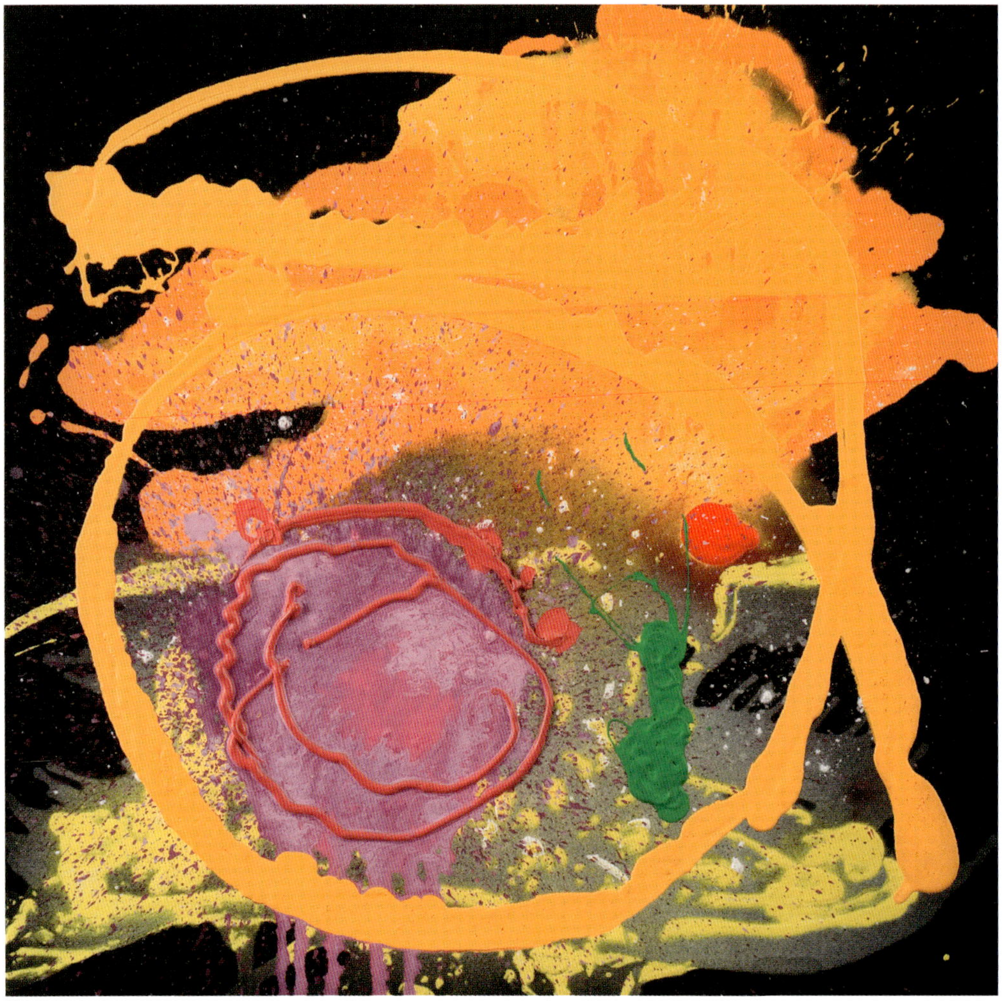

La Dorada, 12.7.89
Acrylic on cotton duck
71 × 71 cm (28 × 28 inches)

In early 1983 Hoyland said in an interview: 'I think there's been terrific pressure on artists in the last 20 years to explain and justify everything that they do ... Maybe it was a necessary thing in the 1960s to be more analytical – but now I think people talk too much. You try to explain too much and most of the time you don't know what you're doing anyway.' This notion of the painting controlling the artist (at least to some extent) is a key element in Hoyland's belief system. He's known, for instance, for saying that 'colour more or less chooses you'. In the 1980s he was constantly re-thinking his art, but refused to give too much away in interviews. He liked to tease or be dismissive: 'I find that it gets harder and harder to paint so you've got to make it as easy as possible.' And: 'I've always kidded myself that I'm going to be a good artist when I'm older ...' Prophetic?

At this point he was no longer making gouache and watercolour studies but little drawings in biro without colour. The emphasis had shifted from painting to drawing, from colour to line. But the full impact of his re-engagement with drawing was not to be felt until the following decade.

1990s

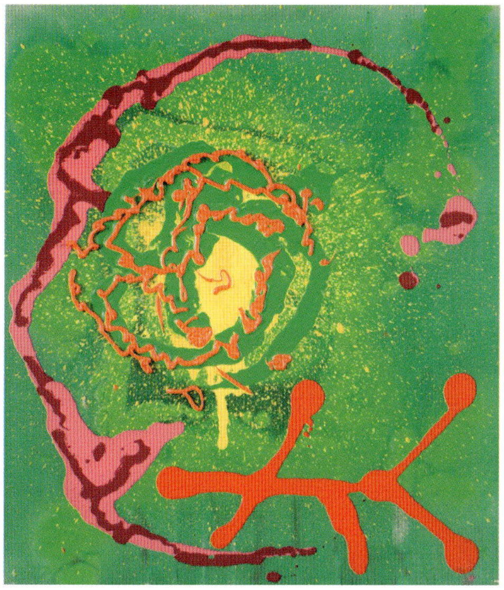

Hydra Cluster, 18.12.91
Acrylic on cotton duck
76 × 66 cm (30 × 26 inches)

This was a key period for Hoyland, almost as important, though in very different ways, as the 1960s. Many far-reaching changes took place in his work. The central motif of the previous decade was dispersed in the 1990s. And two parallel developments which had been gradually evolving, underground as it were, since the 1960s finally came to fruition in the 1990s: the move from a cerebral approach to an instinctual one, and a minimal application to a maximal one.

Writing about an artist-in-residence trip to Thupelo in South Africa in 1993, Hoyland appended a list of *Other Thoughts* to his description of the experience:

1. Mistrust reason.
2. Belief in instinct.
3. Pure of heart.
4. A feeling of holy rage.
5. A sense of isolation.
6. Beyond good and evil.
7. Resignation and understanding.
8. Some irrational absolute.
9. A belief in magic.
10. A kind of paradise.
11. The rationality of superstition.
12. Lust for power.
13. The eye the hand and the heart. And the hard-on.
14. The last primitive act.
15. Felt with the eye.
16. Learn to unlearn.

In an interview with Maurice Cockrill in 1999, Hoyland talked again about the book of Miró's collected writings that Motherwell had given him. Reading it was clearly a milestone for him. 'When I got the book maybe 15 years ago, I was running out of ways of dealing with the formal structures I had been working with. You can't go on

Joan Miró

Joan Miró (1893–1983) tried to define an artist's true reality: 'It is like a secret language made up of magic phrases, a language that comes before words themselves, from a time when the things men imagined and intuited were more real and true than what they saw, when this was the only reality.

'I begin my paintings because something jolts me away from reality. This shock can be caused by a little thread that comes loose from the canvas, a drop of water that falls, the fingerprint my thumb leaves on the shiny surface of this table. In any case I need a point of departure, whether it's a fleck of dust or a burst of light. This form gives birth to a series of things, one thing leading to another.'

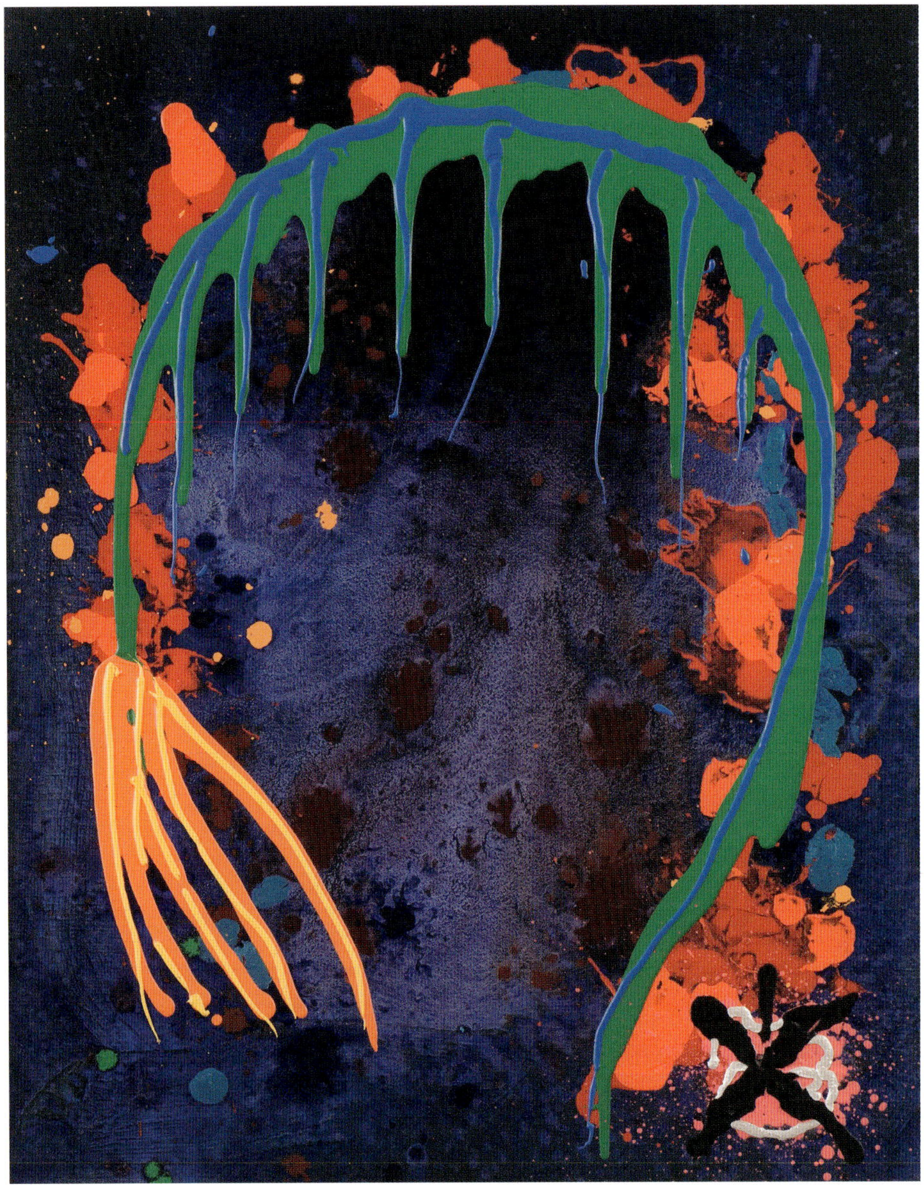

Flames like Rainbows, 20.6.98
Acrylic on cotton duck
90 × 70 cm (35.5 × 27.5 inches)

painting out of your head forever. Often an idea precedes one's discovery of it in nature, if you want to find it.' The key event of this period was visiting Bali in 1994. Hoyland describes it thus: '... a lot of the time you don't know what you're doing, you are just leaping into the dark. But the experiences of going to Bali recently were a bit different because that was where nature seemed to suddenly rear up and confirm ideas I had been reaching towards, confirmed in nature, physically, what I had been looking for in my head.'

The first time he visited Bali was only brief (on the way back from the opening of an exhibition of his paintings in Sydney, Australia), and he had no art materials with him. Deeply impressed by the radiance and sheer beauty of his surroundings, he fell in love with the island. He was particularly drawn to the decorative invention

OPPOSITE
The Pillar, 10.3.95
Acrylic on cotton duck
254 × 216 cm (100 × 85 inches)

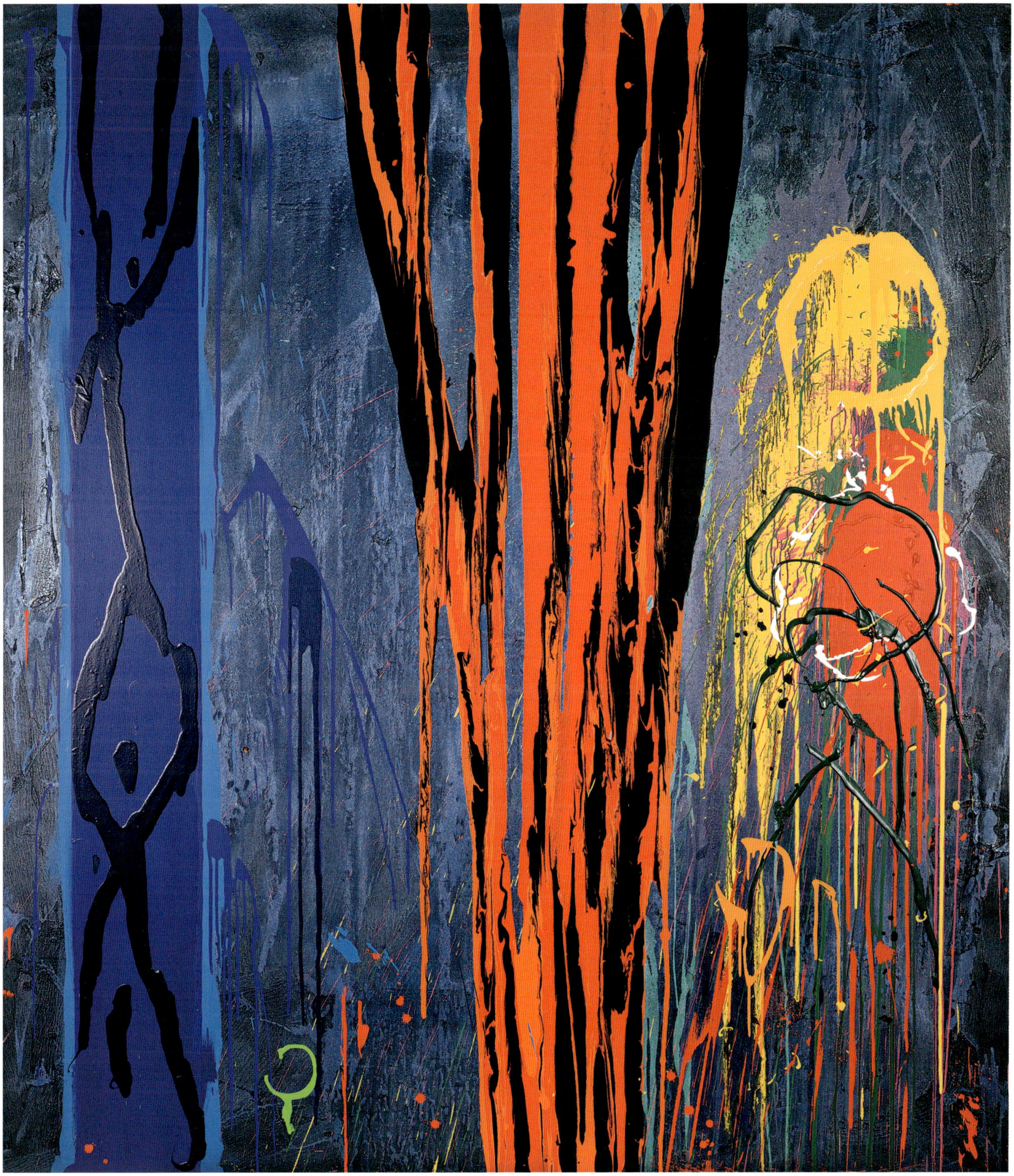

of the people, their use of colour, their strange music and spiritual calm. In response, he made a couple of drawings on the back of an old envelope which he subsequently lost. This upset him so much that he knew he had to return. He did so in the winter of 1995–6 and then again in 1997. That was the first time for decades that he made drawings directly from nature. 'I came back with so many ideas, so many archetypal structures that I could try to hang my thoughts and feelings on.'

Hoyland was mesmerized by the visual splendour of Bali – the strange patterns left by parasites in the bark of trees, the coloured pennants and banners in the streets, the decorations everywhere. He found the lusciousness of it all very compelling: 'There were parasite trees with orange flowers, and then another plant twisted round it with purple blossom. Then there was the sunset as a backdrop.' There were lianas everywhere – rising vegetation in lines and loops, a crazy natural line drawing which inspired Hoyland to emulate it. He drew and drew in coloured inks. He particularly liked the scarecrows in the paddy fields to keep the birds off the rice. 'We've got nothing like this in England. We've only got Robin Hood,' he quipped in a French film made about his work.

The following excerpts from a sketchbook kept while visiting Bali give some idea of his first reactions. He describes structures standing in the rice fields which are 'part scarecrow, part little temple', which he found fascinating. On that trip (July 1997) he made drawings of doorways (*Flames like Rainbows*, page 36), of the wild sprawling wiring on the roof of a house, of a string of neon lights in a restaurant, or the bamboo wind chimes which hang from trees. He wrote: 'Painting is between the noise of bells and running water, between bird and leaf, between the wind and the earth.' Here is the essential hybrid nature of his imagery. In a later sketchbook he wrote: 'In my view new hybrids must be discovered so that the boundaries of the imagination can be expanded.'

Another 1997 note reads: 'Two distinct halves of his divided artistic personality (Gauguin) – on the one hand the liver of pleasure, the creator of images with a frank physical sensuousness, and on the other the searcher after a disappearing spirituality.' I am reminded of Sigmund Freud's favourite joke – 'What is the secret of life? A good liver.'

He loves the abundance of the tropics, the music, the light, the danger. Life is lived far more on the edge in the tropics than it is in nannied and safeguarded Europe. Even human life is less valuable. Hoyland responds to that palpable sense of increased risk with a joyous outpouring of colour and a formal inventiveness that continues to feed him back in England. He loves the sunshine of foreign travel but also the liquid darkness of tropical night.

His work is not all unpremeditated action, he is a thoughtful and constructive painter who gathers material widely that will feed into his imagery. His paintings are half-composed in his head and in notebooks before he lifts up a bottle of paint. But only half. The rest is a collaboration with his materials, the advent of chance, exploiting an unexpected movement or disposition. Hoyland is adept at riding the whirlwind, at recognizing (rather than controlling) chance. Seemingly arbitrary petals of paint, like confetti, are every bit as intended as the most deliberate liquid line drawn in acrylic. His paintings are gloriously orchestrated visual explosions that sometimes have the necessary eye-popping vulgarity of burst balloons at a wedding party. Necessary? Yes, to quell any slight inclination towards good taste. Hoyland always prefers an outbreak of salutary gaudiness to the over-refined niceties of parlour painting.

Hoyland's work of the 1990s and 2000s is more intensely dramatic than anything he's done for 30 years principally because it's more linear. A whole new range of possibilities and contrasts has emerged to enrich his pictorial grammar. Although he paints thickly in some passages, he doesn't use thick paint as a trademark like Frank Auerbach or Leon Kossoff. He employs a wide range of mark

The Yellow Boat, 7.9.98
Acrylic on cotton duck
254 × 236 cm (100 × 93 inches)

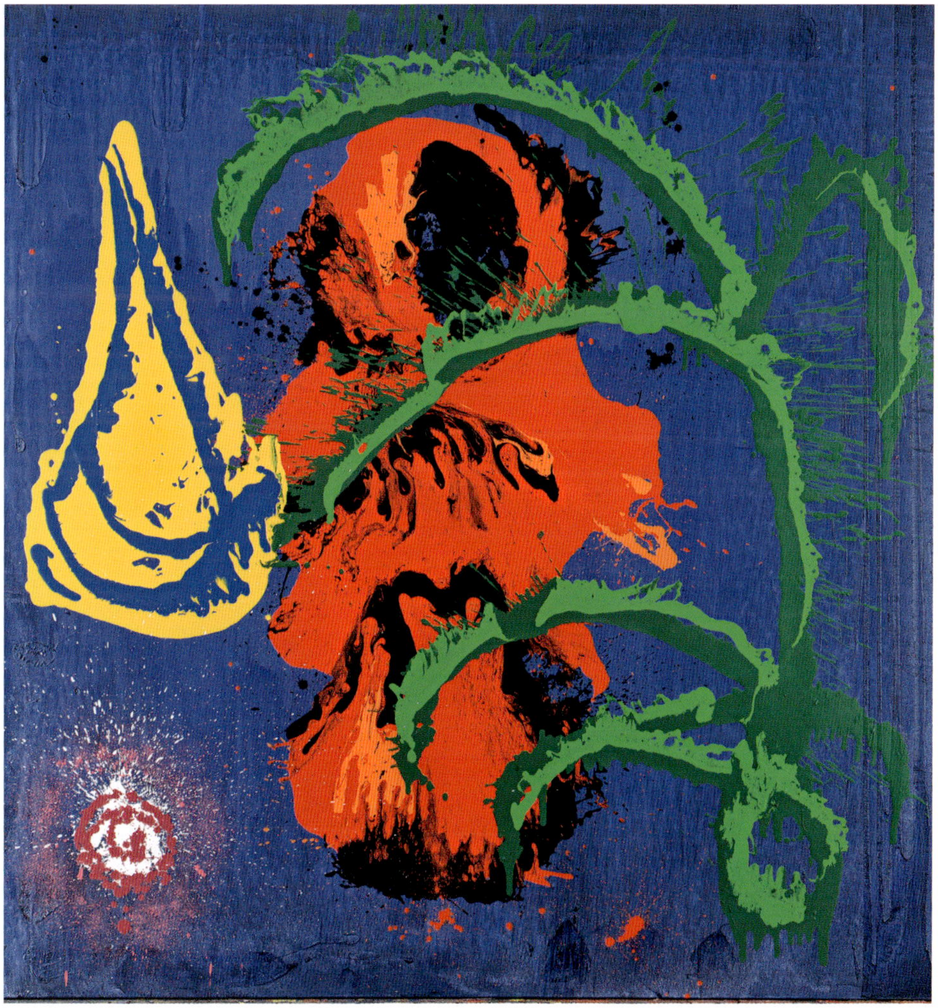

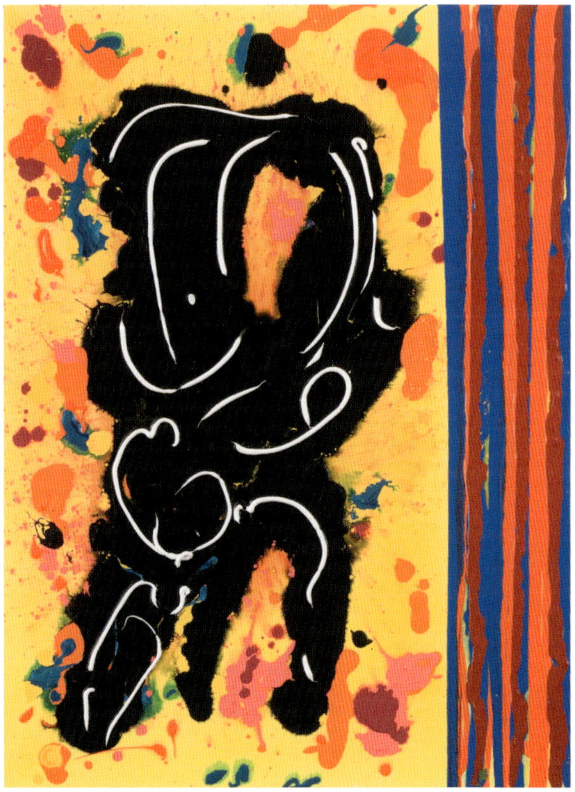

Hovering Angel, 11.12.98
Acrylic on cotton duck
80 × 60 cm (31.5 × 23.75 inches)

and gesture, from the thin glazes of his underpainting – some of which is nearly always visible in the finished work, and quite often considerable expanses of it – to the substantial gouts and tubings of his new linearity. The generosity of paint echoes the generosity of spirit behind these paintings. They depend upon spontaneous, unique actions, gestures which arise from his extensive vocabulary of vital signs, but which are subtly varied from painting to painting, reinterpreted and re-developed to the painting's needs.

There is a close parallel to be noted here between Hoyland and Victor Pasmore (1908–98), who, towards the end of his life conceded that the great Modernist experiment was over and that a new pluralism had arisen in its stead. Pasmore's response to this development was to allow figurative elements to filter back into his work, and although he was still very much an abstract painter, identifiable motifs began to re-appear in his imagery. Chief among these were birds, the fleshy blades of the prickly pear, and a schematized human figure. Hoyland has conducted a similar negotiation with figuration.

However, despite the growing fascination for the natural world, and its direct stimulus, Hoyland remains an abstract painter, whatever qualms he has about the term. 'I've always favoured abstract or non-figurative painting because I think the "withheldness" of it is more profound. I like painting that doesn't tell you all the answers, that leaves you to reflect upon it.'

Kingdom, 2.10.05
Acrylic on cotton duck
152.5 × 127 cm (60 × 50 inches)

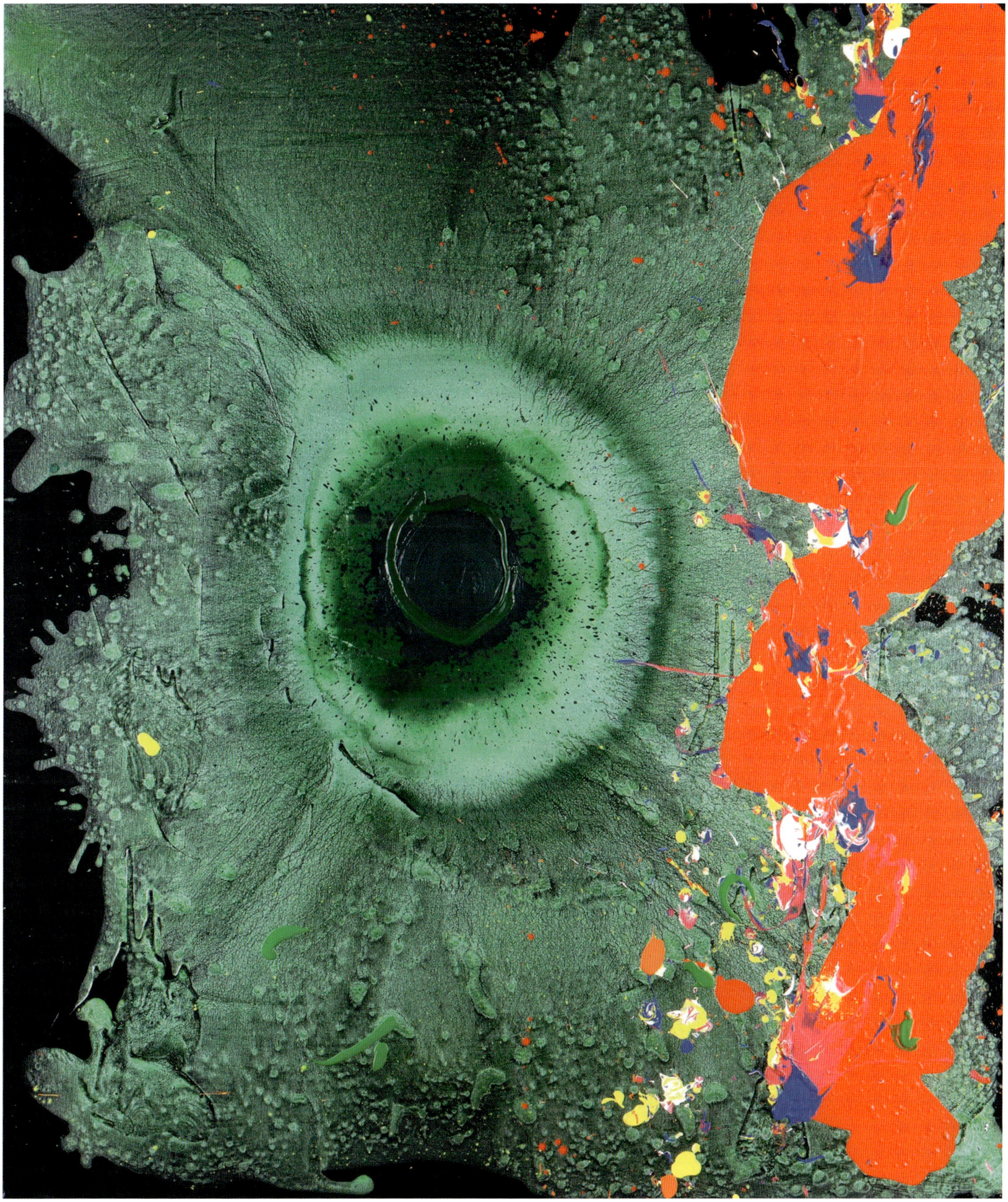

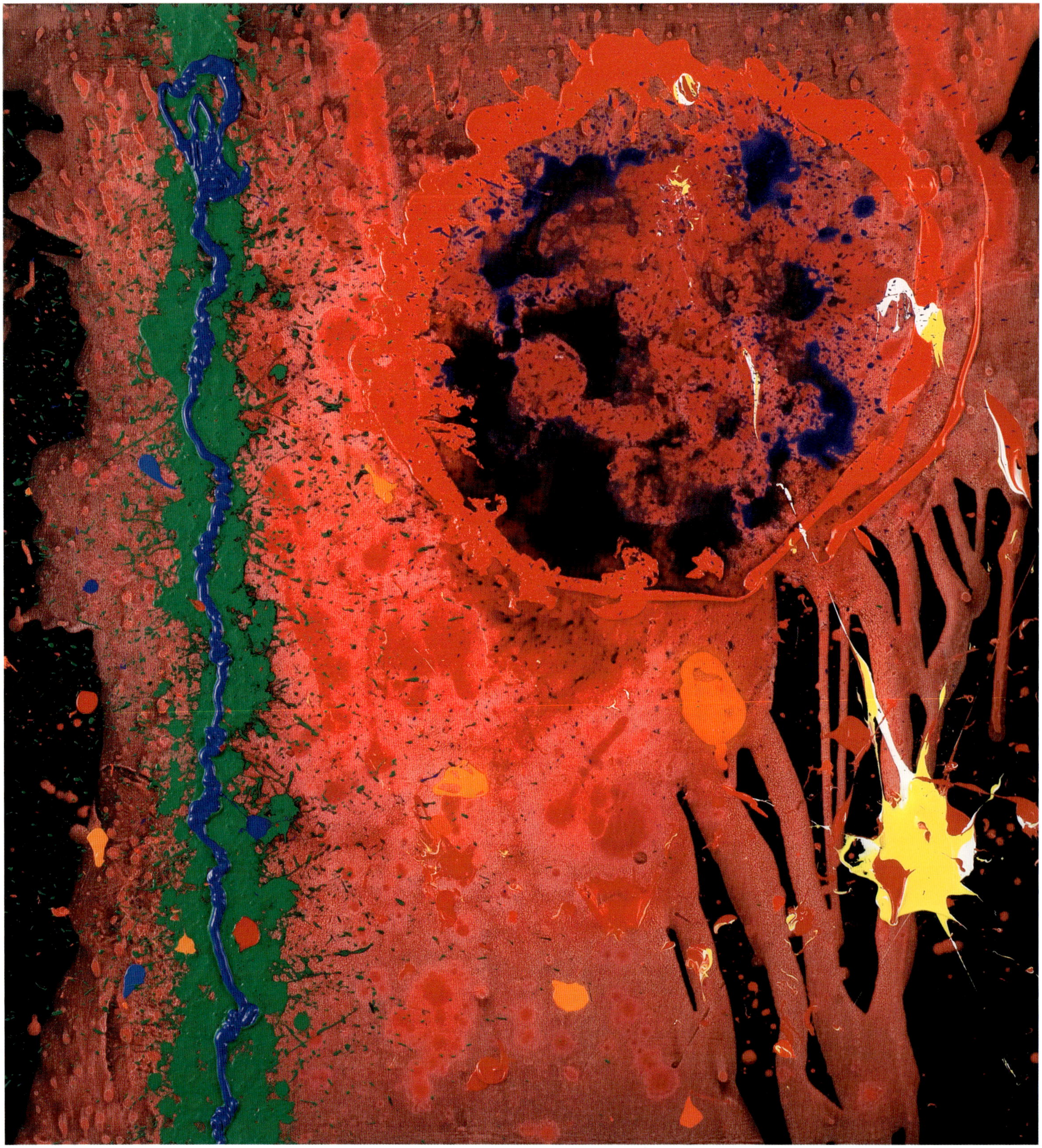

4

Romantic Spirit?

Hoyland has not been afraid to continue, in the great European tradition, a dialogue with history. This is not something the Abstract Expressionists favoured. As a young country, America simply doesn't possess the same relationship with the past as Europe does. A clean slate in America was far easier to achieve. In England, the subversive underground Romantic spirit has never run dry, it consistently nourishes art in this country and erupts forth in strange and unexpected ways. The late work of John Hoyland is one such unpredictable manifestation. The lush imaginative strain that, for instance, surfaced in the 1940s among the so-called Neo-Romantics in a predilection for ruins and agitated landscapes (anathema to Hoyland), also paradoxically informs Hoyland's work. It is a dark energy, an attachment to the chthonic (dwelling deep in the earth) that makes his work utterly different from an art that is of specifically American or undifferentiated international coinage. It encompasses an energetic exchange between the universal and the particular.

Actually, and in spite of their protestations of starting entirely afresh, the Abstract Expressionists were inevitably influenced by their forerunners. Their ideas of the sublime were heavily inflected by the discoveries of the great 19th-century American painters of nature – Albert Pinkham Ryder, Frederic Church or Albert Bierstadt. In much the same way the Romantic strain in English art – with its long tradition of linear invention that reaches back to medieval illuminated manuscripts – exerts an inspiring effect on John Hoyland, however indirect and subconscious.

(Interestingly, the huge size of American Abstract Expressionist paintings was not quite the new development that so many thought it. The painters of the American Sublime had already produced vast acreages of canvas, but so too had various English Romantic painters. Chief among these [if one leaves aside the towering example of Turner] was James Ward, whose landscape masterpiece, *Gordale Scar* [1811–15], measures some 11 feet by 14.)

Despite the genius of Turner and Constable, English landscape painting has often had a poor press abroad. Franz Kline's definition (as told to fellow artist Grace Hartigan) is a case in point: 'You know how it is when you're in the country and

Wild World, 9.9.08
Acrylic on cotton duck
127 × 114 cm (50 × 45 inches)

you're taking a walk, and you're looking at your feet, and it starts to rain and you bump into someone, and you say, "Excuse me!", and he says, "No, excuse *me*!" That's English landscape painting.' An enjoyable dismissal, but a ludicrously uninformed one. Hoyland is surprisingly broad in his interests and can appreciate good art that in taste and discipline is far from his own. He is not the man to follow fashion. He makes his own mind up, and in this case, he has tapped in to the native strengths of English painting. His recent work treads a fine line between abstraction on the one hand and landscape and figure painting on the other. He has created a remarkable hybrid form entirely of his own devising, which is both universal in its application and particular – in that strong strain of English Romantic fantasy – in its origins and demeanour.

In fact, Hoyland is a modern Romantic. He shares the Romantic search for spirit, feeling and symbol behind the everyday appearance of the material world. Although he has no interest in divinity as such, or in accepted religious values (unlike other Romantics, van Gogh included), Hoyland pursues the goal of a higher reality behind the quotidian. Truths about the shifting cares and hopes of human life emerge from the appalling casualness and irregularities of the commonplace world when placed within the larger framework of nature. Nature permeates and brings point and meaning to the shadows and fictions of man's passions. It allows a different perspective. Tap into the passions of nature, the elemental powers, and humanity may for a moment be forgotten. Something larger predominates. Hoyland achieves a translation of direct observation and visual sense data into what can only be called – as it would be in van Gogh – ecstatic spirit. His work approaches, in Robert Rosenblum's phrase, 'the natural on the threshold of the supernatural'.

In Hoyland's work we are challenged anew by the overwhelming, incomprehensible immensity of the universe. Remarkably, if not paradoxically, the effect is dual and opposite: immersion and confrontation. The spatial effects of his paintings – the constellation of voids, the light-laden vistas – draw the eye in, while the surface drawing returns the eye to the picture plane. This complex dialogue continues as the mind grapples with Hoyland's signs and gestures, his potent symbols of flux and diversity, and carries debate further, setting up another conversation between exterior physical space and interior psychological space.

We are not offered a picture of nature, a snapshot, but rather a fervent empathy with the forces of organic growth and the elements, with the microscopic and the telescopic. Here is a new approach to the old Romantic desire to penetrate the secrets and understand the miracles of nature. Science accepts that it can no longer find a solution for everything, an explanation or answer. But art can bridge that gap in different ways, by affording access through metaphor and image. Hoyland's cosmographies reflect the immeasurable, sound the unfathomable. He

Dreamer, 1.6.00
Acrylic on cotton duck
200 × 160 cm (79 × 63 inches)

Ancient Feelings, 17.6.00
Acrylic on cotton duck
91.5 × 61 cm (36 × 24 inches)

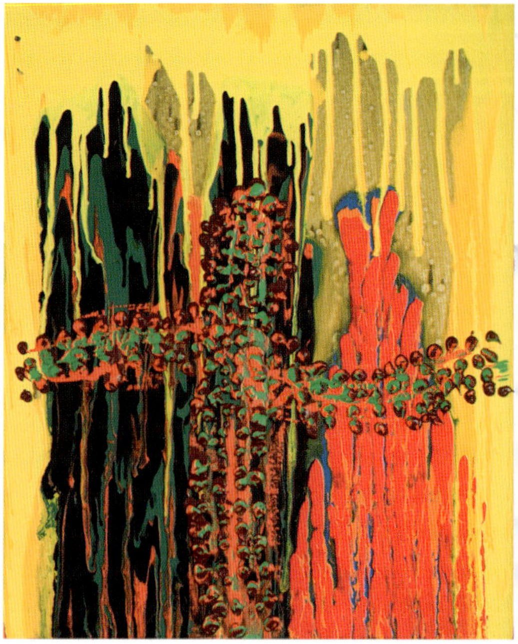

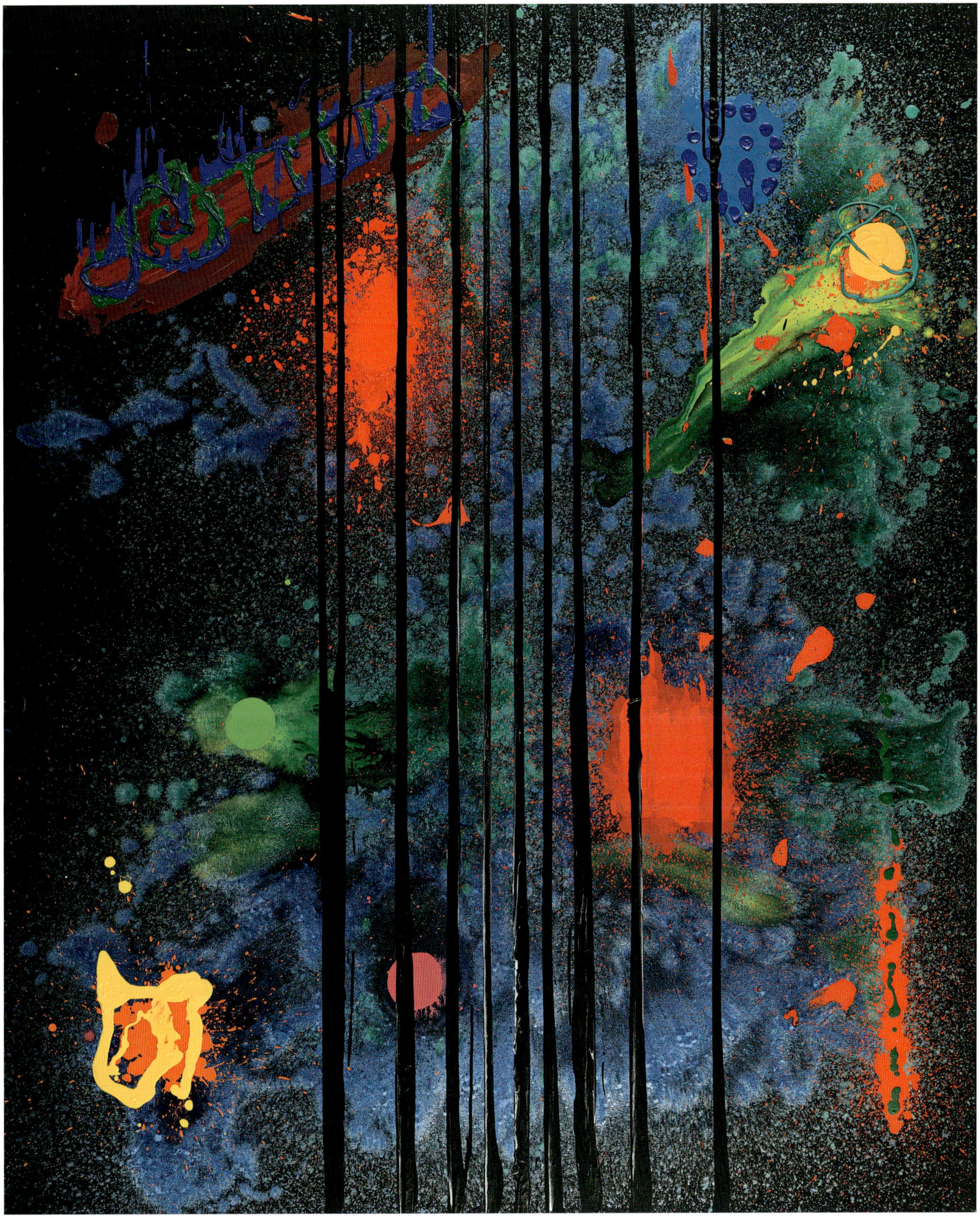

Kinship with William Blake

'There have been men who loved the future like a mistress, and the future mixed her breath into their breath and shook her hair about them, and hid them from the understanding of their times.' This is WB Yeats writing of William Blake, and it gives a clear image of the obscurity into which Blake fell. Hoyland does not suffer quite the same problem, but his work does get marginalized by those unable or unwilling to take the imaginative leap to meet him halfway.

A young artist saw one of Hoyland's small paintings, a moon-scape with red and blue kite-like birds over a dark gold, black and brown land, and immediately identified a reference to Samuel Palmer. Not an obvious link, but an inspired one. He saw the Romantic landscape connection, and the subtle kinship with the visions of Blake. It's not an expected frame of reference, so many tend to miss it. But it provides an approach to the late work of Hoyland which opens up a richness of interpretation which matches his formal inventiveness.

There are many points of contact between Hoyland and Blake. Blake famously said 'the road of excess leads to the palace of wisdom', desired always abundance and exuberance and also cautioned against a generalized treatment ('it is in particulars that wisdom consists'). These are all characteristics which the two artists share. Blake, like Hoyland, hated life drawing, but drew from the imagination with the greatest invention and authority. Both are convinced of the primacy of the imagination. As Blake says: 'The world of imagination is infinite and eternal ...' and, 'imagination divides us from mortality by the immortality of beauty'. Both also favour the action of the head and the heart in unison.

In 1999 Hoyland said: 'You find in nature what you've been looking for in your head. And without wishing to copy nature, one wants to make art that is parallel to it. In the end, nature is too rich to ignore.' Blake said: 'Some see Nature all Ridicule & Deformity, & by these I shall not regulate my proportions; & some scarce see Nature at all. But to the Eyes of the Man of Imagination, Nature is Imagination itself. As a man is, So he sees.'

Blake was above all a linear artist. Pevsner spoke of Blake's 'flaming line', ineluctably sinuous and flowing, while the tenor of his foliate decoration is in the same worshipful tradition as the great manuscript illuminators of the Middle Ages. This predisposition towards what is essentially Celtic ornament can be seen in the wandering vine tendrils and interlacing linear forms that decorate many an illumination and Blakeian illustration alike. It is part of the heritage of British art, reinterpreted superbly by Blake and given a very different twist by Hoyland: line as an expression of energy – as the flow of energy – the signature of life itself.

posits a world of spirit rather than descriptive surfaces, a geography of universal ultimates which yet has real (painted) presence.

We are witness to visions in the mind's eye, not just the outward optic.

On a sheet of his London letterhead Hoyland noted: 'It is easy to be a cynic and appear to gain the upper hand against the poet. His only defence is his dreams, his feelings and his enchantment. He flies beyond the grubby hands of commerce.'

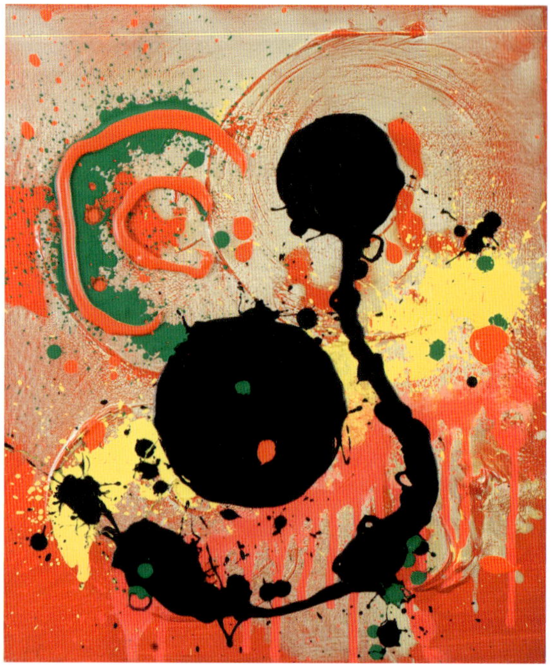

Nature Boy, 12.10.07
Acrylic on cotton duck
61 × 51 cm (24 × 20 inches)

Moon Petals, 4.11.07
Acrylic on cotton duck
91.5 × 76 cm (36 × 30 inches)

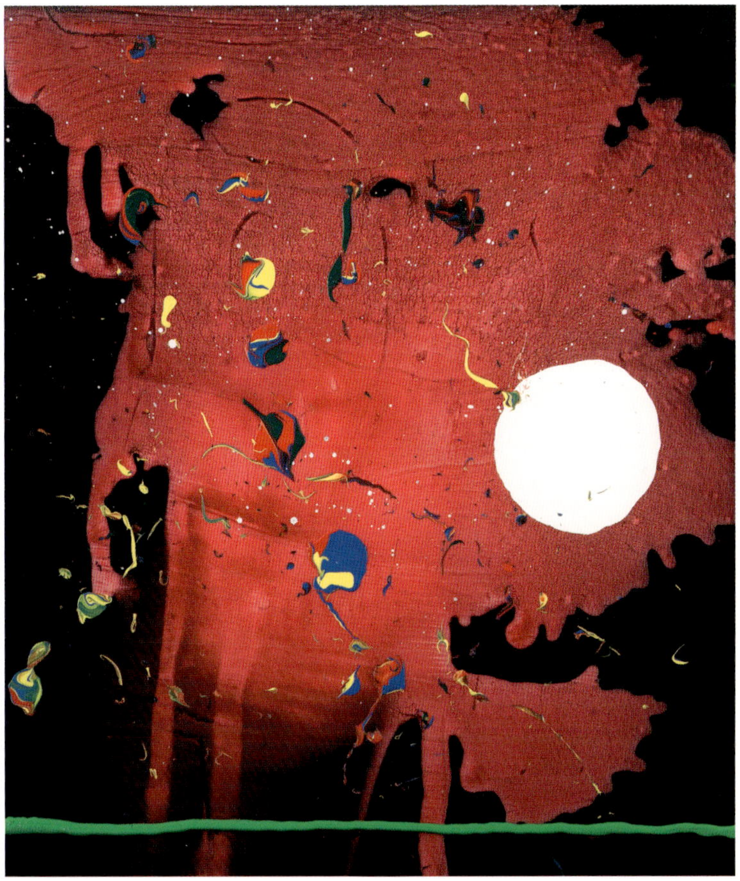

LEFT
Celestial World, 14.1.08
Acrylic on cotton duck
61 × 46 cm (24 × 18 inches)

RIGHT
Cosmic Lady, 25.1.08
Acrylic on cotton duck
61 × 61 cm (24 × 24 inches)

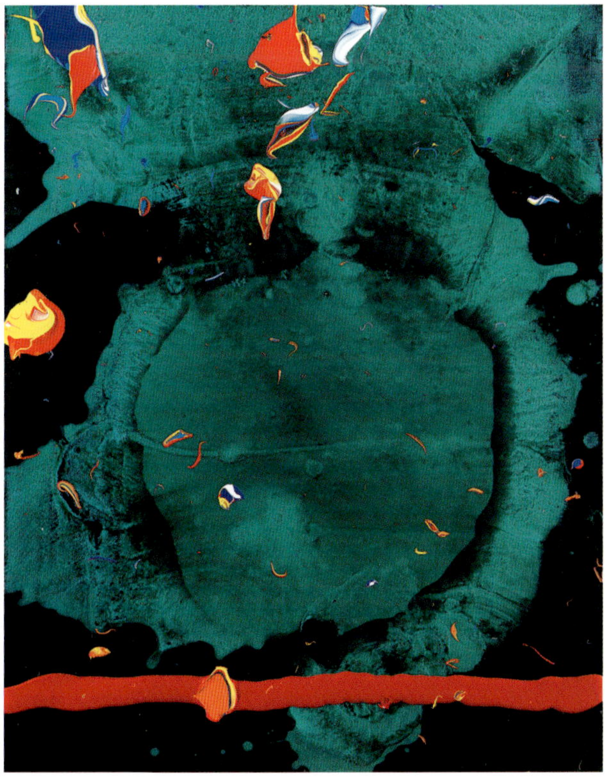

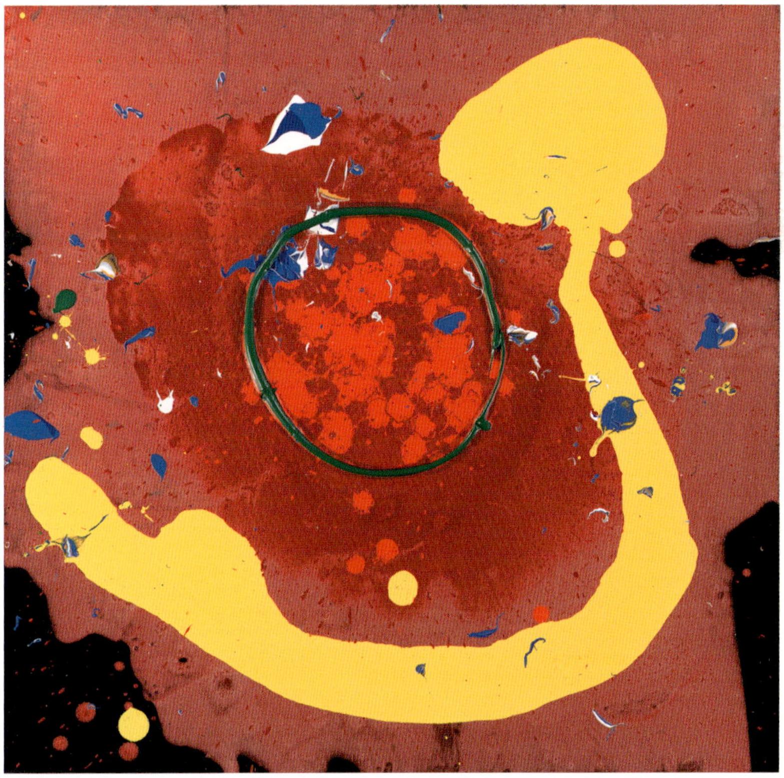

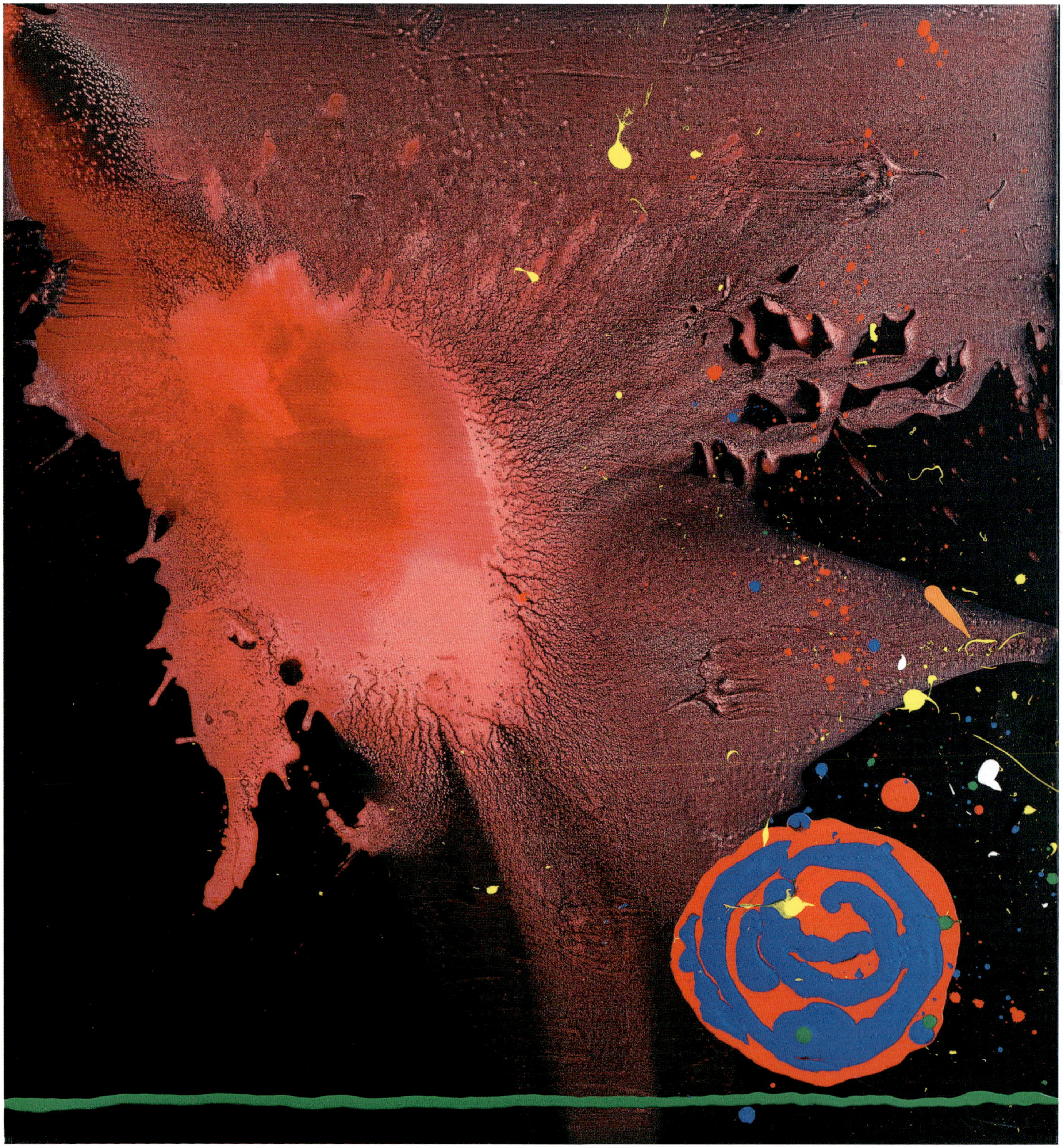

Firelake, 20.7.07
Acrylic on cotton duck
152.5 × 140 cm (60 × 55 inches)

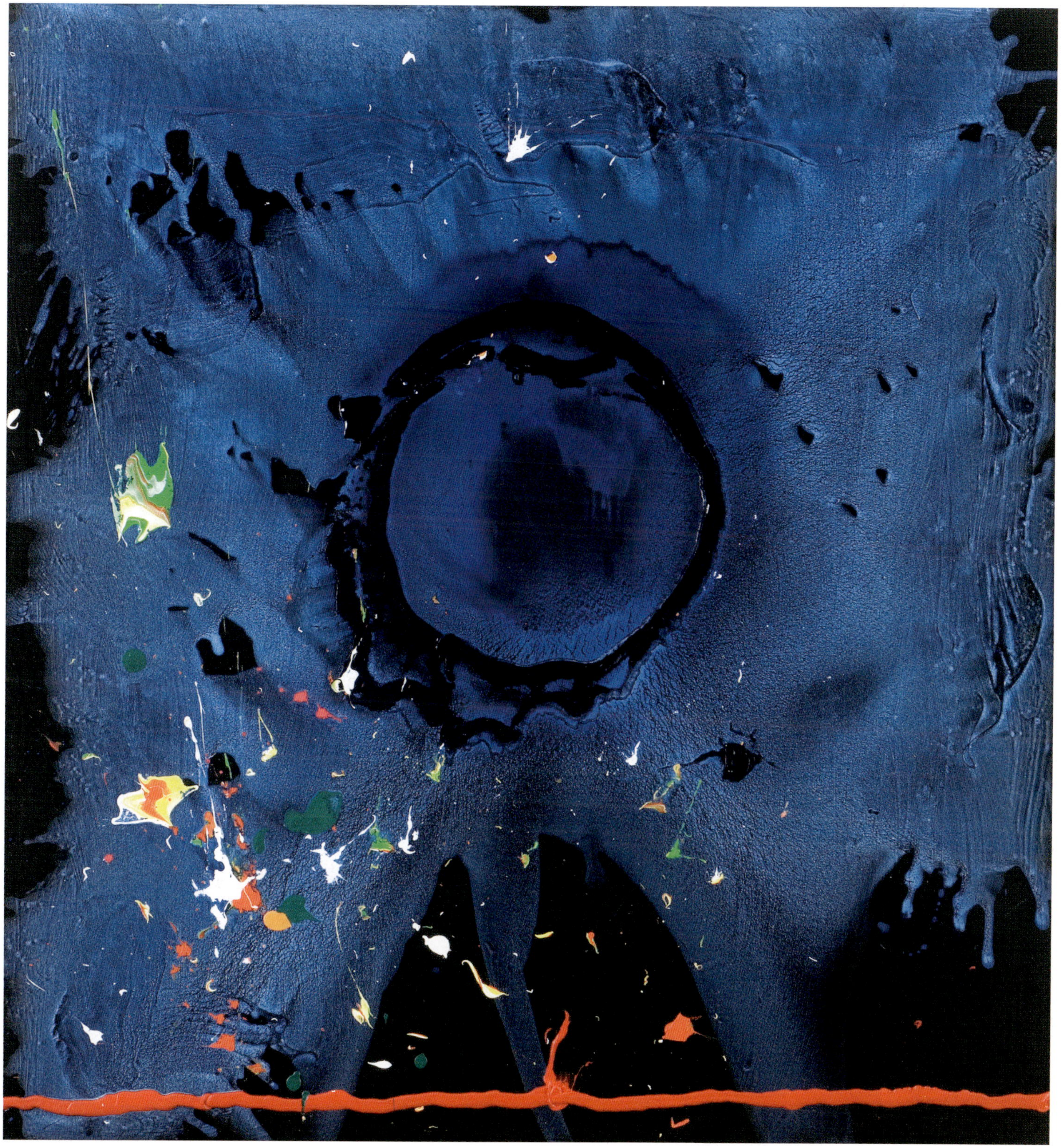

Sky Mirror 2, 29.10.08
Acrylic on cotton duck
152.5 × 140 cm (60 × 55 inches)

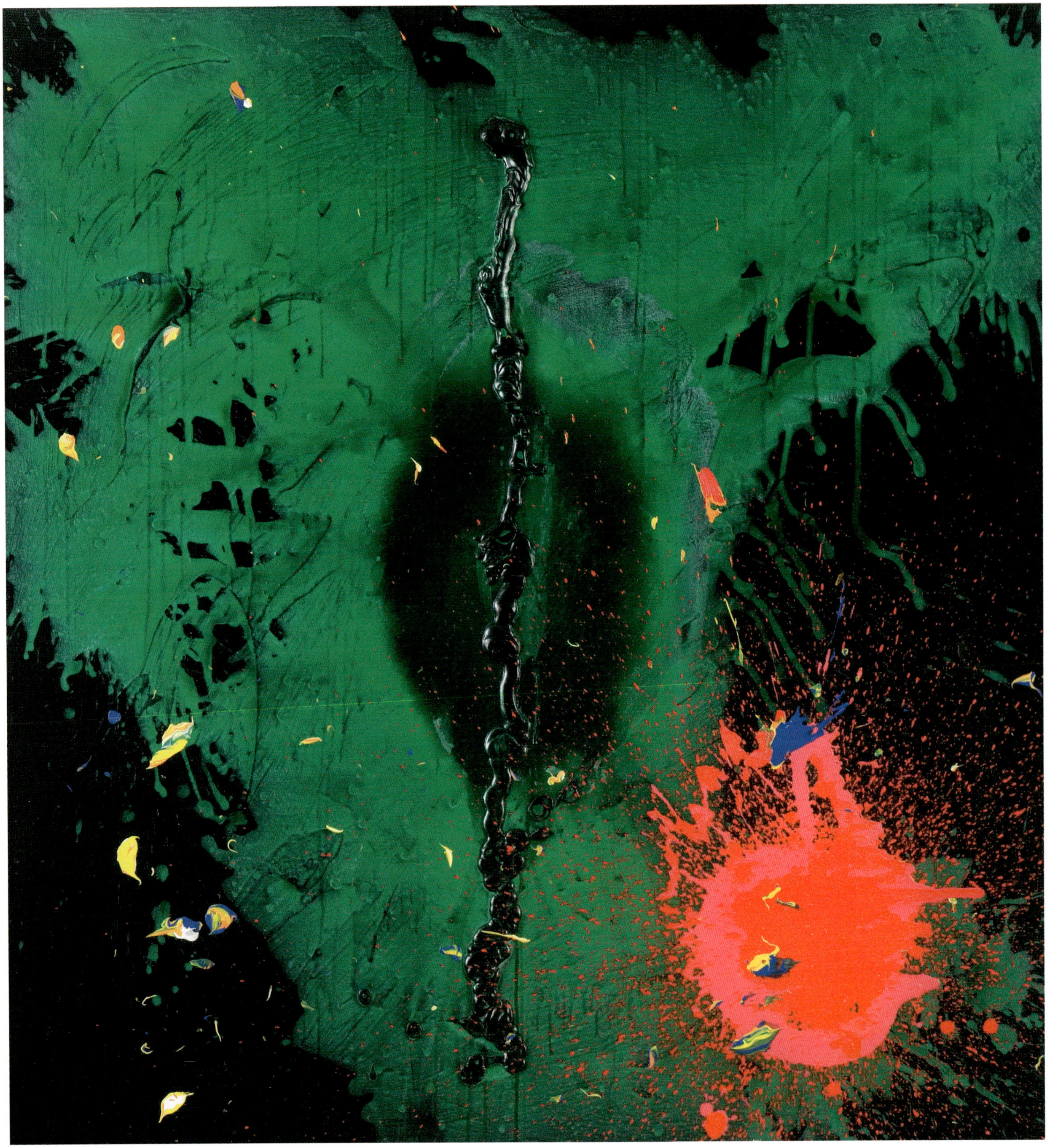

5

Travel

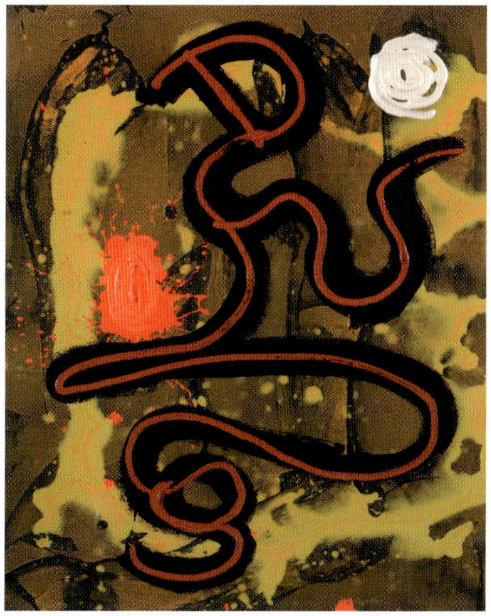

Little Gold Snake, 7.9.92
Acrylic on cotton duck
80 × 63.5 cm (31.5 × 25 inches)

After Jamaica, 9.3.09
Acrylic on cotton duck
152.5 × 140 cm (60 × 55 inches)

Asked if he yearned for the sun as a young man, Hoyland replied, 'Well, I didn't know anything about it – there wasn't any sun! Then a friend of mine, David Smith, knew an Anglophile woman who owned vast tracts of land in the south of France and was willing to lend us a *cabanon* in a deserted valley. We could stay for almost nothing in return for helping out in the market at night in Marseilles, which was quite a long way from where we were staying, near Bandol. Ted Reynolds joined us and we hitch-hiked down with some small canvases and that was the first time I ever saw the South. To me it was like landing in Tahiti. There was still rationing here. Down there were all these brown girls, swimming and diving, and all these grapes. We could only afford bread and tomatoes but we could see the grapes. Then I went back again with David Smith when I was at the Academy school.

'The Academy was good insofar as if I'd been at the Royal College or Slade, I wouldn't have been allowed to go. Henry Rushbury [a fine architectural draughtsman, then Keeper of the RA], who was like Mr Pickwick, bald at the front with long grey-white hair, watch-chain and tummy, said: "Go and paint sunshine, boy." I said, "Thank you very much, sir." You could get away with anything at the RA if you were polite. Then I got that romance with the South, really. The Gauguin syndrome. I went to France a lot. Later I got an Italian dealer and I went to Italy quite a lot in the 70s.'

Hoyland calls Sheffield probably the dirtiest city in the world and maintains that he was scarcely aware of the seasons until he was about 20 – the soot reduced the weather to a terrible sameness. And though he painted a number of landscapes around Sheffield in those early years, the English countryside has not been a great and lasting inspiration – for him it's too gentle and undramatic. He prefers waterfalls and volcanoes. (See his painting *El Misto*, 1.7.06, overleaf. The name was perhaps inspired by the dormant volcano El Misti in southern Peru, apparently sacred to the Incas. Its perfect snow-capped cone has featured strongly in Peruvian

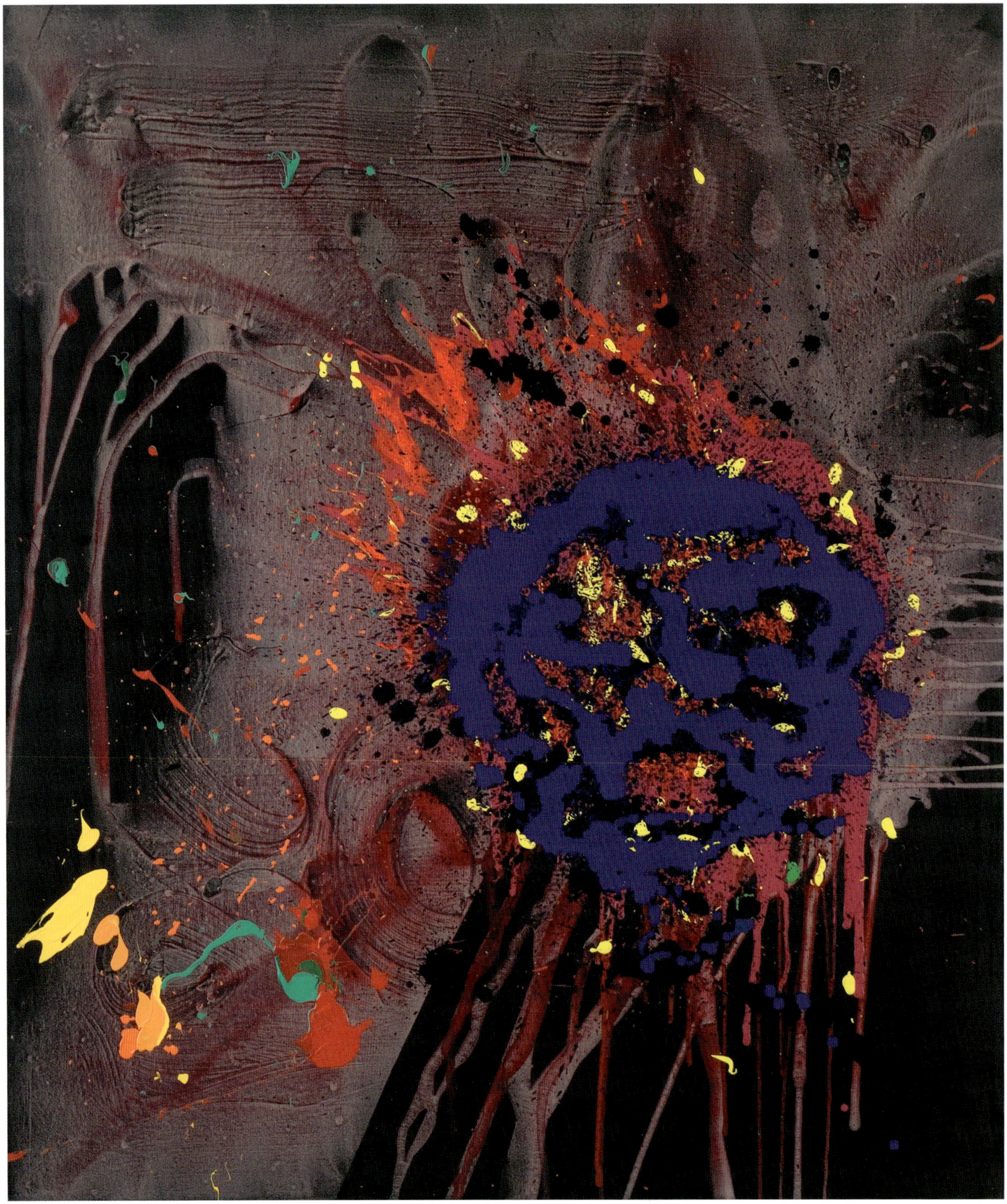

El Misto, 1.7.06
Acrylic on cotton duck
152.5 × 140 cm (60 × 55 inches)

legend and poetry.) Hoyland's love of the exotic, at first satisfied by European travel, soon meant journeying further afield.

America was the first port of call in the 1960s, and then the Caribbean became a favourite destination, first visited in 1969 with Anthony Caro. Since then, Hoyland has travelled widely, taking in Bombay, Hong Kong and Thailand, living for a time in Australia, visiting Trinidad, Antigua and South Africa (where he painted *Little Gold Snake* on page 51), before discovering Indonesia in the 1990s. in recent years, new patterns have emerged, yearly cycles of travel and work. In February, Hoyland tends to go to an apartment on Montego Bay in Jamaica. He travels to a harbour-side flat in southern Spain at various points for short, out-of-season breaks. And he regularly visits his studio in Wiltshire.

Travel is for Hoyland a prime stimulus for work, inasmuch as the unfamiliar and exotic fire up his imagination and feed directly into his art. But the boredom of travel also plays its part – the removal of the traveller from his familiar context in which there is always something to absorb or distract him – and the lack of occupation frequently drives him to work.

On an undated sheet, Hoyland noted at the end of a trip to Jamaica: 'Life is so visually intense here. It's 6.45 in the morning, the ants are rushing around doing what ants do, like hauling off a dead bee the size of a tank. Here I feel surrounded by visual poetry. The humming birds are whizzing around like silent bullets and the vermilion butterflies are bobbing and weaving from bush to bush. The lizards are playing dead. The sun has gently risen and there is no sound except that of a single bird. We leave tomorrow!'

He takes the habit of foreign travel several degrees further, into the imagination. He initiates a journey into the cosmos – far out into deep space, or further in, to examine the microscopic life of cell replication. Hoyland's paintings provide the sensation of being at home in these exotic, even unworldly, terrains. He makes the activity of bringing fire from remote summits seem almost normal.

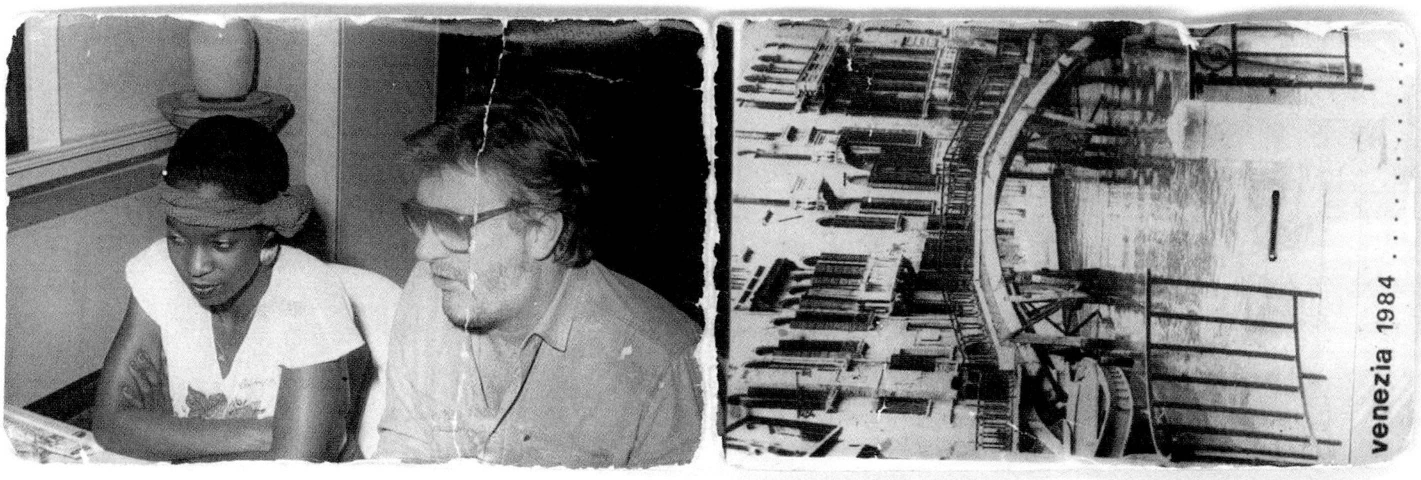

A box of matches: Hoyland with Beverley Heath in Venice in 1984

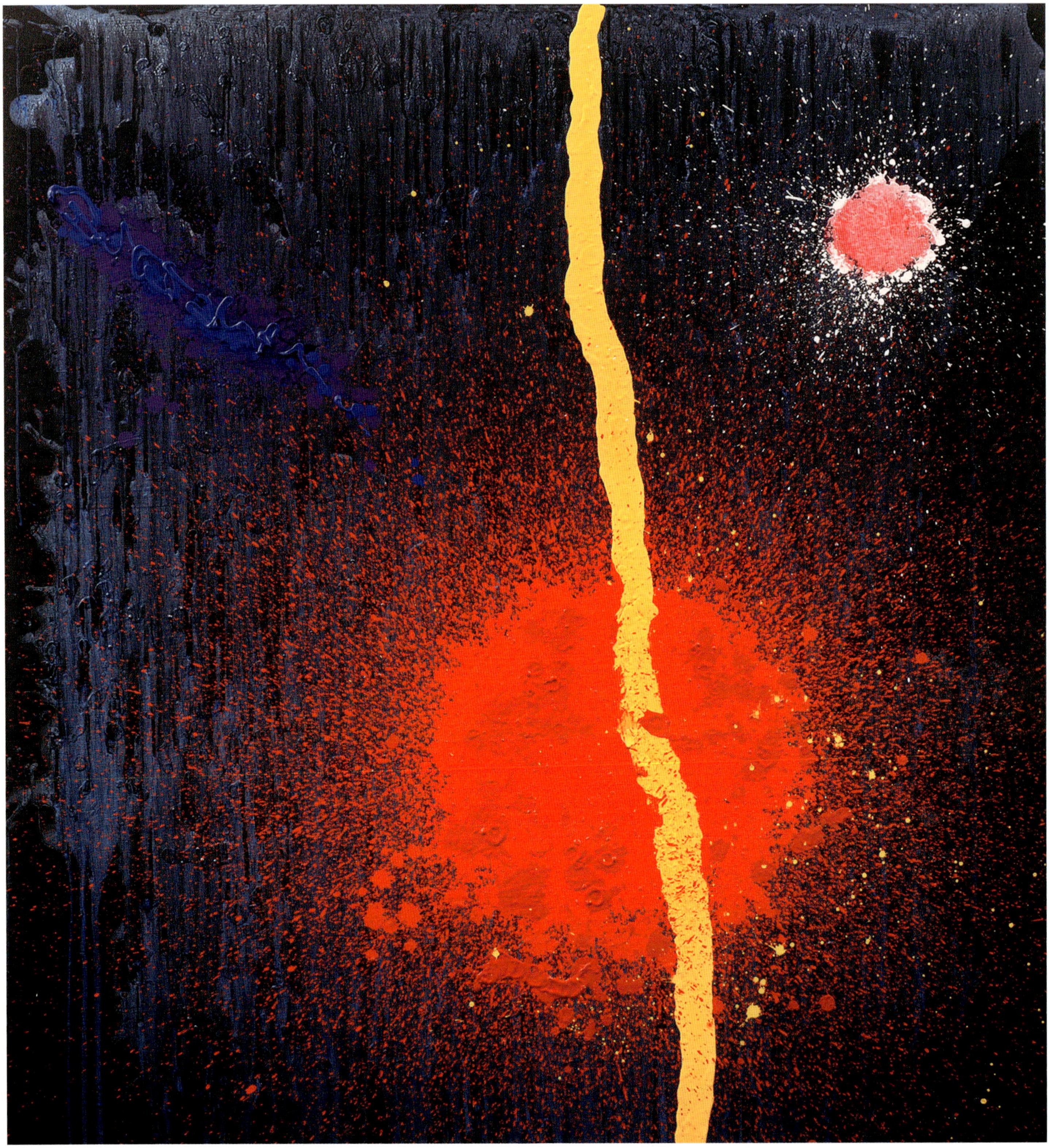

River of Bliss, 24.6.09
Acrylic on cotton duck
152.5 × 140 cm (60 × 55 inches)

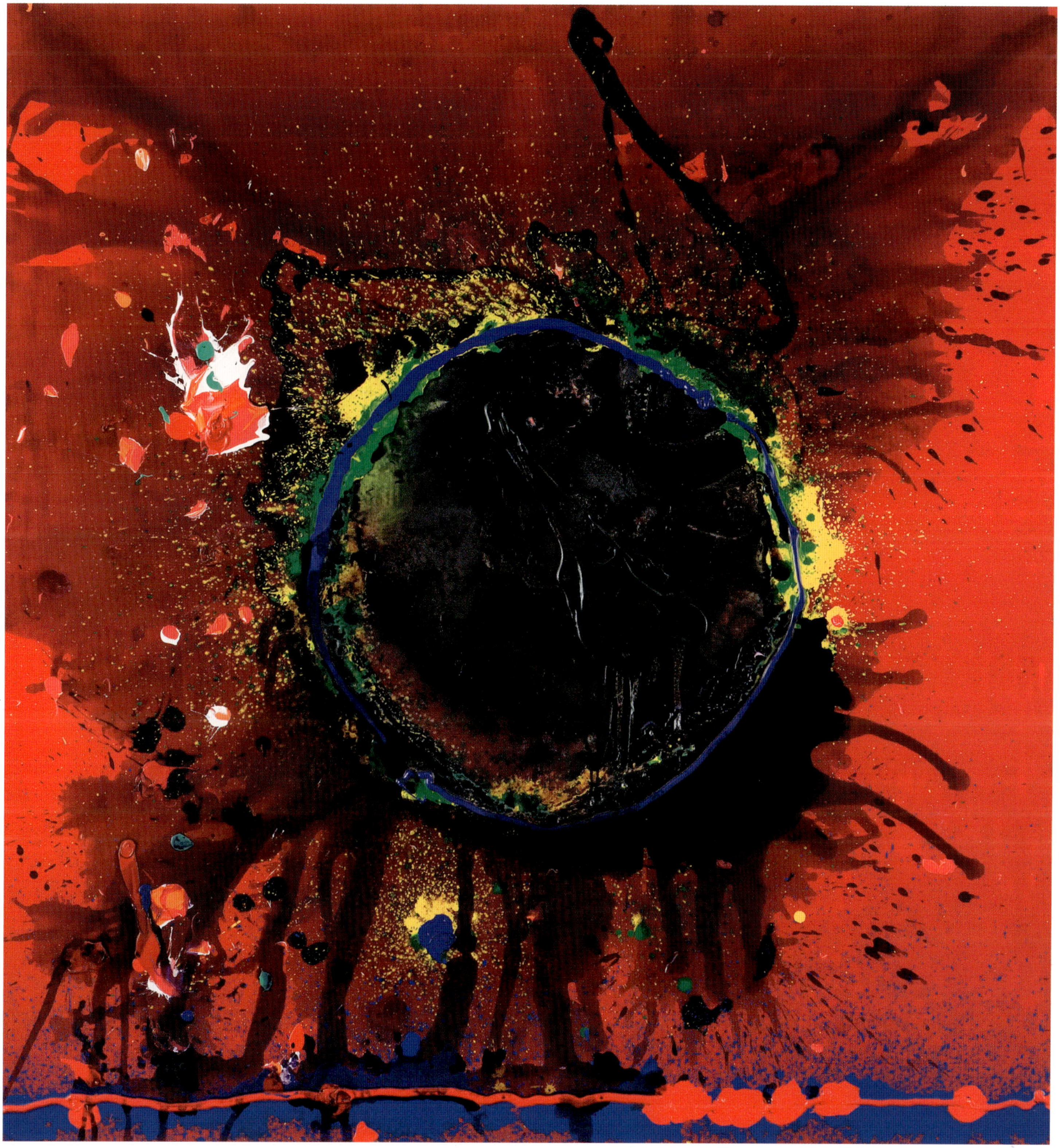

Blind Sun, 24.9.08
Acrylic on cotton duck
152.5 × 140 cm (60 × 55 inches)

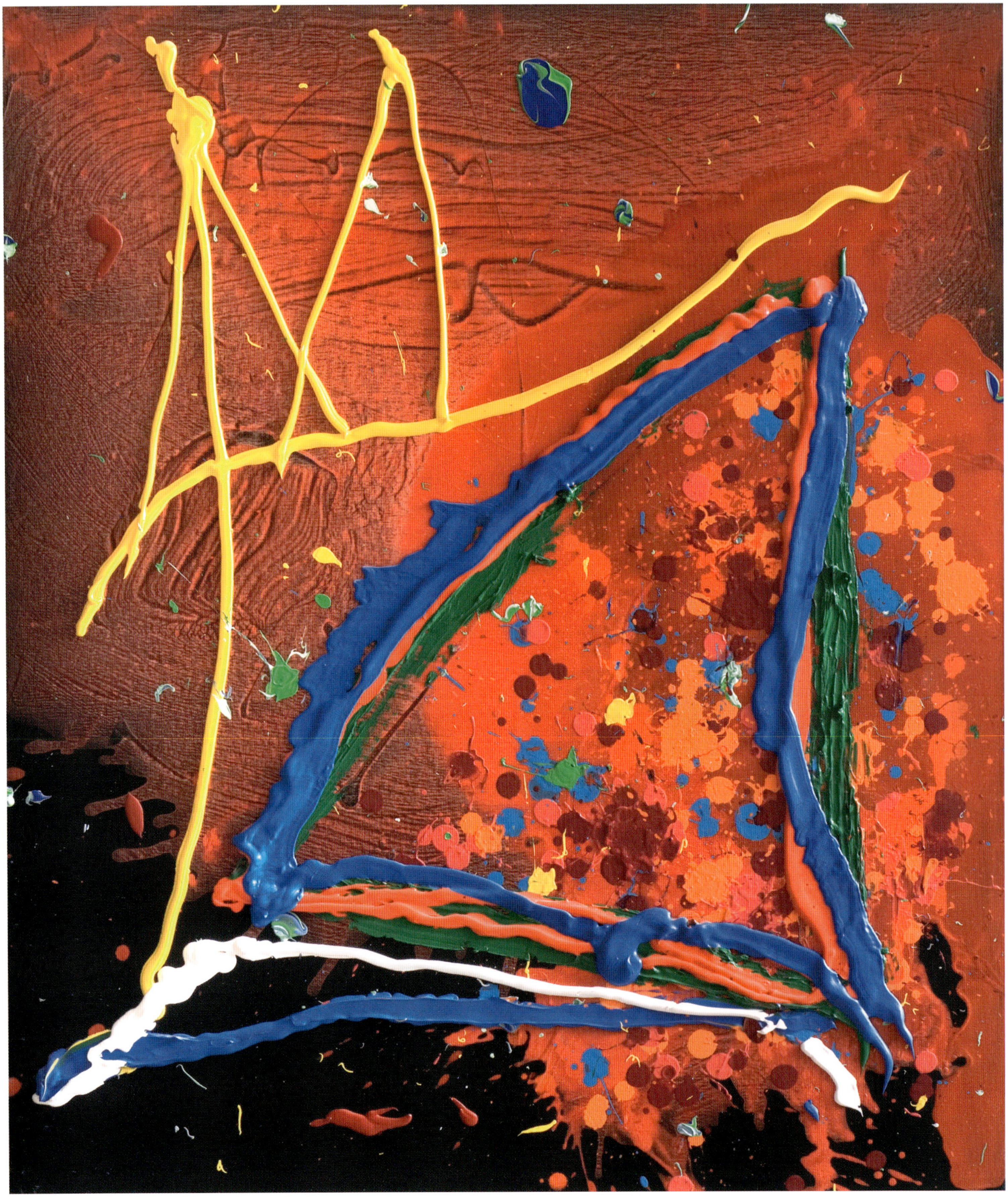

6

Polemic and Belief

Hoyland can be bracingly rude about his contemporaries. He is no respecter of material success or establishment honours, and sees it almost as a duty to deflate the self-important. This is all part-and-parcel of his attitude to art. As he wrote in his introduction to the 1982 Hayward Annual: 'Real art cannot be grasped, learned or understood quickly. Real art evades easy description, discourages amusing anecdotes, confronts glamour and camp with a stony, unblinking eye, and is not welcome in colour supplement land.' So now you know. His seriousness is not to be trifled with.

Hoyland holds strong opinions on most subjects and rarely refrains from expressing them. He gets so angry because he cares passionately. He sees it as his duty to keep informed about contemporary life and would never rely on the political correctitude of the BBC's censored news output. He tunes in to Russian, Chinese and Spanish news channels (with translation) to see how the other half reports. He relishes the cut-and-thrust of debate, and his comments are sharp and to the point and often very funny. But spontaneous wit and repartee, however amusing at the moment of utterance, do not transfer well to the printed page. (As they say: jazz hot, disgusting cold.) Even well-argued invective loses its point when read out of context. For this reason I have decided to confine my quotations of Hoyland's polemic to a couple of examples, leaving aside for the moment his diatribes against insufferably trendy left-wing critics in the 1970s, or the improperly biased selection of the *American Art in the 20th Century* exhibition at the RA in 1993.

But the humour will keep breaking through. A spoof he wrote in Sydney (16.7.94) remorselessly lists what he calls *Museum People's Rights*:

> 'The importance of fashion-driven politically-correct museum people cannot be overstated. They are right on with Women's Rights, Gay Rights, Dolphin Rights, Rights of Whales, Transsexual Rights, We Haven't Made Our Minds Up Yet Rights, Ozone Layer Rights, Nuclear Free Zone Rights, Never In The Office

Rebel Mountain, 22.12.07
Acrylic on cotton duck
91.5 × 76 cm (36 × 30 inches)

Rights, Always At The Party Rights, Send The Free Tickets Rights, Won't Be Back Today Rights, She's Overseas Rights, Choosing A Show Rights, Chairing A Meeting Rights, Could We Have Your Name Rights, Well Just In Case He's Lost It Rights, Could You Spell It Rights, He's Having Lunch Rights, With A Dealer Rights, It's A Wonderful Building Rights, A Wonderful Museum Rights, A Proud Monument Rights, To The Director's Rights, And All The Curators Rights, Waiting For Their Pension Rights, With Free Parking Space Rights, But We Need More Space Rights, To Expand The Gallery Rights, The Art Lovers Are Growing Rights, It's Our Duty To Serve Their Rights, Artists Are Such An Inconvenience, You're Right, But We Can Handle Them Rights, They Have No Rights, That's Right.

'To Be Continued.'

In 2005 he gave a talk in Mauritius which he titled *Invisible Artist or Performing Bear*, itself a version of a talk first given at the Tate Gallery in 1994. The following is extracted from it:

'Artists live in the real world, but most of the time they are invisible. Occasionally they are wheeled out like performing bears, hence this occasion. We all live in a world of information, surrounded by a remorseless torrent of rubbish being poured daily into our minds. The dreariness of calculated processes, bad manners, dishonesty and no respect for the old or young. Lack of leadership in government and the church, the banks, the city, the media, style gurus, Spin Doctors, soundbites, public relations men, advertising, fashion and greed. Publishers who manipulate their readers, art dealers masquerading as collectors rigging the markets, self-important museum directors involved only in power, looking for the main chance under the guise of education, and the torch-bearers of hype, the music and film industry, the men who sold their souls and have carried the young, ignorant and most vulnerable, in their hideous wake. Ethics and business are uncomfortable bedfellows. This is life in Britain.

'As you will see, the only sanctuary left for the artist, or anyone else for that matter, is to escape into the imagination – in my case, through art.

'Art is about making ethical and poetical judgements and developing discerning taste (and by this I don't mean "good taste"), in order to bring together a number of generalities to a concrete formal conclusion, which the artist hopes will make a bridge between him and his audience. Art is about making transformations. This is done through the constant practice of

In March 2002, while holidaying in Havana, Hoyland penned the following satiric ditty:

THE ARTWORLD
CORNER A NICHE IN SEWING
OR INTELLECTUAL GAMES
FAITH IN NEW TECHNOLOGY
IRONY REMAINS
STORY-TELLING PASSION
WHO'S YOUR GURU
BACK TO THE NATIONAL
GALLERY, THAT WILL NEVER DO.
EUPHORIA UNBOUNDED
VISUAL CONCEITS
NURSERY RHYMES AND PICTURE GAMES OR
PRIMITIVE DECEITS
A FOOL'S GOLD OBSESSION FOR
FORMULAS OLD AND NEW
LINES AND DOTS AND CIRCLES
THAT WILL NEVER DO.

Flying Life, 15.3.03
Acrylic on cotton duck
61 × 51 cm (24 × 20 inches)

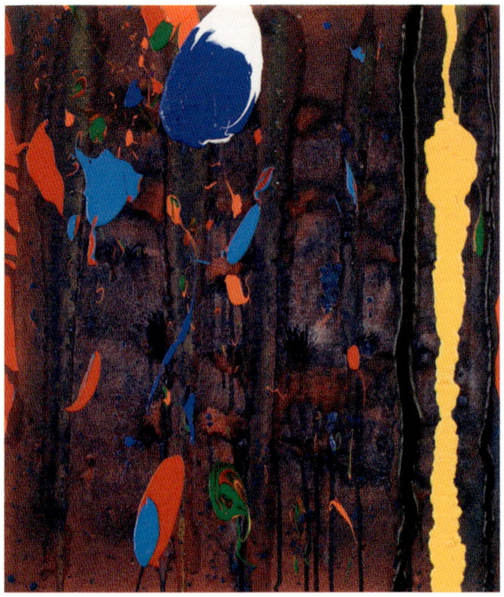

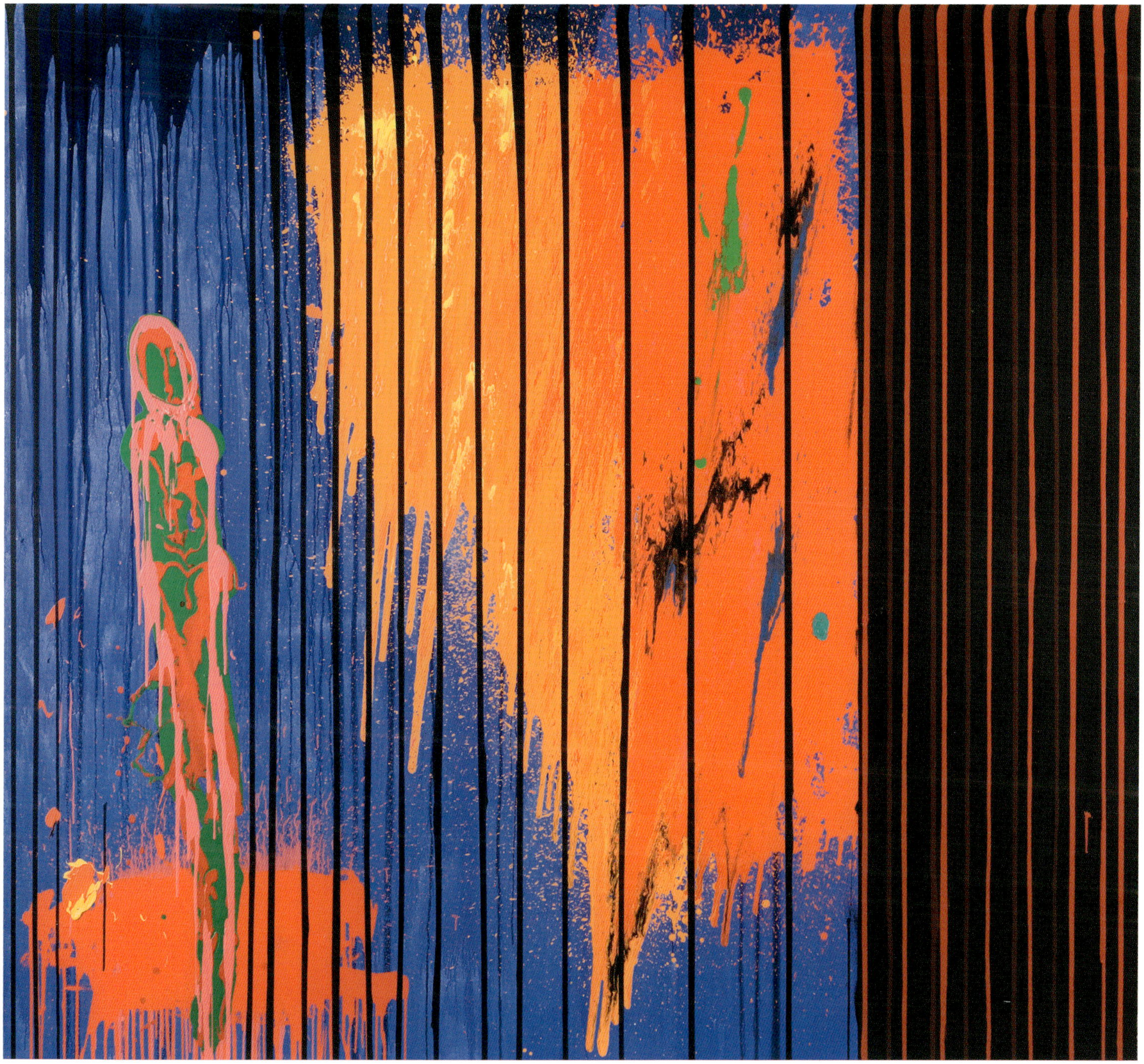

Alone, 21.10.00
Acrylic on cotton duck
236 × 254 cm (93 × 100 inches)

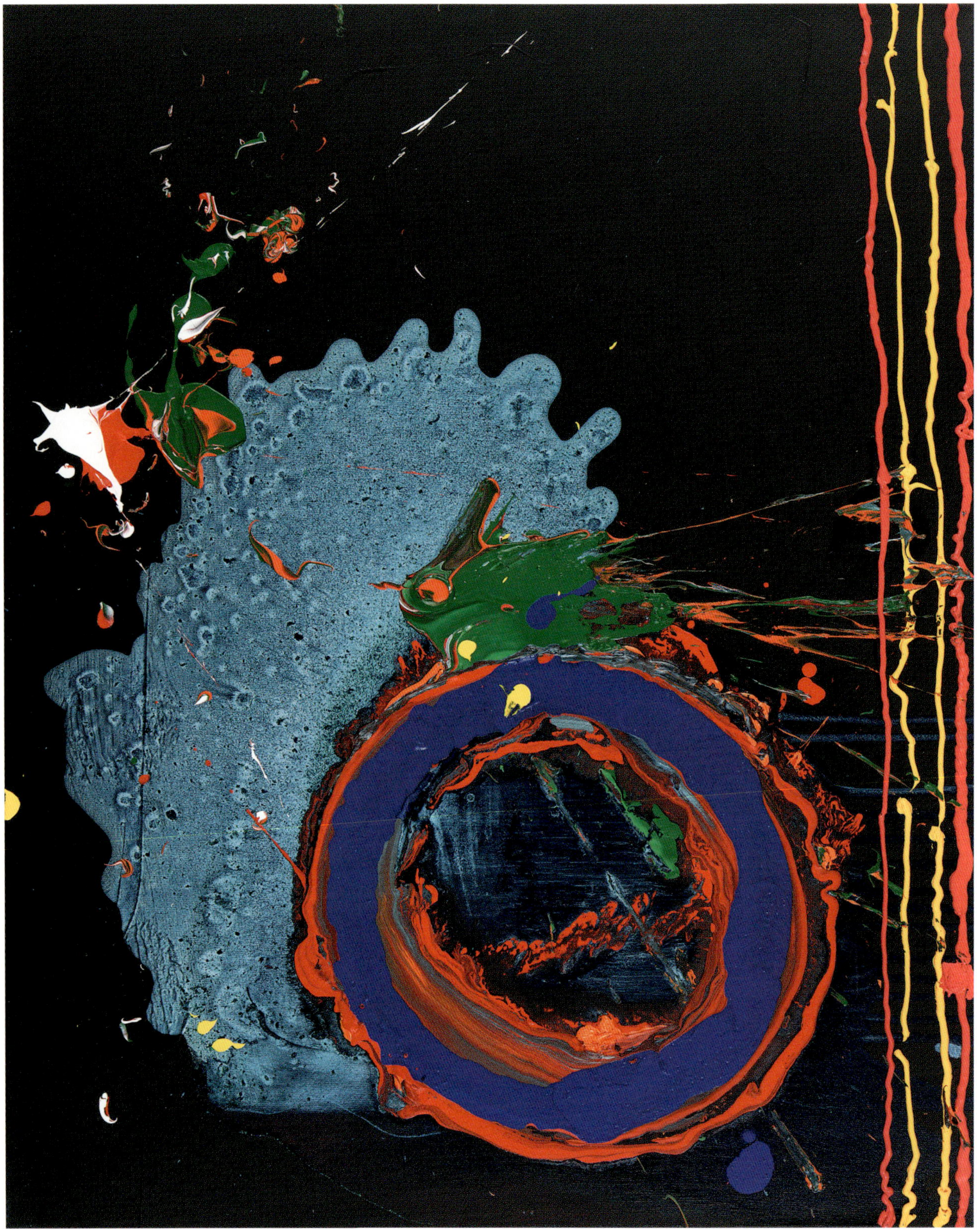

Blue Moon Wind, 1.1.03
Acrylic on cotton duck
127 × 102 cm (50 × 40 inches)

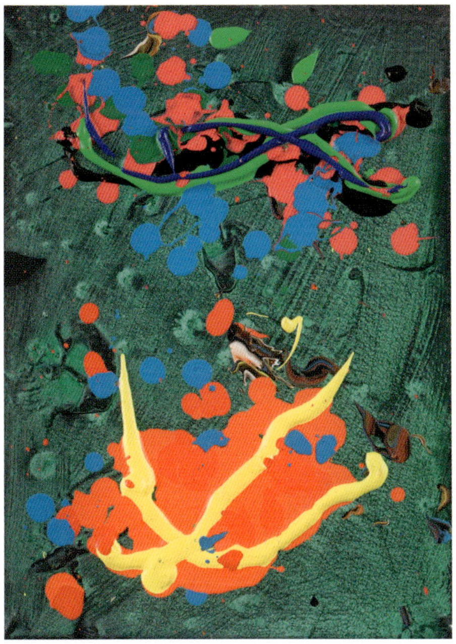

Yellow Bird, 30.12.03
Acrylic on cotton duck
36 × 25.5 cm (14 × 10 inches)

Night Bathers, 25.10.01
Acrylic on cotton duck
56 × 46 cm (22 × 18 inches)

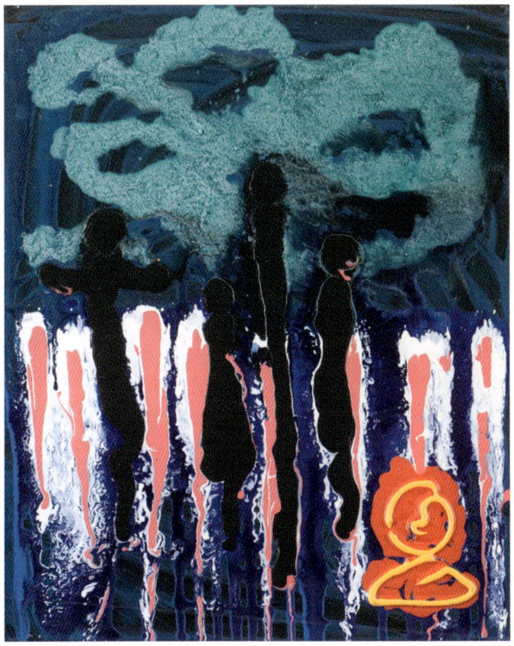

producing art, but it is often the unexpected encounters and intuitive, irrational choices made along the way that bring about the transformation of work. There is also a selective body of knowledge, a context for art, of whatever form. Birthright, one's culture, one's genes, emotional make-up, being working class, middle class or aristocratic etc etc. Education, life's accidents and the light of experience. There is also desire made concrete. Painting is the will and the whole self in harmony, without self-deception but, as Braque said, in the end the problem with art is that you can explain almost anything except the bit that matters.

'I approach my work in a vaguely dialectical way through a form of criticism, trying to investigate a mixture of logic, imagination and empirical accident, trying to break the logical mould.

'Over-valued reason is like political absolutism. Reason sets boundaries, wishing us only to accept the known and live in a framework as if we were sure how far life can extend. The more critical reason dominates, the more we are impoverished. Spontaneity is less about the unconscious and more about inventing new forms, new structures, in which hopefully can be embedded the spirit concealed within the image.

'I would like to make archetypal images of wholeness and have tried to broaden my work over the years, to stretch abstraction, giving it a human face, incorporating the radiance of Matisse and Rothko, the plastic construction of de Staël and Hofmann, and the evocation and innovation of Miró and Picasso – and I'm the first to admit it's a tall order. Picasso saw and learned from African art the freedom to distort, together with formal vitality. Jung said, "vivid colours attract the unconscious", and Matisse spoke of "the beneficent radiation of colour and its power to heal".

'Unfortunately, we are hemmed in by kitsch and novelty, instant gratification and glib posturing, silly nostalgic homages to neo-data, manic conceits and self-aggrandisement, not to mention sexual politics. It is difficult for art to exist in such a low context – survival is threatened.

'Britain is visually uncultivated, cultivation being fine as long as you stick to gardening and you'd better keep it neat. I want an art that has a spiritual dimension, but spirituality or the metaphysical cannot be built to order. We live in a secular, mass culture surrounded by cliché-ridden, so-called advanced art that has become decadent and entirely commercial. Making art for art's sake is the only way that honesty can be achieved. Finding the images that lie behind emotions produced by the mind, hand, eye, memory and heart.

'London – and perhaps the whole of England – for me seems to have little or no poetry. It doesn't encourage a poetic vision of life. Perhaps it's the weather, the light, the vegetation and certainly many of the people.

'Sometimes I hate my anglo-saxonness, the clodhopping, dull mongrelness. Perhaps this is my way to cling to other cultures for sustenance – the exotic in art, place, people and music. I never believed in the dominance of European culture. I want more magic, more drama, black or white but not grey. Not accountants, bank managers, computer programmers, trade unionists, hairdressers and media personalities. I feel swamped by the saturation techniques of the advertising men who more and more have taken over from the artist, the poet and the madman. England is a small, bland, mean little island with manufactured eccentrics, counterfeit emotions and anger – a controlled response as dead as a video. I want the spiritual and the sub-conscious blended with the external world. I have also wanted for a long time to make art that would communicate directly across racial, social, political and linguistic barriers and to pursue an open discussion with art, both old and new, in a diverse cultural context. Here one has to consider whether one's own culture contains the models one needs in order to create new hybrids, because that is what it's all about. Many artists in the past have been indebted to non-European cultural models and in the 21st century it would seem to be logical that this could occur. Otherwise, we shall drown in a sea of mediocrity.'

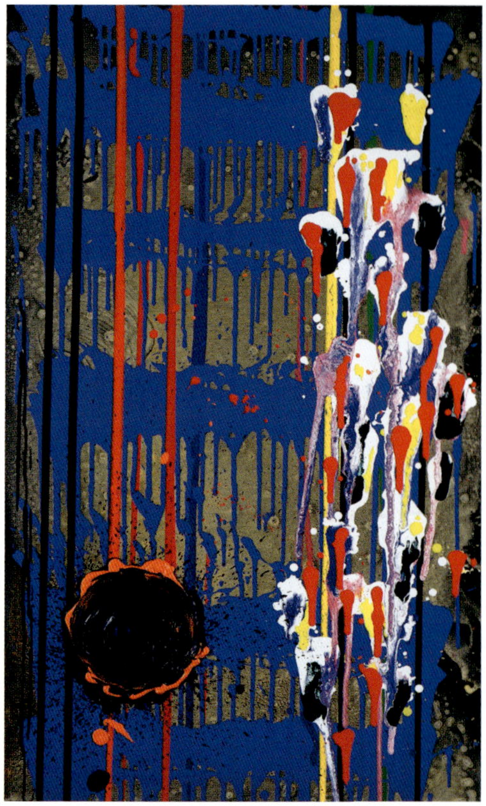

Celebration, 10.2.05
Acrylic on cotton duck
127 × 76 cm (50 × 30 inches)

In his talk, Hoyland also mentioned visiting a Biennale of contemporary art in Sharjah in the Arab Emirates. 'I attended a conference with one of the selectors of this show, and we could not understand the arguments and things being discussed. They were conducted in a language of jargon, art speak, politics, power games and, frankly, "Art Bollocks". This situation is a very difficult one for young artists as they are easily drawn into the mire of fashion, politics and money. Never have I seen less love or spirituality under one large roof. There were endless tedious videos – I call them bad home movies – posturing and naïve, no joy or youthful enthusiasm, no celebration of life, of nature or of love, but no shortage of gimmicks. I regard them as the Theatre of Impotence. To me they are a fashionable form of nihilism.'

In an evocative phrase, Hoyland refers to 'the ancient and shifting language of painting and sculpture'. Thankfully, he cannot resist the opportunity to say something more positive about making art, our hope for the future.

'Perhaps I might take the liberty of offering some advice to young artists: Look at things until you can see what else they are, or might become. Try to develop a pattern of awareness by creating in your minds gardens of pictures. Tune into their rivers of association. Fragments of association can become the tools of mysticism even with all its inherent dangers.

'Imagine if one could bring about an experience in others from atoms, suns, space, time, light and darkness, and most of all colour. Finally, avoid all doctrines.

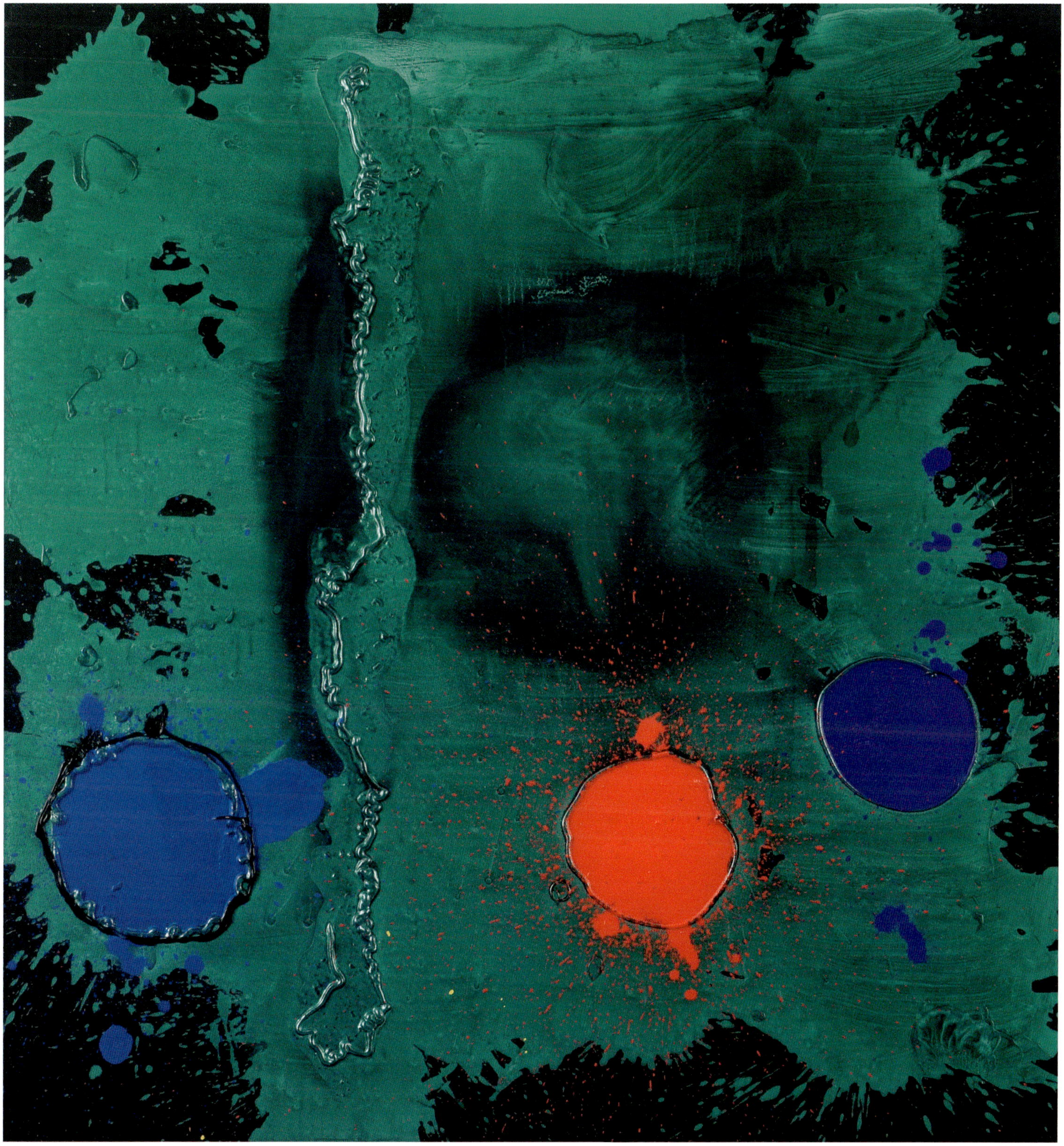

Moment, 2.1.09
Acrylic on cotton duck
152.5 × 140 cm (60 × 55 inches)

'Paintings are a seduction, one develops a relationship with these inanimate objects which becomes a bond like a living person, a mirror, a realm of elusive power. Art plays a game of structural truthfulness, it becomes alive. It contains and understands ecstasy through colour as light. The artist must try to make every song sing and push beyond the fixing of appearances. There is no place for cynicism, only joy, passion and wonderment, clarity and eagerness. Painting should be made to look easy, painting as the embodiment of what it is to be human. Paintings are a kind of dream language, and like music they propose a new reality. Simplicity can give them their greatest power.'

Hoyland then turns from the general to the particular. 'In my own work I am trying to accept the forces of nature, and the power of the human spirit. They have allowed me to grow and to experience a view of both the simplicity and the overwhelming complexity of nature and man. In daring to imagine there are no straightforward answers, perhaps it's an illusion daring to dream but this is what makes art so exciting.

'Finally, what is the subject of my work? I can only hazard a guess, but I can give you a list of things: masks, mirrors, Avebury Circle, views from planes, mountains, waterfalls, graffiti, damp walls, cracked pavements, the cosmos, tropical fruit, drink, sex, music, the tropical light, oceanic light, Mediterranean light, tribal art, Indian, Japanese and Chinese art, drums, jazz, Africa Highlife music, reggae, soul, latin and classical, modern dance, magic realism, Borges, the metaphysical, dawn, sunset, atolls, flowers, The Book of Imaginary Beings, The Dictionary of Angels, Bangkok, Rio de Janeiro, Montego Bay, Cuba and Bali and Mauritius.

'In order to create a sense of magic, trying to transform the commonplace into the real to make paradise.'

Here's a poem Hoyland began in Mauritius in April 2005 and then re-wrote in London during the year. It's like a catechism or a series of injunctions to himself, to be repeated into the shaving mirror before entering the studio, a daily affirmation of belief:

PAINTING IS A LIFETIME'S EFFORT
LIGHTNESS AND DEPTH
CREATED FROM THE BODY
NATURE, POETRY, SILENCE
THE ELEMENTAL
FIND YOUR OWN NATURE
PAINT THE OCEAN AFLAME AND THE RIPENED SKY
CHANGE THOSE WHO STAND BEFORE YOUR IMAGES
YOU WALK THE EARTH ALONE
THE TROPICS ARE CLOSER TO THE ESSENCE OF THINGS
PAINTING IS BEYOND EARTHLY MATTERS
BEYOND THE PHYSICAL
IT IS THE ENDGAME
ONLY FOR THE GENIUS OF A FEW

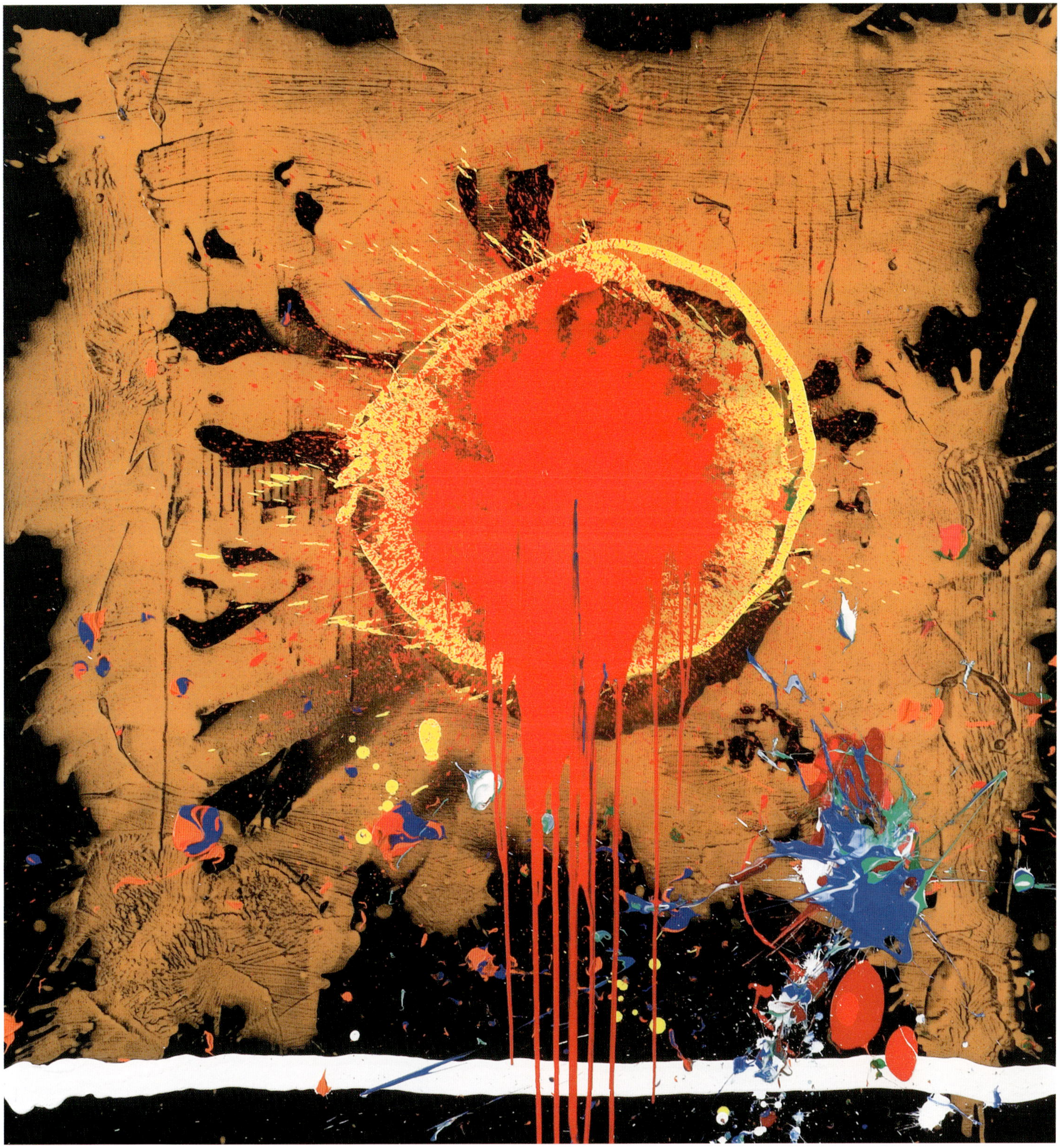

Blood Song, 24.11.08
Acrylic on cotton duck
152.5 × 140 cm (60 × 55 inches)

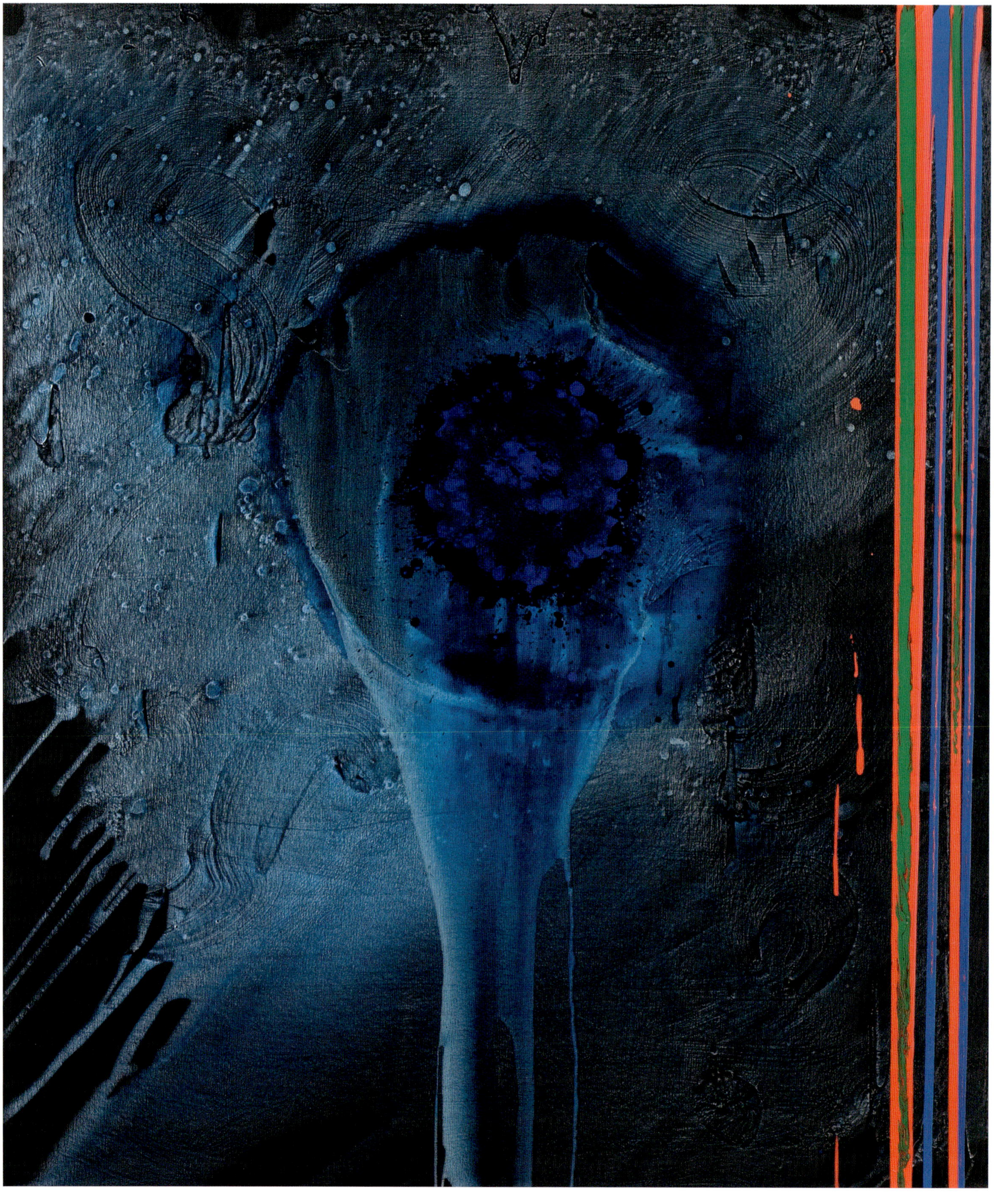

7

Progenitors

Among the great historical English artists, Hoyland has been especially drawn to Turner. 'He is wonderful. Some of the first great paintings I saw were Turner watercolours in the Graves Art Gallery in Sheffield. And Cotman and Peter de Wint. The Junior Art School was very near there – 200 yards away.

'I started out painting a lot of landscapes. When you're young you paint what you know, what you've seen. You paint the garden, you paint your Dad, you paint the dog, you paint your girlfriend. When you're old you don't care what the fuck you do! You're more free to just dive in and take risks and you can always dip back into your earlier work. What Picasso called the "unlearning process".' Hoyland admires Picasso highly and is shrewdly observant of his work. (He also admires Matisse but mentions him less.) He comments of Picasso: 'I've thought for years that in a way his work is so well constructed that if instead of a third sculptor, two-thirds painter, he'd been the other way round, he might have been even greater. They look like blueprints for sculpture, a lot of his paintings.'

Hoyland feels free to make reference to his early work in his current paintings just as he likes to salute key figures who have influenced him, such as Vincent van Gogh, Chaim Soutine or Nicolas de Staël. Each artist builds up a personal tradition of artists who have been important or inspirational. As Ben Nicholson observed, looking back on his earlier life: 'One finds only the influences one is looking for …' One of the key early figures for Hoyland was de Staël, an artist also interested in his progenitors. De Staël made many drawings analysing the Old Masters, a habit that Hans Hofmann shared too, and, just to keep the interconnectedness going, Hoyland observes that Hofmann himself was influenced by de Staël. This all chimes with T S Eliot's belief that there can be no originality without a basis in tradition. Or as Varvara Stepanova, the Constructivist visionary, noted in the title of a *c.*1919 drawing: *Study the old, but create the new.*

One of his earliest and most abiding interests has been in van Gogh. In recent years Hoyland has made a whole series of paintings in homage to the Dutch master. As he says: 'Van Gogh was always at the back of my mind. Sheffield Art School had

Bouquet for Vincent, 3.4.06
Acrylic on cotton duck
152.5 × 127 cm (60 × 50 inches)

such a poor representation of anything around the turn of the century, but there were these little Skira books. (I've still got one.) In one of those I first saw *Starry Night*, and *The Café at Night* and I read about him. I re-read his letters not too long ago and then I read Martin Gayford's book *The Yellow House*, which is an imaginative reconstruction of his life with Gauguin. It started me thinking nostalgically of Vincent, but he's always been one of my great heroes. And Gauguin.'

Among the paintings that Hoyland has produced that reference van Gogh, *Bouquet for Vincent* (3.4.06) is one of the most splendid, with its poured banks of colour down the right side of the painting. The iridescent paint changes as you walk past it. Green was poured wet over the red, in a burst of almost Fauvist fervour. In one way this painting marks a return to the red/green combinations of the 1960s, and in another is a pure 2006 salute to van Gogh. Others in the series are *Letter to Vincent* (8.7.06) and the cobalt raptures of *For Vincent* (21.10.08).

John McEwen wrote in 1979 of Hoyland that 'only Matthew Smith, of English modernists, has used colour so lavishly.' In 1997 Hoyland reviewed a new biography of Matthew Smith by Malcolm Yorke for *The Spectator*. His review is an excellent assessment of an unfairly neglected artist. It is also fascinating for what it reveals about the writer. Here it is, quoted in full:

> 'I remember Clement Greenberg saying in the mid Sixties that the worst painters in New York were better than the best painters in England. To me this was a red rag to a bull; how dare this egotistical, insensitive critic make such an outlandish, xenophobic claim? It couldn't be true, and it wasn't, quite, but in retrospect I know what he meant. In the Sixties American art, for those of us who spent the majority of our time over there, lifted our work and our spirits. Something was in the air: Rothko, Motherwell, Newman, Kline and de Kooning were painting there, Pollock and Louis had just died.
>
> 'Several decades earlier, this had happened to Matthew Smith, born in 1879. After leaving the Slade, he was in France – in the right place at the right time. He exhibited in the Salon des Indépendants alongside Matisse, Derain, Dufy, Vlaminck and others. He knew them, or of them; his role may have been minor but showing amongst artists of such stature is a great confidence-builder and would have given him an opportunity to make comparisons, and for self-criticism. Perhaps in the artist's mind there is an imagined golden thread attaching him to the great artists of the past and to his idols. He had only worked briefly in the Matisse school but three weeks listening to Matisse, I would guess, would be more valuable than four years in Manchester and three years at the Slade. This would have given him the opportunity to see Matisse the man. A man like himself, not a god, a man experimenting and asking questions, a man who worshipped his own gods.

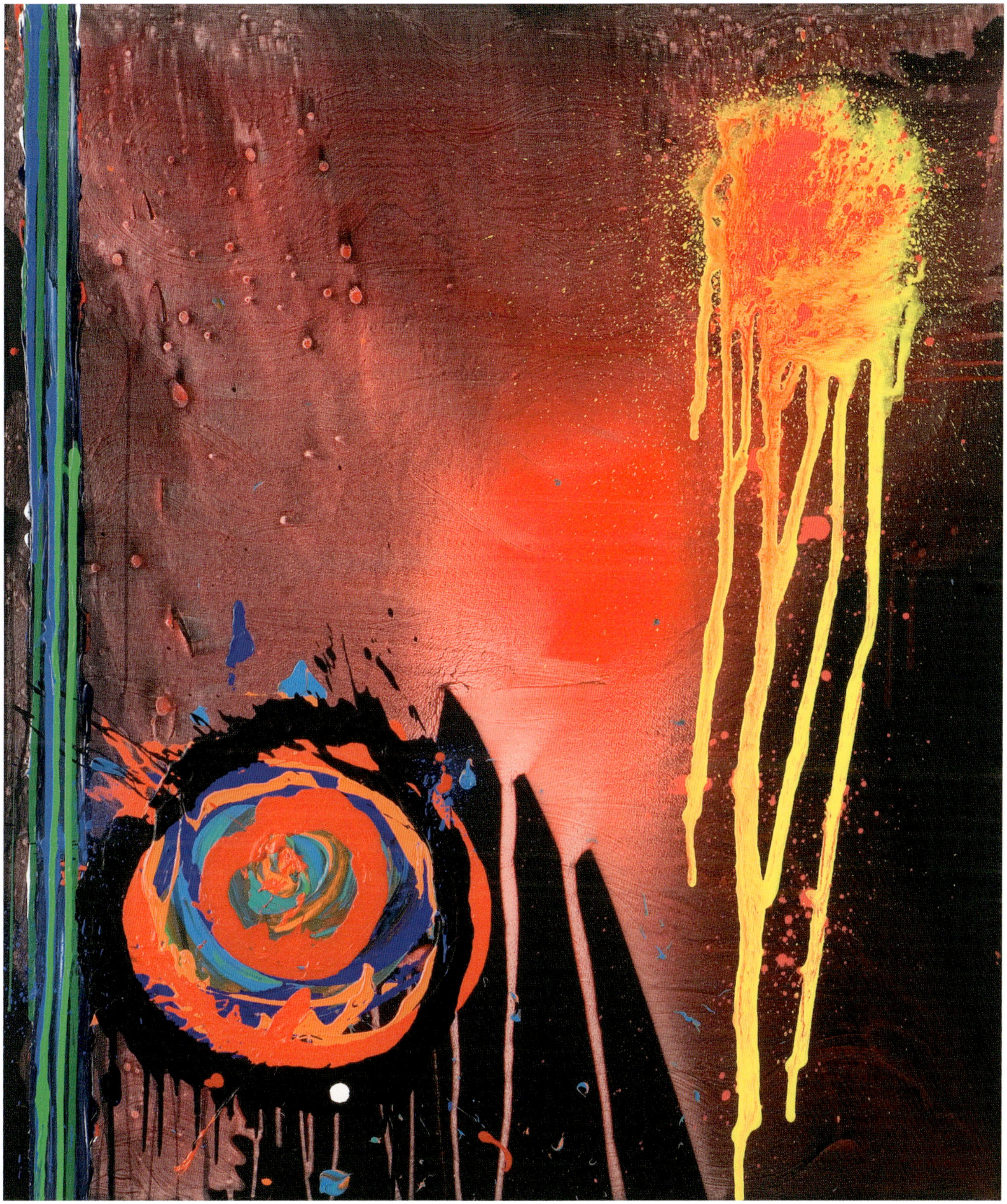

Letter to Vincent, 8.7.06
Acrylic on cotton duck
152.5 × 127 cm (60 × 50 inches)

'Matthew Smith was born into a typically Victorian family in Halifax, Yorkshire, where his father was a successful factory owner; a stern but good man considered to be highly intelligent, he pursued refined taste within the limited possibilities of provincial Victorian England. Naturally he wished his sons to succeed and prosper and in his view there was no way that this could be done as an artist. Art was for leisure. Matthew was the oddball, shy and awkward, and seemingly physically weak with troublesome eyes and a record of failure at the jobs his father found for him. There was a showdown. Matthew had decided he wanted to study art and won. This showed steel behind the timid exterior. After art at Manchester Municipal School of Technology (father still hedging his bets) he was placed, comfortably, at the Slade School. I was entertained by Yorke's collection of anecdotes about the Slade, the Royal Academy and the heroes of the day. Wilson Steer pronounced on van Gogh ("shouted too loud"); Sickert advised Gauguin to stick to painting as a hobby; Tonks, the Slade professor, taught students to hate French painting and how to draw with a plumb line. The public wanted detail, high finish, stories and melodrama, painted painstakingly with consummate skill. Art schools taught the English disease of over-refinement ("I don't think you have quite resolved the nose"). Not much has changed.

'Smith was lucky; he had a rich daddy who, though reluctant, paid for everything, including travel. He lived an enviable life, wining and dining with interesting people and if they weren't interesting they were rich and supportive. Smith was a hypochondriac (a professional one); the type who complains that he is worn out from attending his friends' funerals, always moaning about something to divert people from his innate selfishness, while driving others to despair, but this was perhaps his only protection. His shield against self-doubt. Smith became very successful in England. By the time he was 40, his colourfully robust work set him apart from his contemporaries. Smith had managed to do something that few English painters achieve. He painted light with colour through colour volume, paint was paint and paint was form, but the paint also had a life of its own. There is none of the illustrational melodrama and theatricality of Bacon, nor the timid expressionism of some of our "leading" or is it "leaden" painters; his best works were a pure force. He was a northerner; like van Gogh and Matisse he lusted for the sun, the wine and the women (with whom he seems to have been very successful) and though his manners were impeccable, his nickname was "the Moth" – we see him trying to pick up waitresses, feeling up secretaries in galleries and seducing friends' wives. The fact that he always "had a few bob" may have facilitated his many successes. He had what I would describe as canniness, which others might see as Yorkshire meanness: generous when it was to his benefit. Being a

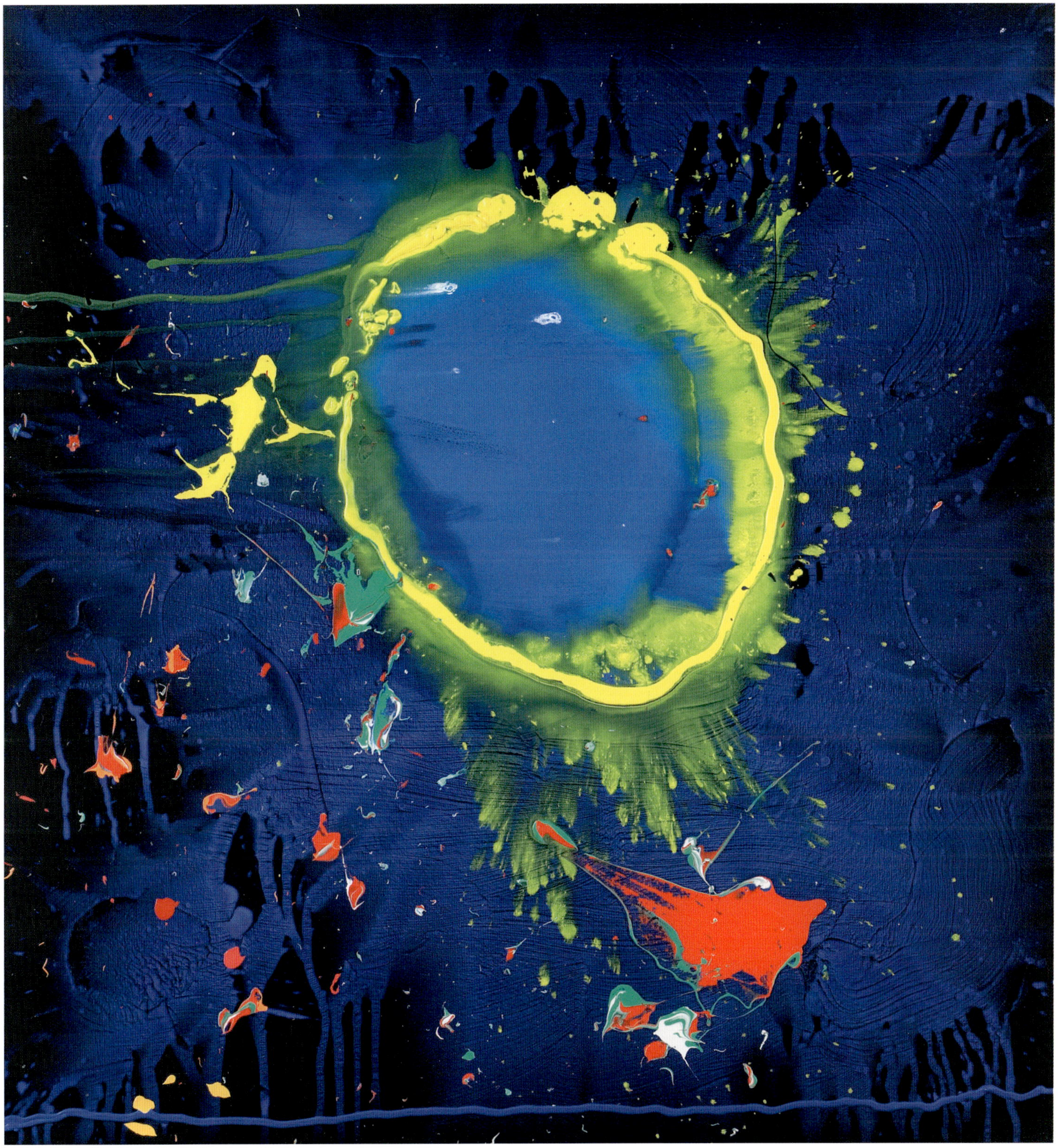

For Vincent, 21.10.08
Acrylic on cotton duck
152.5 × 140 cm (60 × 55 inches)

> Yorkshire man, he didn't like being taken for a ride and this was his form of natural justice.
>
> 'As a painter, Matthew Smith never had a "big idea" and lacked the physical and intellectual rigour of the greatest artists that he admired. He didn't have the breadth of ambition. Nevertheless, he achieved moments of great beauty in his finest works. He was not a Gauguin, whom he admired, but there are some parallels. Thinking of Gauguin in Tahiti, all these events took place over the past one hundred years. Smith's achievements took place fifty years later and today it seems that little has changed, not in art, the establishment or public attitude. But in art one hundred years is a drop in the ocean.
>
> 'When an artist enters his studio, no matter how much money he has – he still has to confront himself through the painting – he is alone; money is of no importance. Before I read Malcolm Yorke's book I knew nothing about Matthew Smith the man. This is a lively, well-researched book full of amazing anecdotes, background detail, and cross-references to the historical context and it paints a wonderful picture of the life and times of Matthew Smith. Mr Yorke displays an understanding of how painting works and how we all develop in different ways. Malcolm Yorke's life of Matthew Smith helps convincingly to explain what made him tick.'

There are a number of key passages here. Firstly: 'Perhaps in the artist's mind there is an imagined golden thread attaching him to the great artists of the past and to his idols.' This surely is the way Hoyland thinks in terms of his own artistic progenitors. Secondly: he writes of the importance of getting to know great artists in person. For Matthew Smith this was Matisse, for Hoyland it was Rothko, Newman, Motherwell and the rest of the Americans. Thirdly: the English disease of over-refinement crops up again – 'I don't think you have quite resolved the nose.' And finally: 'By the time he was 40, his colourfully robust work set him apart from his contemporaries. Smith had managed to do something that few English painters achieve. He painted light with colour through colour volume, paint was paint and paint was form, but the paint also had a life of its own.' This could be an assessment of Hoyland's own work.

8

Hoyland as Curator

In 1980, Hoyland selected the Hayward Annual, a review of contemporary painting and sculpture more usually the choice of a committee. It was a signal honour to be asked, offering real recognition of his place in the art world. Hoyland made no pretence of the show being a comprehensive survey of current British painting, this was to be a personal selection. It focused on 18 painters, with a contextual addition of other artists. The painters included Gillian Ayres, Basil Beattie, Brian Fielding, Clyde Hopkins, Albert Irvin, John McLean and Terry Setch. The contextual figures included Anthony Caro, Patrick Caulfield, Terry Frost, Roger Hilton, Ivon Hitchens, Ben Nicholson, William Scott and Matthew Smith. The critic Tim Hilton called it 'the first major group show of serious painting to be held in England since the "Situation" exhibition in 1960.'

In his introduction to the catalogue, Hoyland paid tribute to the sculptors, and especially to Caro, whose 1963 Whitechapel show 'marked a turning point for art in this country'. As Tim Hilton wrote about Caro in his catalogue essay: 'The fact that his sculpture was radical was not as important to painters as was the fact that he represented high art, and also internationalism. Through him there was a direct route to American achievements.'

The real reason for giving the exhibition space here is for the light it casts on Hoyland's thought processes. As he admitted in the catalogue: 'Painting is not easy to write about and I cannot describe or explain these works. I would suggest that their very nature and seriousness denies instant communication. They will not reveal all their secrets immediately. If approached with caution and curiosity, gradually their true identity will be recognized. Some will remain elusive, a dusty mirror withholding secrets, that is their essence. Don't expect instant gratification. Look at these paintings as you would listen to music. Hearing music is abstract, but we are more conditioned to sounds. Perhaps we have been too literal, too object-orientated. We have refused to look and enjoy abstract relationships, harmonies of colour and form which we do without question in music. No one surely would ask, "Does music have meaning?" It appeals to the emotions but we don't attempt to specify these feelings. Music doesn't illustrate emotion. Though a title may suggest the direction of the composer's thoughts. So it is with painting.

'What the painters also share in common is their "belief" in the medium of painting, in its directness, its responsiveness both illusive and allusive, infinitely variable in behaviour, and alchemic in its magical fusions. Painting doesn't need any gadgetry and disallows gimmickry. It survives unaided as a pure force.'

Hoyland goes on to attack the failure of many influential critics to believe in British Art. 'This represents a major failure of responsibility', he writes. 'A failure of nerve and imagination to recognise and pull together a complex and fragmented situation.' He concludes with a plea for understanding. 'We are still developing, gaining in understanding and confidence. It is the only way. Be patient, and try to make that connection, find that bridge which the artist is building between himself and you. Painters know that the choices are never simple.'

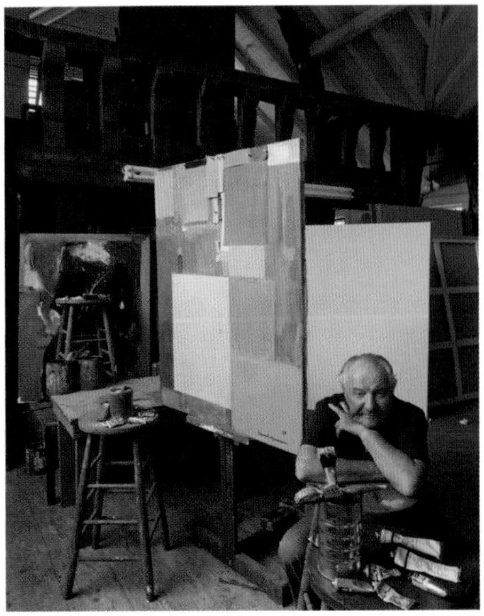

Hofmann in his studio in 1956

The other exhibition that Hoyland curated in the 1980s which was also of immense relevance to his own work as a painter was *Hans Hofmann: Late Paintings* at the Tate Gallery (March–May 1988). Hofmann had not been included in either of the Tate surveys of the New American Painting in 1956 and 1959, and was probably the least known of the great Abstract Expressionists, and to some extent remains so even today. Hoyland had first encountered Hofmann's work in New York in 1964, in the company of Clement Greenberg, and was immediately impressed. He had continued to look out for his work.

In the catalogue he wrote: 'During those years, the early sixties, we were regularly bombarded by American Art and we awaited each new instalment like food parcels to a half-starved community. I had been fortunate to meet Motherwell, Rothko, Reinhardt, Newman, Frankenthaler, Noland and Olitski, both here and in the USA; and was very much in awe of them, particularly the older generation. They were my Gods and seemed to be remote and unreachable, with the exception of "Barney" (Newman) as he was known to his friends. He loved being with people and especially young ones. Hofmann however was by this time something of an outsider, living in Provincetown.'

Hoyland discusses the *Situation* show of 1960. 'We were trying to make a new urban, more uncompromisingly abstract, art based on rational thinking and visual perception. Until the end of the 1950s, we had felt starved of an intellectual and perceptual *raison d'être* for our work and were reacting against what we saw as the quasi-Romantic English tradition; what we saw as compromise and also the violent excesses of post de Kooning abstraction. I felt, as did many others, that the most uncompromising new art of the time was the work of Rothko, Still, Newman and Motherwell. It was powerful, huge, overwhelming and mysterious, and for those of us who had a passing interest in Zen, Zen calligraphy and the Beat Poets had a spiritual content we had not experienced before. It must be remembered that all but a few in Britain after the war were familiar with what had taken place in Paris and most who knew either hated it or didn't tell.'

The catalogue introduction is a useful index of Hoyland's artistic development. Here he reminisces about his influences: 'My student loves – Rembrandt, van Gogh, the Fauves, Monet, Cézanne, Matisse, with Munch, German Expressionism (and a touch of Synthetic Cubism lower down the list) led me on to de Staël and Poliakoff in Paris, whose work I had seen at the Whitechapel. Then Soutine and Rouault, to whom I was drawn more than, say, to Bonnard or Vuillard. This group for me was the melting pot, seeing Hofmann was confirmation.'

It was Hofmann's European roots which Hoyland felt so at home with. 'Hofmann seized the initiative from Mondrian's division of the canvas into rectangles and inspired by Matisse's palette marked an art full of reverence to the masters but unfettered by their towering achievements.' Hoyland notes that by 1958 the rectangle had become the anchor and main form in Hofmann's spatial articulation. He writes: 'Hofmann's years of painting from observation, now firmly absorbed into his subconscious, began to give him the mastery and freedom his inner compulsion desired. He still was heard to say, "I bring the landscape home with me", and quote Cézanne's "Where colour is fullest form is richest"; though by now it was Hofmann who more fully realised Cézanne's ambition.' [Actually Hofmann quoted Cézanne as saying, 'When colour is richest, form is fullest', but the burden is much the same.]

Hoyland observes that Hofmann would sometimes use 'puddling and dripping combined with strongly impastoed surfaces integrating the watery puddles with rectangles, a seemingly impossible juxtaposition of colour and form'. Just as Hofmann wanted to unify the plastic qualities of a painting with its psychological effect, so did Hoyland. A brief examination of some of Hofmann's remarks about what he called 'paint, holy paint' reveals the many parallels between the two artists. This is less a matter of Hofmann influencing Hoyland than the individually-discovered parallel paths of fellow artists.

Hofmann spoke of wanting 'to swim in colour through mysterious regions and express everything'. He called nature 'the source of all inspiration. Whether the artist works directly from nature, from memory, or from fantasy, nature is always the source of his creative impulses.' Creation was 'a synthesis, from the artist's standpoint, of matter, space and color. Creation is not a reproduction of observed fact.' He defined spirituality as 'the emotional and intellectual synthesis of relationships perceived in nature, rationally, or intuitively.' He noted: 'Spirituality in an artistic sense should not be confused with religious meaning.' Hoyland agrees. He personally is not interested in any kind of religion. 'I can't stand the idea of being told what to do', he says.

Hofmann believed in colour as an element in itself capable of expressing the most profound moods and emotions, in a rather Expressionist manner, but he was also involved with form and structure in the tradition of Cézanne and Cubism. He said that to him abstract art meant 'to discover myself as well as I can'. He also said: 'One shape in relation to other shapes makes the "expression"; not one shape or another, but the relationship between the two makes the "meaning". As long as a means is only used for itself, it cannot lead to anything. Construction consists of the use of one thing in relation to another, which then relates to a third, and higher, value.'

According to the British artist Fred Pollock, American painters were interested in how far Hofmann was prepared to go, to see what crazy things he would do in a painting. It was his extremism that appealed, along with the physicality of his paintings and his strength and variety of colour. There was never anything slick or suave, nor did Hofmann ever seem to take the easy route. Hoyland admires Hofmann's breadth – 'he could go anywhere from day to day'. He aspires to that degree of freedom in his own art, and in his late work has taken possession of a similar liberty.

In a discussion with other artists printed in the catalogue to the Hofmann exhibition, Hoyland says: 'What makes painting vital for me is that volume can be perceived through colour, and colour perceived as light, radiance. Hofmann's are like walls of light; pigment can have radiance. Hofmann said, "Light in the natural world reveals form. Colour is revealed through light, but in the painted world it's the other way round, light is revealed through colour."'

Some commentators have become defensive about Hoyland's relationship with Hofmann, as if it were necessary to disprove the passage of influence from older artist to younger. This is a mistake of emphasis. Of course Hoyland was interested in Hofmann – passionately so. After all, he took on the largely thankless and immensely time-consuming task of organizing an exhibition in celebration of his work, and you don't do that as a practising artist unless you think the painter in question worth studying. Undoubtedly, Hofmann was undervalued and little known in England and Hoyland helped to change that. And what is also clear is that Hofmann offered crucial inspiration and confirmation for Hoyland, though he was never 'a role model'.

He comments: 'If you look at Hofmann's space, although it's non-perspectival, it's actually very much to do with a kind of diminishing perspective due to the size of the forms. So you get foreground, middle ground and background quite a lot, which can go backwards and forwards because he held that surface by the heavy impasto of the pictures. I think my paintings are much more an imagined space, they're more like Morris Louis, more like a dreamlike space than a physical one. Hofmann painted a very physical space.'

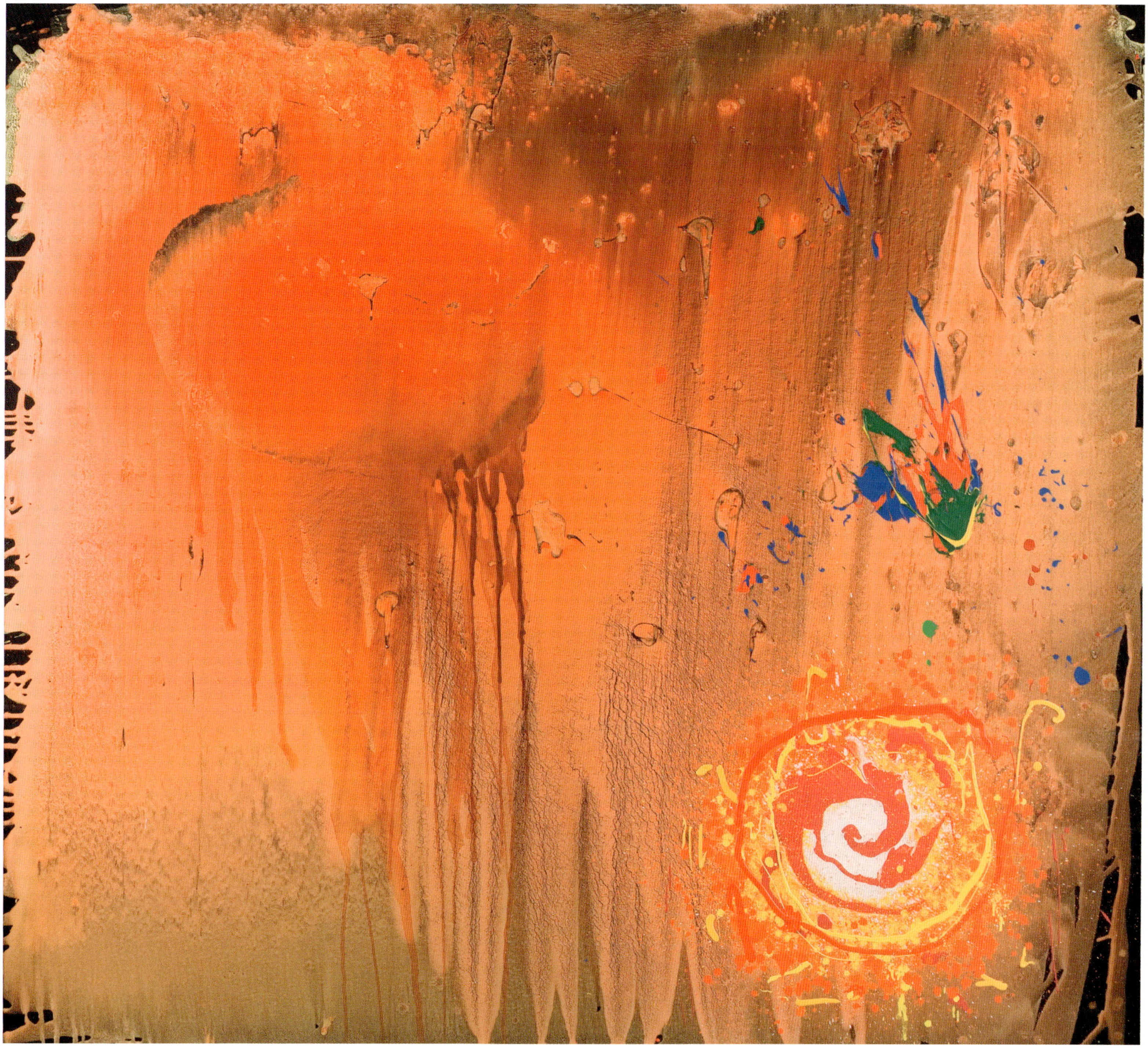

The Golden Traveller, 21.3.04
Acrylic on cotton duck
236 × 254 cm (93 × 100 inches)

9

In the Studio

To maintain the steady output of work he has made over half a century, Hoyland has to be ferociously disciplined. His hours in the studio begin early in the day, and he tends to paint mostly in the mornings, but since he has occupied a live-work loft on the edge of the City of London since 1980, he can just walk into the studio from his living quarters to look at a picture at any hour of the day or night. Life and art are thus closely aligned and the studio is actually bigger than the living area, a proportion and sense of priority important to him.

Early on, Hoyland reacted against the easel convention by working on a vast scale and using methods of application which required the canvas be worked on flat, on the paint-spattered arena of the studio floor. The only easel he has is a large one in the centre of the room for displaying finished paintings. No trace of the original floor is visible. Hoyland thinks it was made of wood with a covering of scrim, but this has been so overlaid with splashes and daubs of paint (it's Hoyland's

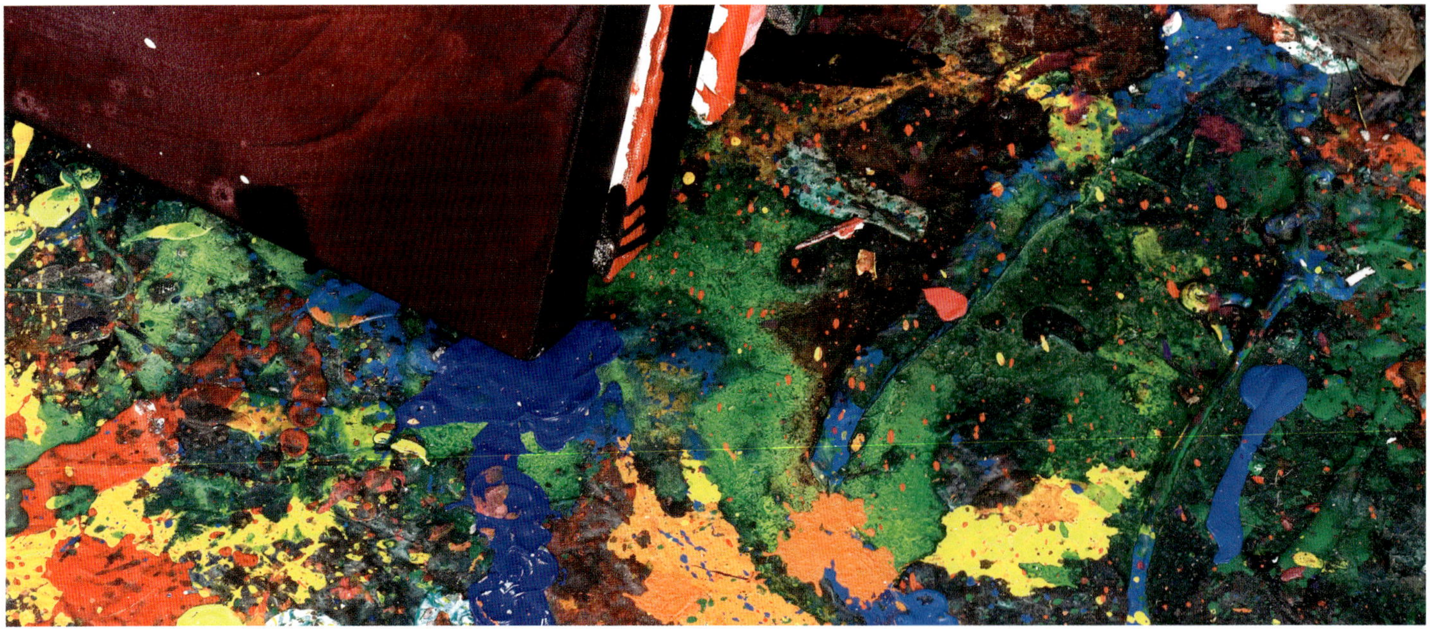

The paint-daubed floor of Hoyland's London studio, 2009

habit to test colour mixes by flicking or squeezing paint onto the floor) that the substructure has been hidden for years.

Whether visceral or celestial in intent, active or contemplative, the element of surprise is a crucial component in Hoyland's form-composing. His time is divided between research – which can involve nothing more exciting than a walk in his local neighbourhood, or at the other extreme, continental travel – and exploring new experiences in colour and formal relationships. Hoyland's art is sustained by his unquenchable vitality, by his honesty as much as his painterly attack. His job is to shape the chaos and impose a structural lucidity on his sense impressions, his perceptions of the infinities of nature and man's relation with it. Colour creates light, and Hoyland's paintings light up from within. Their radiance is balanced by the quality of revelation offered. Increasingly, looking at Hoyland's paintings is like engaging with a force of nature.

Hoyland has been using acrylic paints since they came onto the market in 1963. 'With acrylic, you can draw from the shoulder as opposed to the wrist. The movements are almost balletic. You have to rehearse them.' He loves those mazy swirls, the sarabands and curlicues he can deliver on the button. His own skill – which he constantly tests and pushes to new heights – is less a source of satisfaction than anxiety. Each painting is a trial of strength, a combat with inert and often recalcitrant materials to imbue them with life and the refulgent energy which sparks effortlessly from his best paintings. Will he succeed this time? There is no room for complacency.

He uses a variety of formats, though he tends to favour the upright or 'portrait', and a whole range of sizes, from a small, hand-sized canvas to large expanses measuring 100 × 93 inches. ('I've always liked doing big pictures', he says.) Hoyland always works on pre-stretched canvas, ordering the sizes he needs, and then relating his painting to the edges decreed by the stretchers. Barnett Newman did the same. This is a very different approach to that of painting on unstretched canvas and then cropping the best bit to make a painting – a strategy adopted by rather too many American artists. Newman said derisively of this tendency: 'That's not painting, that's photography.'

The grounds are generally put on when the canvas is upright against the studio wall or on the easel. His recent favouring of black for underpainting is not because of its sorrowful, funereal qualities (despite its use in the elegy paintings) but simply because other colours look so good against it. Hoyland likes the resonance it gives. He also likes to use black and white as colours. The actual painting of the imagery is done when the canvas is laid flat on the floor, though it might be lifted or propped up to make the paint run in a certain direction. Hoyland arranges a plank on bricks so that he can get to the centre of the big paintings and work wet into wet.

Hoyland lays down such beautiful and subtly-modulated grounds these days that sometimes it must be an enormous temptation to leave the painting simply at that. And the responsibility of painting on top of such exquisite groundwork must be correspondingly heavy. A false move may result in ruining the painting, though Hoyland has become adept at erasing mistakes and directing our attention away from pentimenti. But often he has to psych himself up to putting on paint and moving to the next stage, and the painting may well progress via a series of crises.

One of the great discoveries of recent years is a whole range of iridescent acrylics, which has enabled Hoyland to bring an unprecedented degree of radiance to his work, along with a suggestion of planetary landscapes and deep galactic space. Vertiginous abysses open up out of a wilderness of stars. The sidereal now plays a large part in his imagery: his paintings are generously star-scattered. He is doing for the age of space exploration what Turner did for his day: exploring the outer limits of radiance, and how form can be almost dissolved in light without losing all meaning and definition.

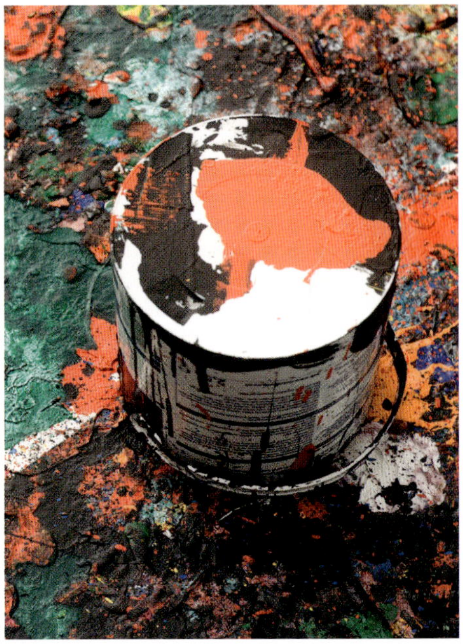

Hoyland uses standard matt acrylic to build up the underpainting

The process of working in the studio enables Hoyland to compare what he is working on with other recent paintings, partly to test the quality of the new work against previous achievements and partly to reaffirm a kinship of imagery and intent. In much the same way, Hoyland encourages the viewer's eye to roam across his paintings, not get stuck on a focal point, but to move about through the

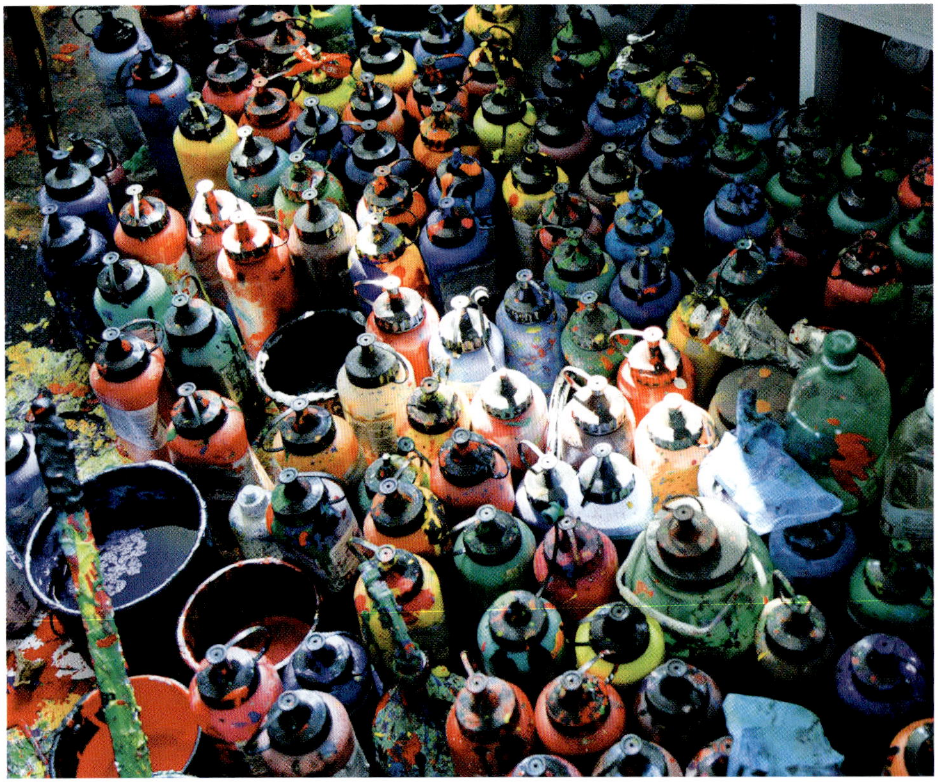

Tools of the trade: Hoyland is constantly trying out new ways of applying paint

different layers and levels, the clusters of incidents, the various areas of interest. It's a process of diversifying relationships, and it underscores his entire approach.

He makes sophisticated use of what might be called 'automatic' techniques in recognition of their discovery and appropriation by the Surrealists, who wanted to leave everything to the dictates of the subconscious. (Fat chance.) He favours pouring, staining, flicking, throwing, but these activities are always controlled, not random acts of the unconscious. He also explores new ways of applying paint. In a notebook dated November 2004 he writes: 'Find a way to make better marks. (Rag? Stick?)' He comments later that you can never get enough paint on a stick.

Hoyland emphasizes the importance of learning the language of painting. 'So many painters don't understand colour', he told John McEwen. 'They make all the shapes the same size. My paintings are induced. By throwing and splashing paint you can get all the effects of movement. You can't do that with a brush. They create a sensation of water or air. Life vitality. It's an extension of Pollock with greater refinement. Put a blob of paint on a knife and throw them until they get right, as Pollock did. These little characters, these minute details, have their own little lives in the galaxy. They're not about image really. That is what I like, that the paintings can be explored endlessly after the first impact. They're not emblematic. The minor characters can be major characters.'

A detail of Hoyland's studio wall, 2009

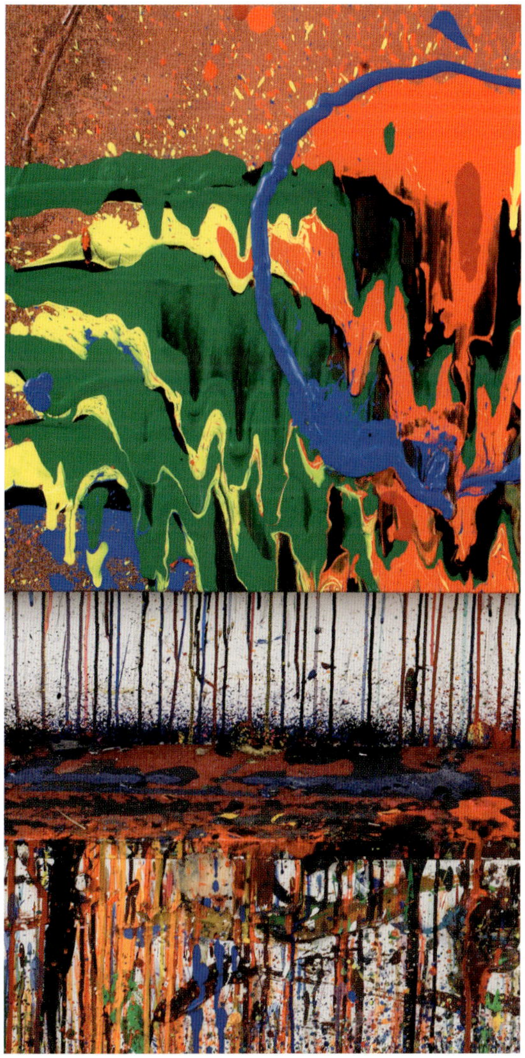

And he stresses the importance of glazing – laying a thin coat of colour over another colour – a technique the Old Masters relied upon, but which has been rather marginalized in recent decades by the popular *alla prima* approach of walloping down the paint with spontaneity and abandon. The key to Hoyland's practice is that he adopts a great many *alla prima* devices of applying the paint, while also developing a more thoughtful, layered approach. This is part of his originality: impetuosity underscored by structure.

He is self-deprecating. 'When you do it, half the time you don't know what you're doing, you're in too much of a panic. You just dive in and try something out. You can have a strategy but painting is still an event: something demanded by the process and what the work is teaching you while you're making it.' He talks of 'catching' it when he is describing the making of a painting. As if he is chasing some elusive beast, the mythical unicorn of art. 'I think I just caught it', he says of a painting he is pleased with.

Images of flight wheel through his work. The birds that appear as dynamic cruciform ideograms echo the soaring and scything of seagulls in front of his studio windows in London. The swooping flight of birds, the airborne arabesques, the flow back and away: it's not so much a bird he paints as an equivalent, a potent sign of speed and movement. It's also a useful excuse for an impetuous gesture, should he ever need one. Just as the sunrises he loves to watch in Spain and the Caribbean are the seed of the chromatic audaciousness that distinguishes his latest paintings.

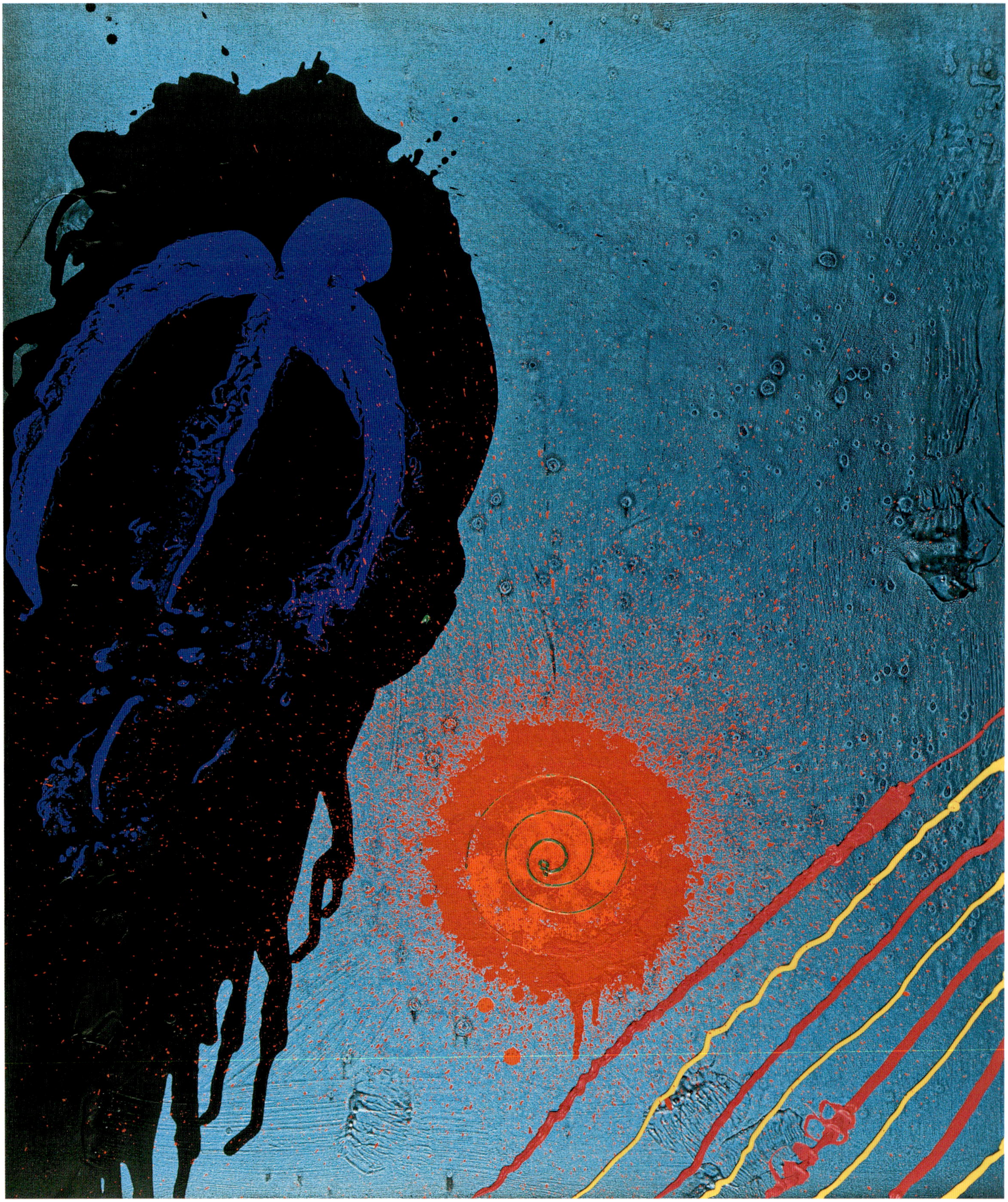

10

The Elegiac Impulse

For most of his career, Hoyland has made paintings whose mood has been predominantly affirmative and up-beat. Rarely has he made a melancholy picture. One of the most distinctive and moving developments in Hoyland's work of recent years has been the loosely-associated group of elegies painted since the new millennium. These are paintings inspired by loss, often by the death of friends, and propose a different side of Hoyland, an aspect of the sensitivity he has long kept hidden. Of course, it was always to be suspected that the main reason he was such a good painter, and so inventive a colourist, was the depth of finely-nuanced responsiveness beneath the tough-guy exterior. But he has until now been careful not to let it show. His approach to painting has been complex: it involves alternately exposing and cloaking his innate sensitivity, and taking a series of readings from the range of his responses. This process is aided and abetted by drink: by the attendant breaking-down of doubts and inhibitions, and the heady freedom incurred by alcoholic consumption. Also by its corollary – the lacerating or euphoric clarity of hang-over, and the subsequent withdrawal into hyper-sensitivity and nervous irresolution.

If Hoyland uses alcohol to achieve the various states of highly-charged receptivity he needs (what might be called the drinking mind), he has been exceptionally protective of this essential and deeply personal dialogue taking place within him. He has been an adept of disguise, masking the delicate interior life behind a brash and worldly persona. It is as if he feared the roots of his inspiration could not safely be revealed without risking serious damage to the whole plant. But now he has thrown caution out the window and is prepared in a subtle and unostentatious way to wear his heart on his sleeve. The elegy paintings are directly confessional, even autobiographical, in a manner that we have not seen before in Hoyland's work. These statements of feeling have an unaccustomed directness that yet avoids sentimentality. They draw the viewer into an embrace which is both lamentation and celebration.

The years since the turn of the century have been filled with leave-takings. One of Hoyland's first friends and supporters to die was the ever-loyal Bryan Robertson. Robertson had been such an influential figure in the postwar English art world and

Elegy, 6.1.03
Acrylic on cotton duck
152.5 × 127 cm (60 × 50 inches)

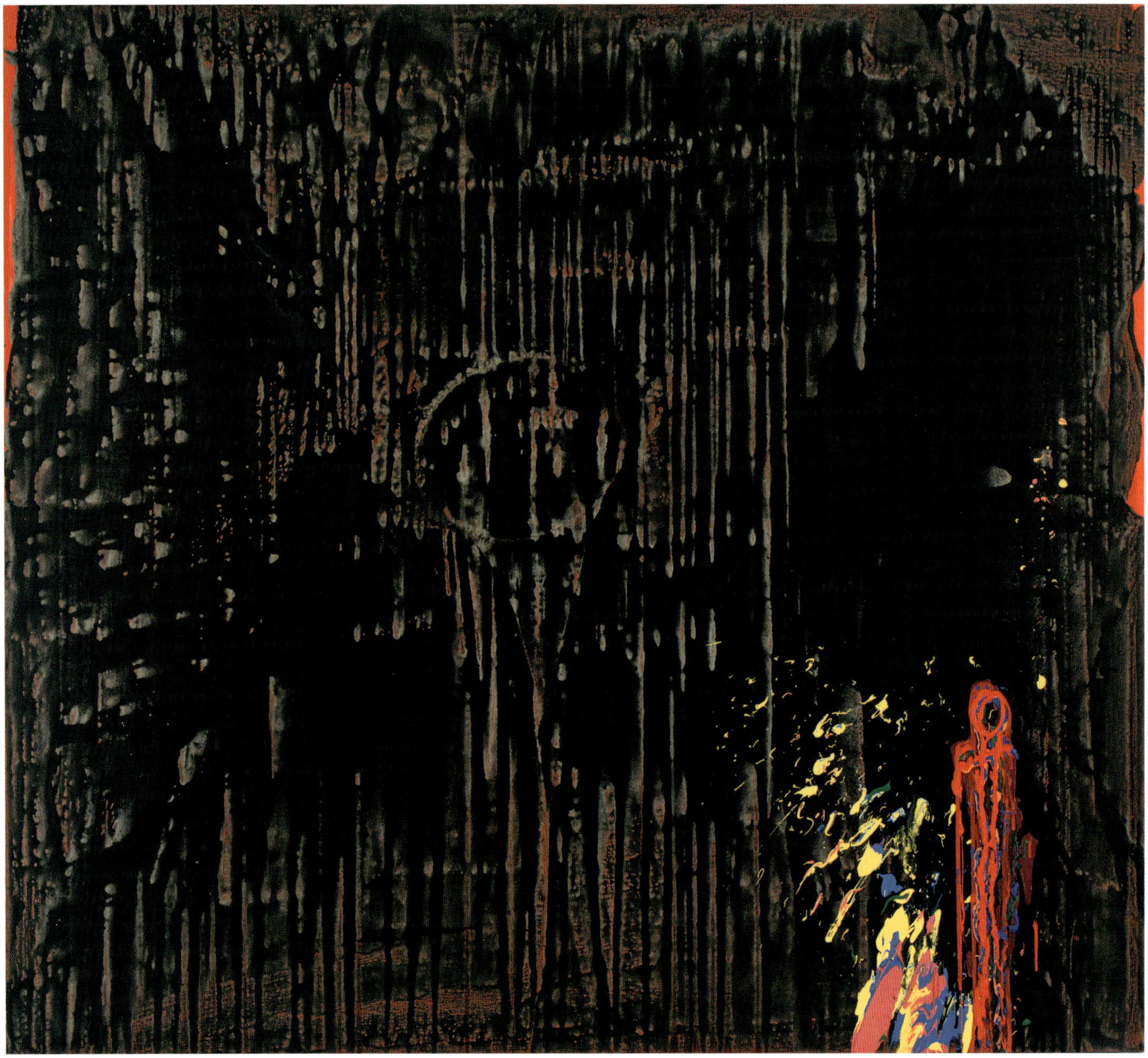

yet few properly acknowledge his contribution to our cultural life. Hoyland painted an appropriately ambitious and complex tribute to him. *Master Weaver: Homage to Bryan Robertson* (2.11.02) is a painting of large impact, predominantly sombre (though beautifully modulated in greys and browns) yet with incidents of colour bright with possibility. I asked Hoyland why he called Robertson the Master Weaver. 'I don't know. It's just one of my titles that I picked up from reading somewhere. But in a way Bryan was a kind of weaver – he wove people together. He was a great catalyst. He opened up that dialogue with America. Weaver – weaving a spell – my titles are not literal.'

Master Weaver: Homage to Bryan Robertson, 2.11.02
Acrylic on cotton duck
236 × 254 cm (93 × 100 inches)

Master Weaver was not the only tribute that Hoyland painted to Bryan Robertson. At the beginning of 2003, he composed the first of his elegies. Entitled simply *Elegy* (6.1.03), on page 82, it is a rich deep turquoise against which various motifs disport. A ragged dark cloud edges in from the right, with a deep blue flying form within it, like a bird as swift outrider of the storm. Below, a red explosion of colour and light, with a greeny-gold spiral inside, leads to a series of crimson and yellow diagonals. Despatches from the front-line of visual pleasure: a fitting tribute to Robertson's passion for art which demonstrated imaginative energy, radiance and the ability to soar above life.

Produced later that year, *Elegy for Terry Frost* (24.9.03), overleaf, contains one of the most luminous and seraphic of Hoyland's underpaintings. Against a tenebral

Hoyland wrote the following appreciation of his friend Terry Frost (1915–2003):

'How many people does one remember, who automatically bring a smile to one's face, even in brief recollection? Someone told me recently that Terry Frost reminded her of her father, who had also been a prisoner of war, and subsequently seemed to enjoy each experience with a vividness beyond the normal. What a great joy it was occasionally to find Terry sitting in Mulligan's Bar in Cork Street, red beret, green glasses perched on his nose, with a pint of Guinness which he would dilute with a bottle of champagne. He would be talking wide-eyed about the moonlight coming through the trees on a hillside in Provence. He would be talking of ellipses and eclipses, the sun, the moon and the stars – and about last night at the Chelsea Arts Club. He would also be telling everyone that I poisoned him with Thai fish soup, a smokescreen for his own mildly delinquent ways. The sheer excitement, the rage, the joy and the honesty, and also the deadly seriousness – all things one experienced with Terry … and that was only after the first bottle …

'Terry delighted in life. His sense of fun and wonder belied the subtlety of his mind and eye, the poetry and love captured in his distinctive vocabulary of universal signs where space, time, construction and colour capture what he had experienced through nature, and more importantly in reverie. His perceptions flowed from him, like an ever-running river.

'Terry's paintings are a kind of dream language, and like music, they propose a new reality. When Terry condensed the image he had created, simplicity gave his work great power. His techniques of painting and collage were simple, almost primitive – but no painting of reality can move one like the revelation of its underlying structure. His paintings weave a dream language, a landscape and therefore have a metaphoric power. They float high above the pitfalls of reality. Terry embraced the informal and the irrational, together with the spontaneous and the unknown. As a painter, he was able to let go: to jump into the dark.

'Terry's paintings are a seduction. One develops a relationship with these inanimate objects which becomes a bond with the living person, a mirror, a realm of illusive power. He developed an inner eye. He understood the ecstasy of colour as light, and as a bridge to the metaphysical. Terry

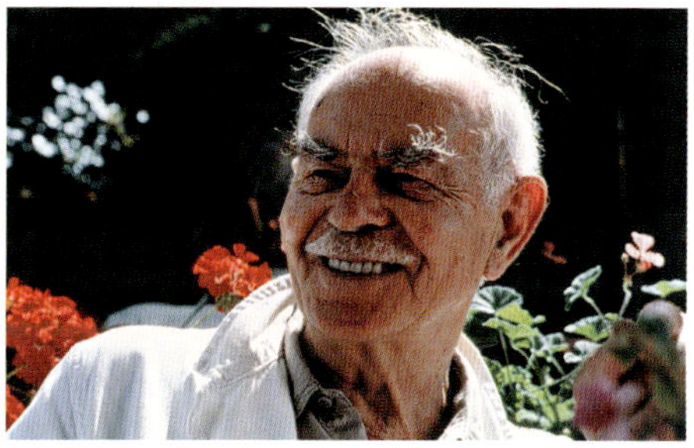

was a model of how to live in order to make art, his own heroes never far from his mind. Towards the end, there was a great liberation of knowledge, of risk and of spontaneity. His works play a game of structural truthfulness: they are alive. Terry strove to make every song sing. Terry also pushed way beyond the fixing of appearances. As Jung said, his "art, like life, called not for perfection but for completeness".

'Terry loved life and family, always relying on the strength of Kath his wife. His almost childlike wonder at the world was also a revelation to the thousands of students he taught over many decades. There is no irony in Terry's work; there may be humour and wit, but there is no place for cynicism. Only joy, passion and wonderment, clarity and passionate eagerness. It is painting made to look easy: painting as the embodiment of what it is to be human.'

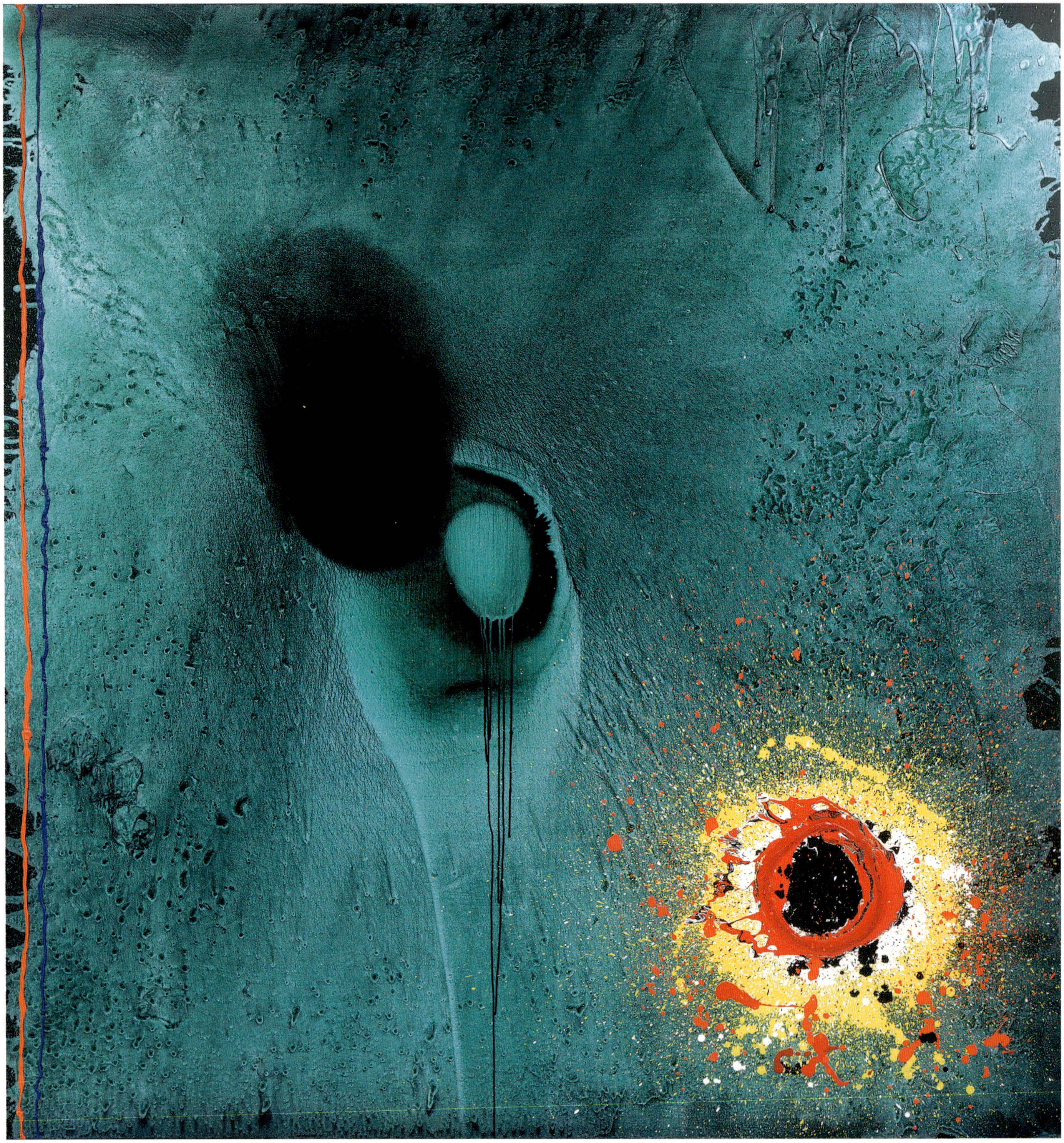

Elegy for Terry Frost, 24.9.03
Acrylic on cotton duck
254 × 236 cm (100 × 93 inches)

but surprisingly unthreatening black hole, the central area of the canvas is irradiated with a tarn of silver light. Lines of colour (orange and blue) trace the exteme of the left perimeter, while ravening circles of yellow, white, red and black suggest a final salute from the departing spirit. (Hoyland cleverly avoids using a spiral here though it was one of Frost's favourite motifs.) The whole painting is most beautifully pitched, formally as well as emotionally, lament balanced by celebration, surface activity against deep space.

Again, in *Lament* (1.6.06), Hoyland uses the circle within a circle motif. It rotates like a Catherine wheel at bottom right, throwing off sparks of colour as energetically as a dynamo. The distinctive purple line drawled down the left side of the canvas, with pale yellow flecks and blips scattered over and around it gives the vertical emphasis necessary to balance the cavernous blues laid over the black of

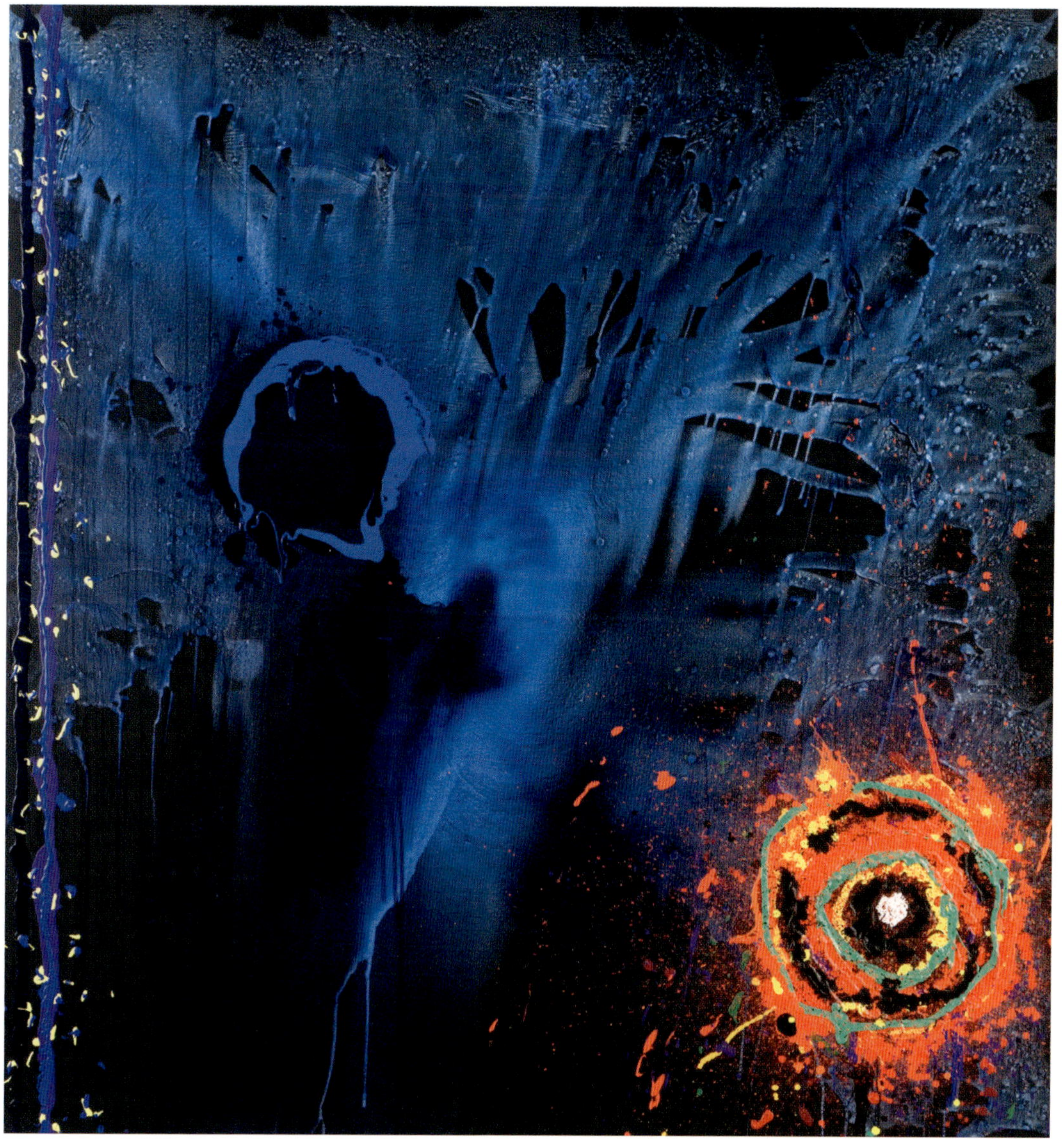

Lament, 1.6.06
Acrylic on cotton duck
254 × 236 cm (100 × 93 inches)

deep space. *Souvenir (for Patrick)* (2.4.06) is one of the finest of a very strong series, and is Hoyland's lament for his friend Patrick Caulfield (1936–2005). The carefully drawn lines on the right-hand side pay tribute to the graphic crispness of Caulfield's work, while the dilating gold and orange at the painting's heart tell of an exceptional human being. As John McEwen has written: 'the graceful and falling tangle of midnight blue at its edge is a sad and eloquent gesture of farewell'.

Hoyland calls Patrick Caulfield 'my greatest friend'. They met at the *Young Contemporaries* exhibition in 1959, and soon after were both employed to teach at Chelsea School of Art. They enjoyed each other's company and spent a lot of time together over the years, though there was always a healthy competitiveness between them. As Hoyland recalls, when they were younger he had to adopt alternative methods to the usual chatting-up of girls, because Caulfield could simply out-chat and out-charm him every time. Caulfield painted painfully slowly, in contrast to Hoyland's prolific output. On one occasion, having declined the offer of seeing Hoyland's new paintings in the studio, Caulfield said: 'You depress me. I wish you'd stop painting for several years.' All this is recounted with great good humour by Hoyland. In typical fashion, he sums up their differences in temperament in a vivid image. He refers to Caulfield as 'the dark stream', and to himself as 'the plundering river'.

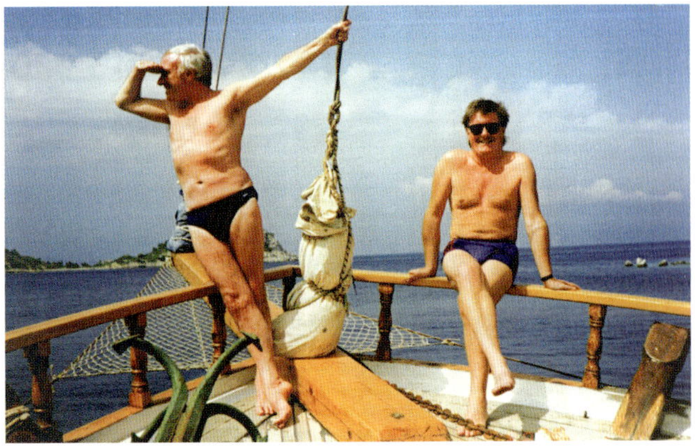

Hoyland (right) with Patrick Caulfield holidaying together in Turkey, 1988

Hoyland recalls Caulfield saying he always wanted to be a sheep-shearer when he lived in Acton as a boy. So when Hoyland was appointed artist-in-residence at Melbourne University (1979–80), and was living for several months in Australia, it

The following is taken from Hoyland's address at Patrick Caulfield's funeral in 2005:

'The most inexplicable thing about Patrick was his work: it was and remains an enigma. Patrick was unbelievably clear-sighted and subtle and he possessed a formidable willpower; Bryan Robertson described him affectionately as "the man with the iron whim".

'Patrick was always polite, without showing any sense of obligation to anyone. He concealed everything that mattered to him from all but a few. He was charming, graceful and seemingly impassive; he rarely showed his inner passions. Patrick did not attach himself to movements or theories and had no interest in politics. He could not understand why anyone else should. He continued to explore the idiosyncrasies of his inner mind until the end, which was all he needed to sustain his growth.

'Patrick loved deeply but never expressed it overtly except in his eyes and the warmth of his handshake. He possessed huge reserves of stoicism in his life and his art, and for me was more his own man than anyone I have ever known.

'Perhaps I may be permitted to tell a small anecdote. One day we went for lunch at the old Tate, and Patrick ordered the wine. "I think we should have something really good", he said. I agreed. We quickly finished the first bottle. "I think we should have something better." I concurred and by this time we were the only people left in the restaurant. The second bottle was then dispatched. "I think we should have something really special", he said. I looked into his blue eyes and said, "Patrick, we can't afford this". He looked straight back. "Of course we can't, but it's never stopped us yet", he said.'

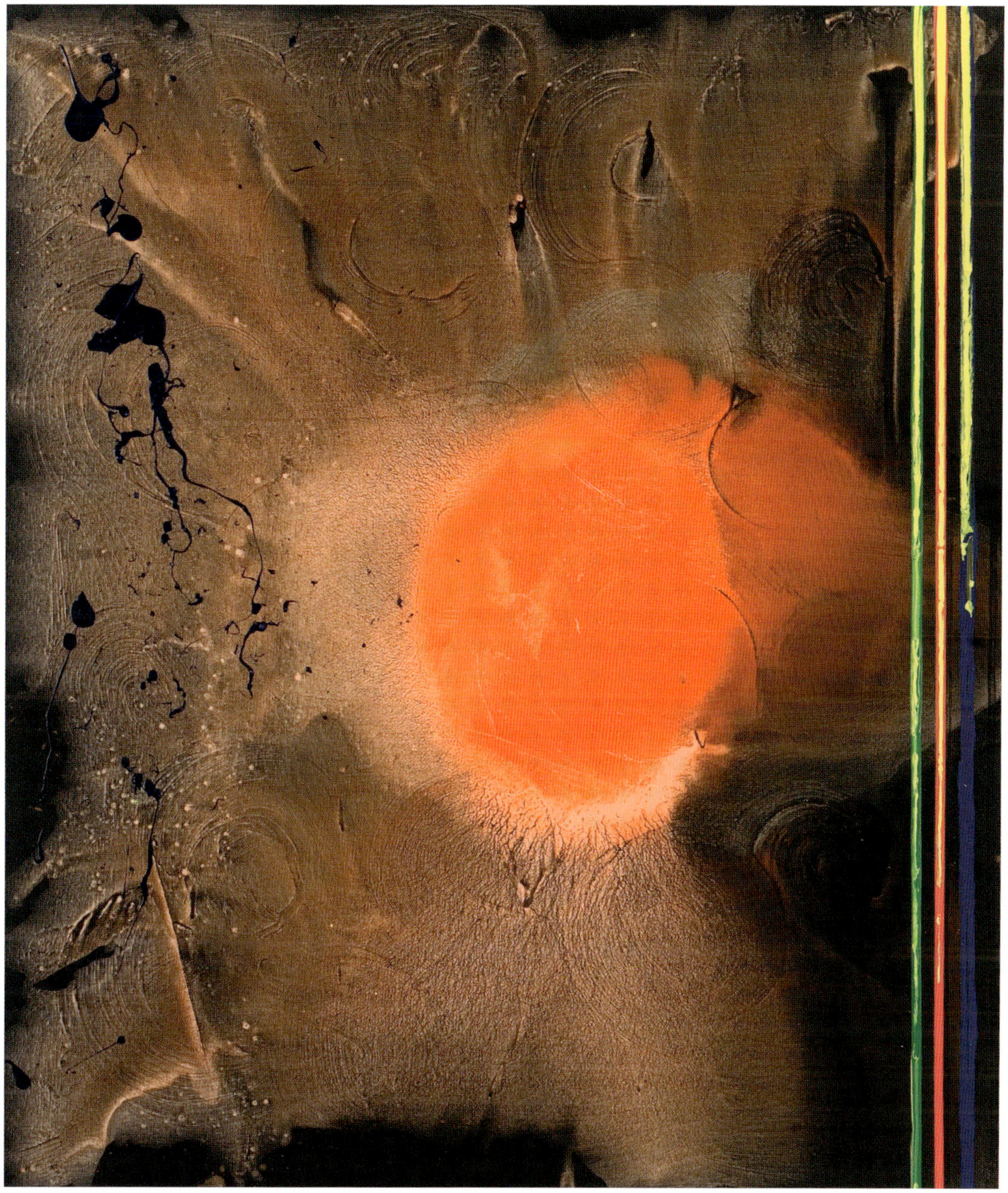

Souvenir (for Patrick), 2.4.06
Acrylic on cotton duck
152.5 × 127 cm (60 × 50 inches)

was expected that Caulfield would make him an extended visit. In fact Caulfield stayed some seven weeks and enjoyed himself immensely. Hoyland would drive the pair of them into town, drop Caulfield at a welcoming hostelry and continue on to his studio at the University, where he would do some painting before returning to find Caulfield and have lunch. Lunch was a leisurely affair and would sometimes extend for hours into the afternoon, as bottle succeeded bottle and the conversation roamed widely across time and continents. On occasion, Hoyland and Caulfield would still be sitting at their lunch table as dinner guests began to arrive, and one meal would segue liquidly into another.

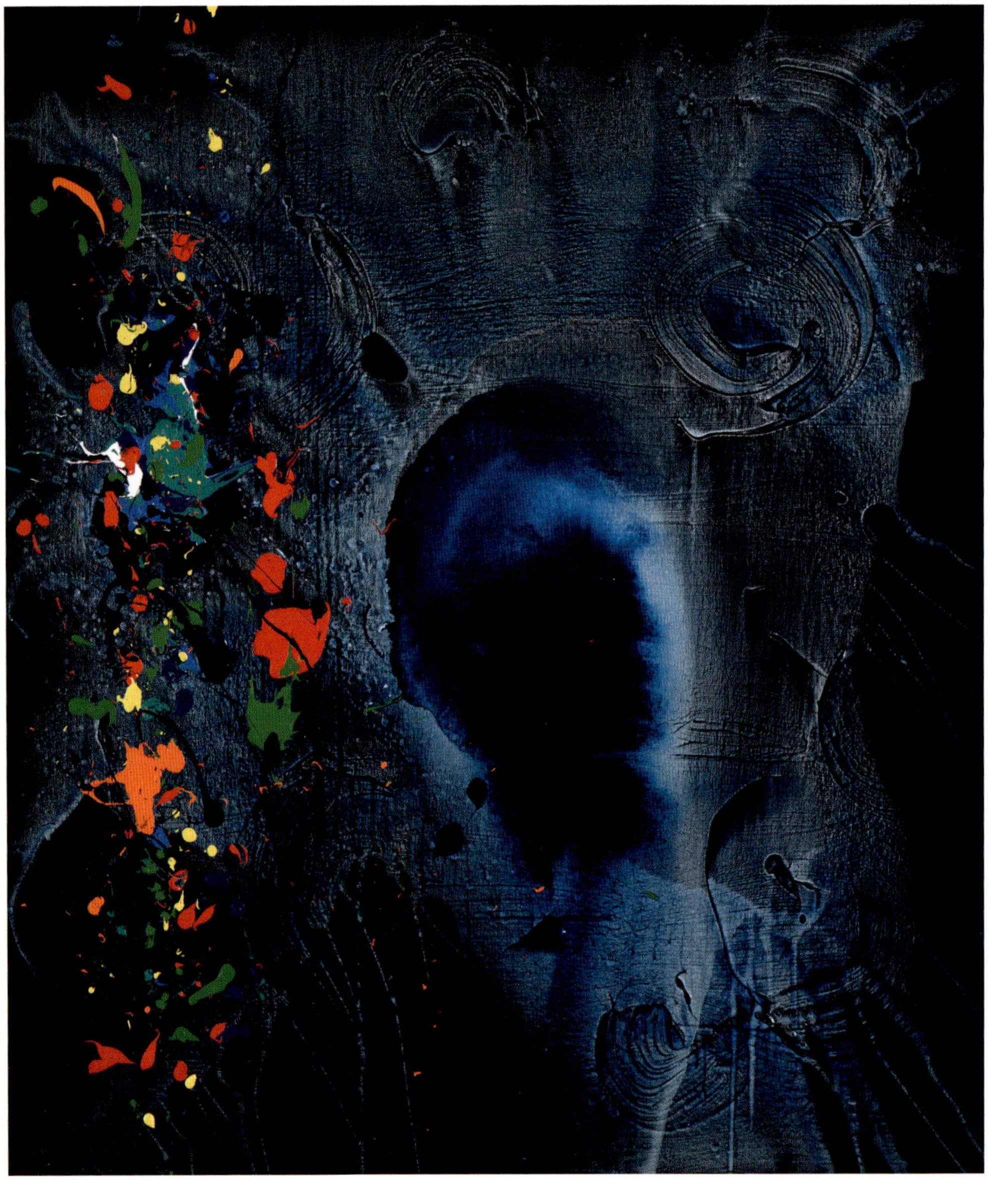

Love and Grief, 5.4.06
Acrylic on cotton duck
152.5 × 127 cm (60 × 50 inches)

Love and Grief (5.4.06) is one of the most poignant of this unofficial series or sequence of elegiac paintings. It is perhaps more potent because it does not focus on the death of any particular individual, but rather expresses a universal sense of loss and the balancing power of love which makes it bearable. Hoyland plays provocative spatial games, bringing the black hole at the centre of the painting forward and making it head-shaped so that it reads like a shadowy profile. This motif is surrounded by intricate patterns of worked paint, glazed with paler blue-greens. The downward drift is countered by centring swirls. And then blazing down the left side is a fabulous coruscation of colour: vivid green, blues, orange, red, splashes of white. This vertical passage, typical of recent Hoyland, redeems the monochrome intensity of the image, and renders it more pleasurable and less searingly melancholy. Here is the love that warms the heart, as indeed it warms this majestic painting.

Mind Horizon (5.6.07) is another painting in the elegy group, though less specifically oriented towards an individual. It has a pervasive melancholy despite its lambent colour. The mood is shaped and directed by the flooding of iridescent red, watered down over black. Note the unusual use of a jagged line of blue and violet over white along the bottom. Hoyland has developed and refined a remarkable

Mind Horizon, 5.6.07
Acrylic on cotton duck
254 × 236 cm (100 × 93 inches)

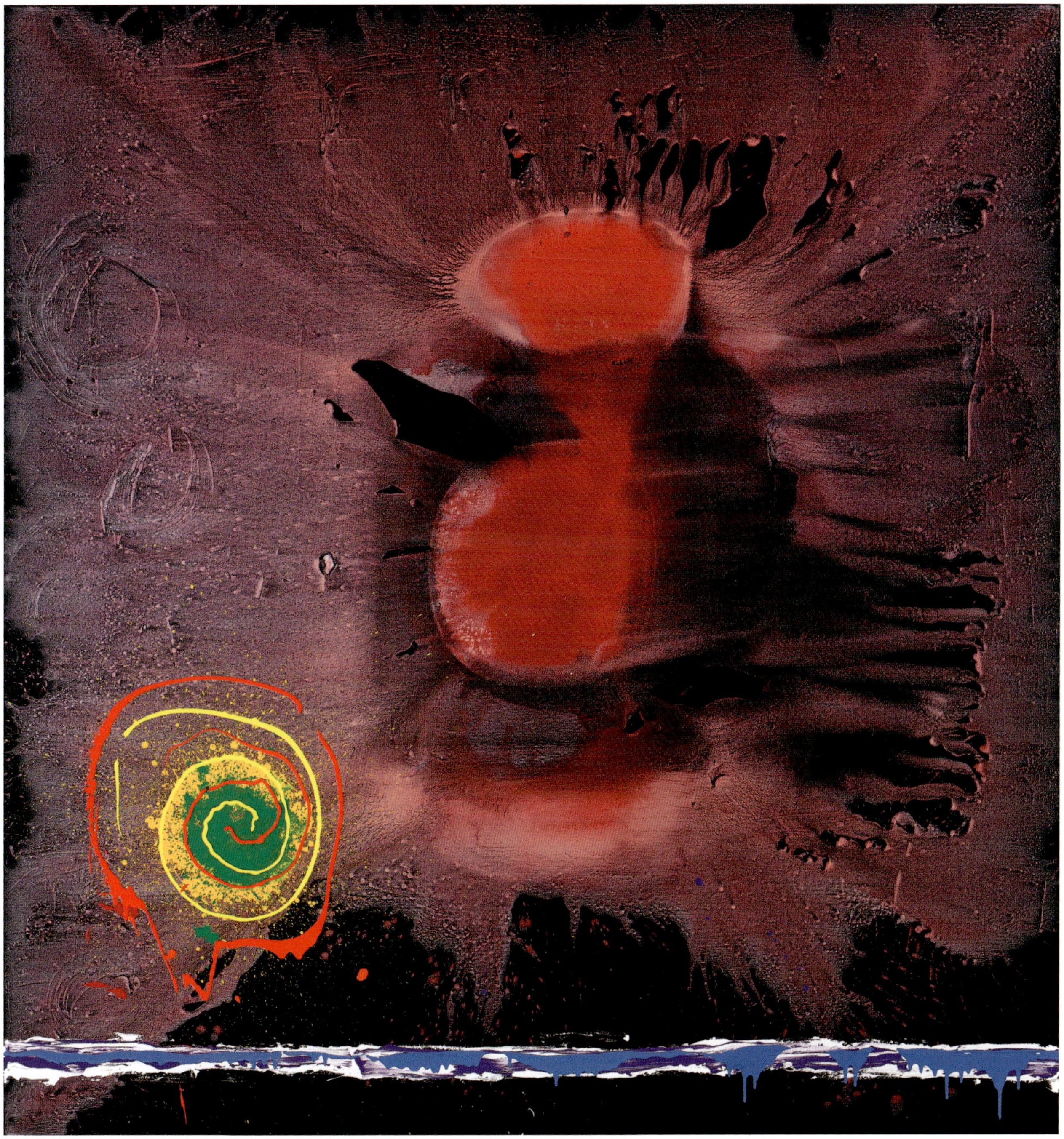

technique of collaborating with chance. He knows a great deal about how his materials will behave but there are always imponderables. It is impossible to calculate precisely what thrown and run paint will do, and Hoyland does not attempt to. ('You can do as much research as you like and it can still surprise you.') Instead, he remains open and alert to possibilities.

If something happens in the flow of paint which he can use, rather than have to attempt to curb or alter, he will act upon it with all despatch. As he says: 'you can't plan those things, you can only take advantage of them.' For Hoyland, this is how nature behaves, in its larger-than-man rhythms and patterns. For him, painting evolves in the same way, as a natural process, like rain falling or bark growing. In this painting, the last bit of paint to go on was the spiral at bottom left – predominantly yellow and orange on a patch of green. It's like the last punch in a fight, or indeed like a signature in the form of the artist's thumbprint.

He comments: 'You can't dominate or control a painting or it will have no life. Once you get heavy with a painting, you generally lose it.' This form of language again suggests collaboration – the similar sort of alert agreement as that between a spirited horse and its rider. But for Hoyland there's nothing like mixing your metaphors and enriching your imagery, and he also talks about the '*coup de grâce* – the opportunity to nail it', as if the act of painting were now a contest, like a bull-fight or big game fishing.

The problem of deciding whether a painting is any good continually exercises him. He recalls with much amusement one of Bryan Robertson's periodic visits to his studio to view new work. As Hoyland pulled out large canvas after large canvas and showed them to Robertson, he prefaced each new arrival with comments like 'Here's a good one', or 'This one I really like.' Robertson eventually remarked tartly: 'Well, you certainly seem to have a high opinion of your own work.'

Hoyland agrees – he does. And partly this is because he knows that it's often difficult to determine whether a painting is good or not when it's just been painted. Sometimes weaknesses will appear swiftly and 'you have to go back and have another go'. But more often than not, it takes months or years for the true value of a work to emerge. As a consequence he destroys little, though he often re-works a painting, provided he can achieve a finish that still looks spontaneous. Greenberg used to say that a painting that begins by looking ugly is actually the most beautiful, but you can't see it straightaway. Hoyland also likes to quote Socrates: 'Beauty is a brief tyranny.' The painting that seems most beautiful to begin with may not last.

It's usually a mistake to get too literary about Hoyland's work. The title of *Dominion* (16.7.07) may indeed contain a reference to Dylan Thomas' marvellously bardic line 'And death shall have no dominion', but, if it did, as some commentators have suggested, would it not be called 'No Dominion'? Anyway, Hoyland neither confirms nor rejects the reference, which suggests that in this case he is happy to

Dominion, 16.7.07
Acrylic on cotton duck
152.5 × 140 cm (60 × 55 inches)

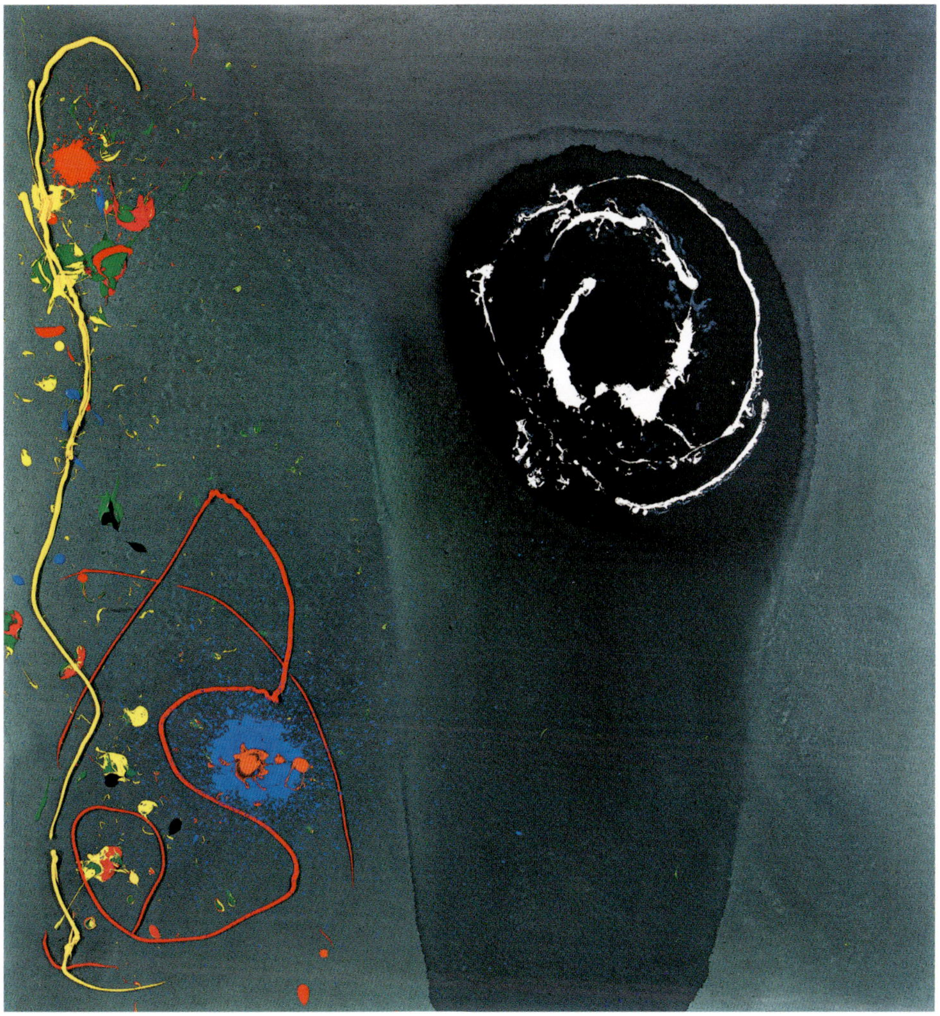

let it stand. It certainly appears to be much too positive a painting to be about death, the great absence. It's one of those paintings the artist himself is left wondering at. The beautiful underpainting or background was done in one go, and then Hoyland left the painting for quite a considerable time because he was fearful of wrecking the perfection of that first stage. Then he summoned his courage (not to mention his audacity) and executed the lyrical passage on the left in a short burst of intense activity. Its joyful shorthand in staccato and then extended red and yellow bursts offer a potent counterpoint to the swirling mists of the underpainting and the starshine of the eddying circular emblem at mid-top right.

Poem for Piero (28.9.07) has again the glaze of iridescent sea-green over black, with here a series of circular patterns like crop circles or brushing in the sand. Veils of green dominate the right, while down the left side reaches a great thunderbolt of red, at one point interrupted by blue, scattering red seeds prodigally to either side. Its title implies less of a lament than a celebration, and offers an intensely painterly and affirmative tribute to Hoyland's friend, the Italian painter Piero Dorazio. It also

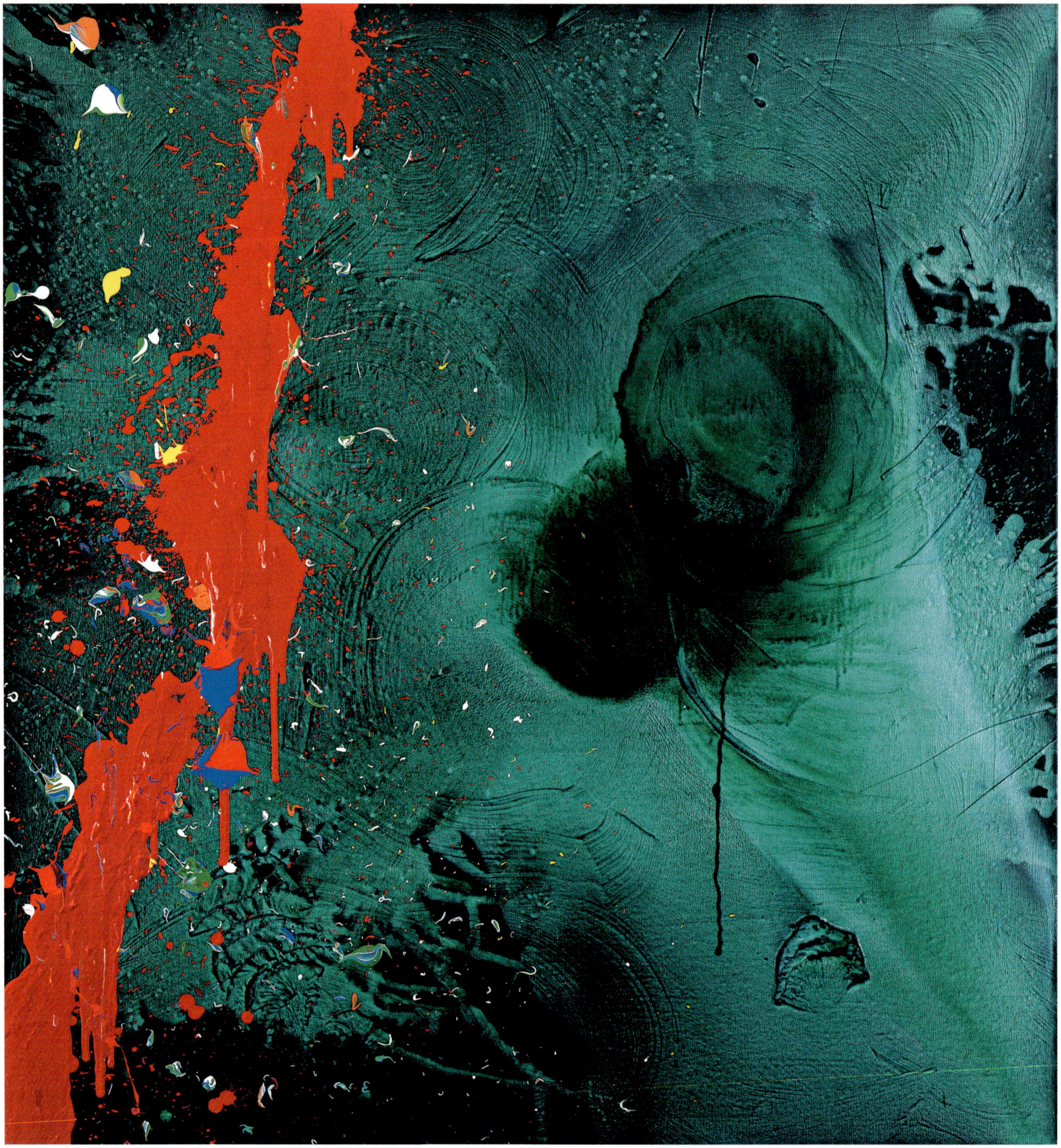

Poem for Piero, 28.9.07
Acrylic on cotton duck
152.5 × 140 cm (60 × 55 inches)

Piero Dorazio

Piero Dorazio (1927–2005) was a distinguished abstract painter, an important innovator of Modernism in Italy, celebrated for his geometric meshes of coloured lines. His work explored the relationship between lyrical sensuality and rigorous formalist design. 'For me,' he said, 'colour is an instrument not a means of expression.' He lived for a year in Paris (1947), meeting Matisse, Picabia and Braque, before returning to Rome. In 1953 he was invited to Harvard to teach and stayed on in America, meeting Pollock and befriending de Kooning, Kline, Rauschenberg and Frankenthaler. From 1961–9 he taught at the Graduate School of Fine Arts at the University of Pennsylvania. In 1970 he returned to Italy and took up residence in a former monastery in the Umbrian hill town of Todi. Dorazio, who was refreshingly outspoken and independent, was once described by an Italian critic as 'the exact opposite of politically correct'.

In November 1993 Dorazio wrote to Hoyland after making a visit to his studio. He'd been impressed by the intensity and power of Hoyland's work and referred to his 'epic' paintings. He also discussed the RA American art exhibition and its strange exclusion of Roberto Matta, commenting, 'he was in the 40s the most influential painter and mind in NY.' Dorazio goes on: 'This art world rotates around Duchamp, who, were he alive, would not like it at all. [Those] who knew Duchamp know[s] how much he admired Cézanne and Matisse with whom he could not compete, that's why he invented his own art. But he resented followers. This is how art critics can misquote art and its history! Fuck them.'

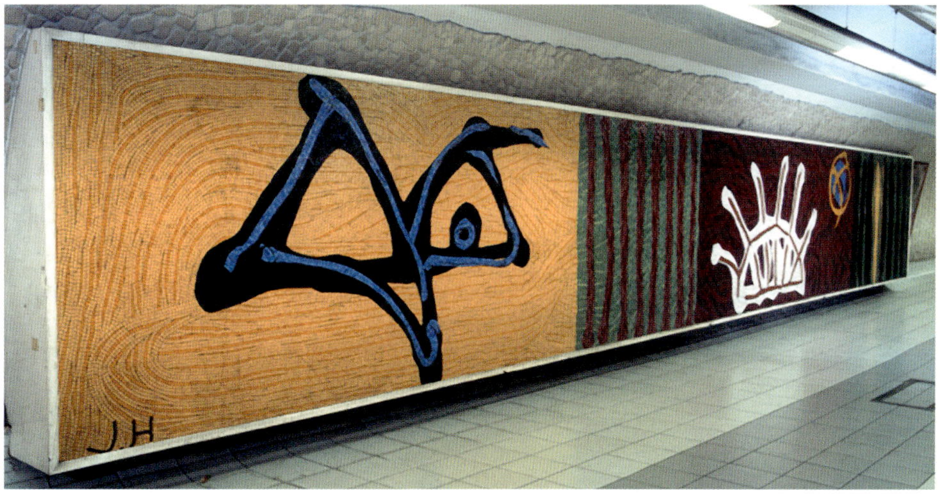

The mosaic mural Hoyland designed for the Rome metro in 2001

Hoyland comments: 'I met Piero Dorazio through a Dutch guy called Bob Postmo who was one of his students and a big admirer of mine who brought us together. Piero was a professor at Pennsylvania University and had seen my work at the Elkon Gallery [in New York], the first American gallery I showed with, and we became friends very quickly. Subsequently I visited him quite a lot in the 60s and 70s.'

One of Hoyland's most important public statements is little known even to his admirers. It consists of a large mosaic mural on the Rome metro. The commission was part of a major project involving other artists, mostly Italian (Dorazio among them), but also included Patrick Caulfield. The scheme was masterminded by Dorazio's cousin. Hoyland recalls his part. 'I did two or three designs in the proportion of the thing, picked out the best one and sent it off. I heard nothing. Then six years later I got a phone call asking me to come to Rome tomorrow! We managed to get a flight. I hadn't seen this thing and I had to be photographed pulling the rope with the mayor to unveil it. It was bloody fabulous! It was a lot better than the original. They put in four yellows to my one, or three blacks. I actually got paid, and I would have done it for nothing! Mine is between the Spanish Steps and the Borghese Gardens, which is like Bond Street meets Green Park. Patrick's is out in the equivalent of Morden. It's the biggest thing I've ever done.'

relates back to an earlier painting, *Scatter the Devils* (30.4.03), shown on page 2. This contains a reference to Dorazio's own wine, made from his vines at Todi (Dorazio's grandfather was a wine-maker), which was called *Scaccia Diavolo* and apparently had a similar effect on the stomach the morning after. A title thus echoes a private joke while suggesting on another level combat or at the very least disputation.

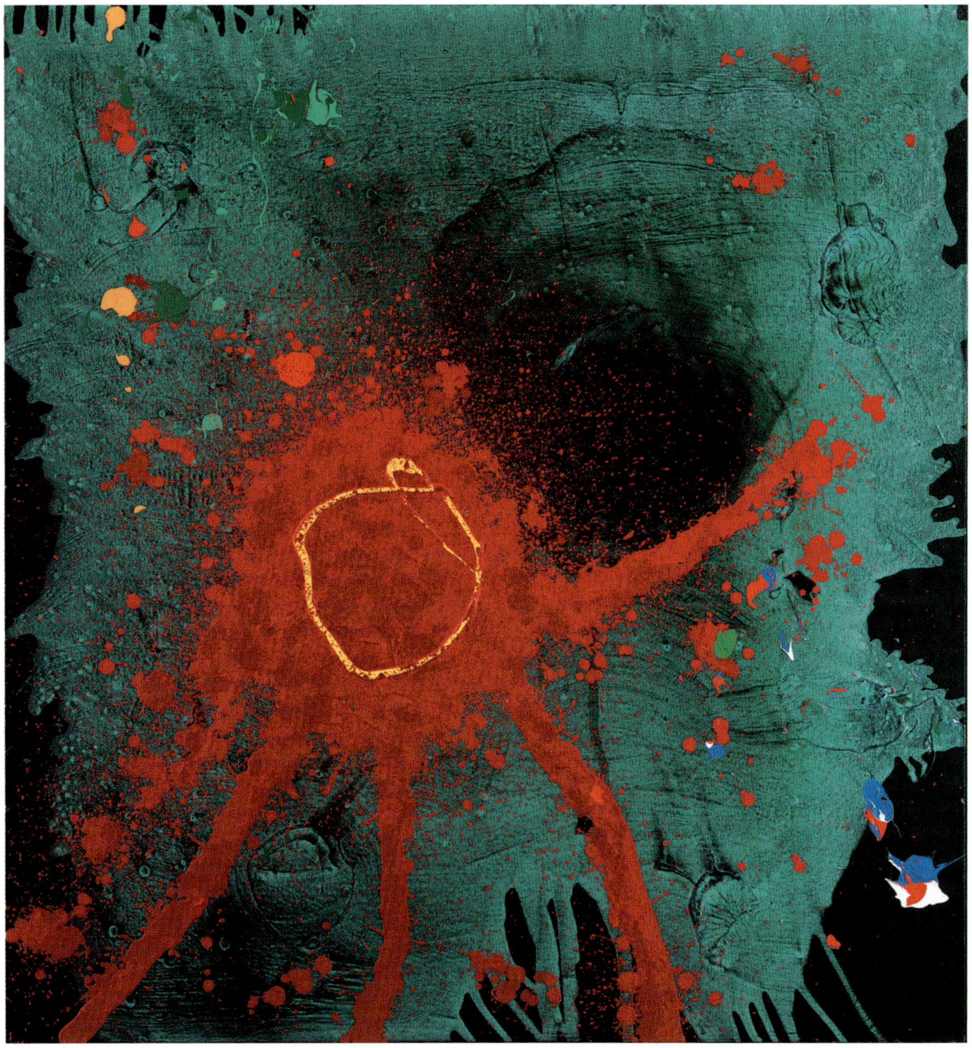

Lebanon, 17.10.07
Acrylic on cotton duck
152.5 × 140 cm (60 × 55 inches)

Lebanon (17.10.07) has a contemporary context it's both possible and useful to identify. It was originally inspired by a photograph accompanying an article written in August 2007 by *The Independent*'s Robert Fisk, a journalist Hoyland admires. The photo was of a large splash of blood on the tiled floor of the main hospital in Tyre, and had been taken by the Italian photographer Paolo Pellegrin. Hoyland was struck by the photo because he thought 'it looked just like one of my paintings'. Interviewed about his painting in 2008, Hoyland commented: 'I don't see *Lebanon* as a political piece, although the title would indicate that. I was simply struck by the constant threat to people living in the Middle East and the sheer horror of the things that happen. I suppose my sympathies would always be with the victims and the underdog, so I suppose that in that way it is political.'

Lebanon is a painting which stands in two camps – it is a prime example of one of Hoyland's inventive, imaginative, active paintings, but it is also a reflective, elegiac statement, lamenting the waste of war. The palette explores further the

OPPOSITE TOP LEFT
Blood Line, 7.10.07
Acrylic on cotton duck
91.5 × 76 cm (36 × 30 inches)

OPPOSITE TOP RIGHT
Blood Feud, 28.8.07
Acrylic on cotton duck
91.5 × 76 cm (36 × 30 inches)

OPPOSITE BOTTOM
Happy Safe?, 12.9.07
Acrylic on cotton duck
91.5 × 76 cm (36 × 30 inches)

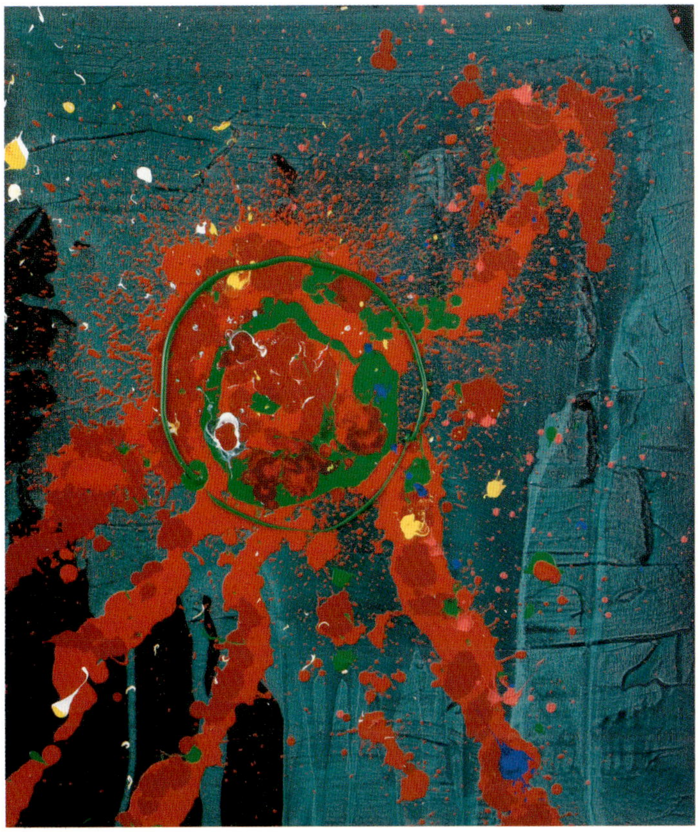

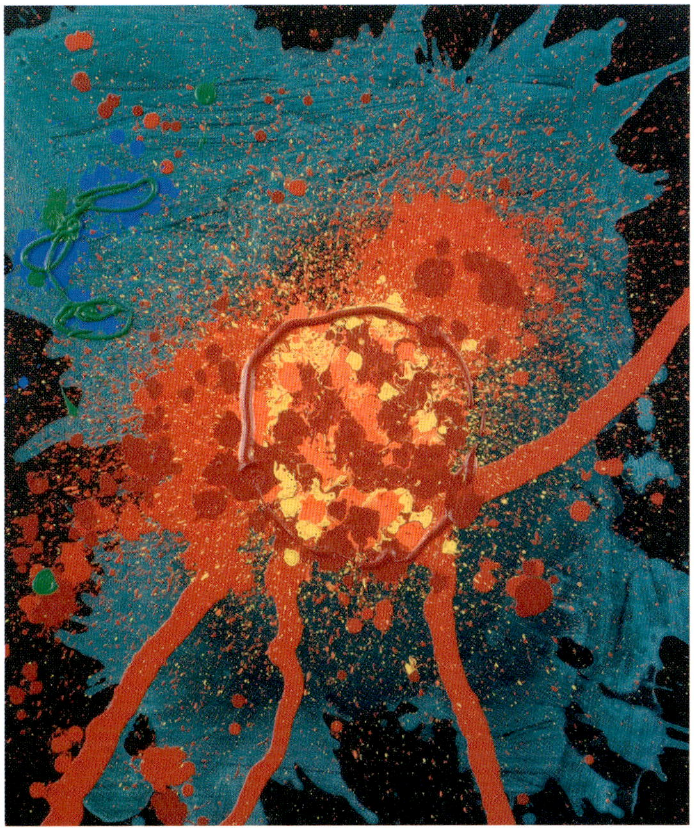

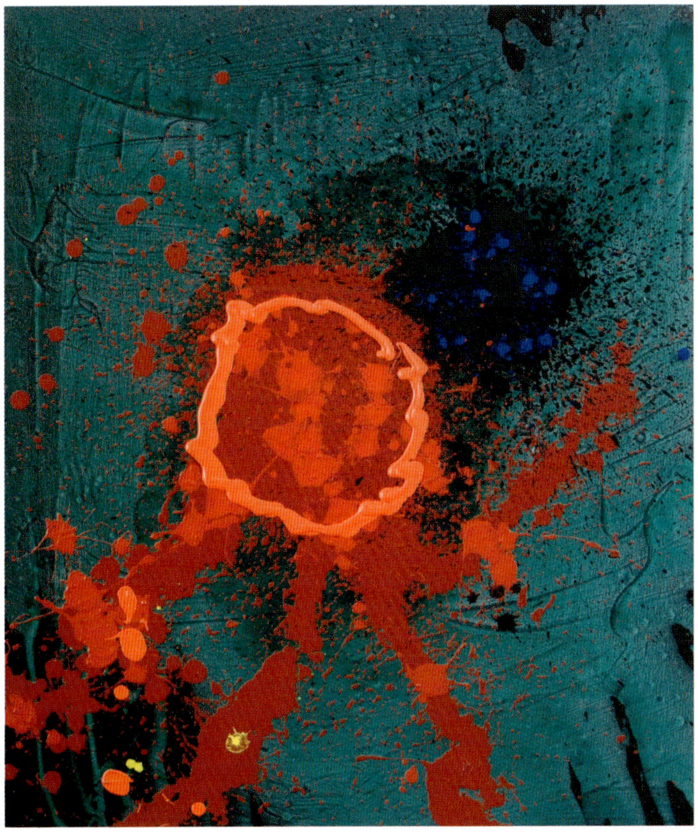

thinned green over black that Hoyland has used for many of his elegy paintings, though it takes further the intense red/green opposition. It is a striking and provocative painting: the yellow line at its heart is like a chalked positioning mark on a blood-stained pavement. Hoyland takes the battle back out onto the streets.

Other paintings explore the subject further. Three smaller pictures, though painted separately, make a kind of informal triptych on the same subject – *Blood Line* (7.10.07), *Blood Feud* (28.8.07) and *Happy Safe?* (12.9.07). A canvas like *Blood and Flowers* (20.11.07) has moved the imagery one step further away from the obvious disputes of war, and submerged political topicality in a luscious invention of colour that is not only more optimistic (because less specific) but also altogether grander and more magnificent in its disposition.

It would be misleading to compile a list of dead friends Hoyland has not elegized, but one notable absence is Robert Motherwell (1915–91). As yet, there is no homage or elegy to Motherwell, and when I asked Hoyland why, he replied, 'I was

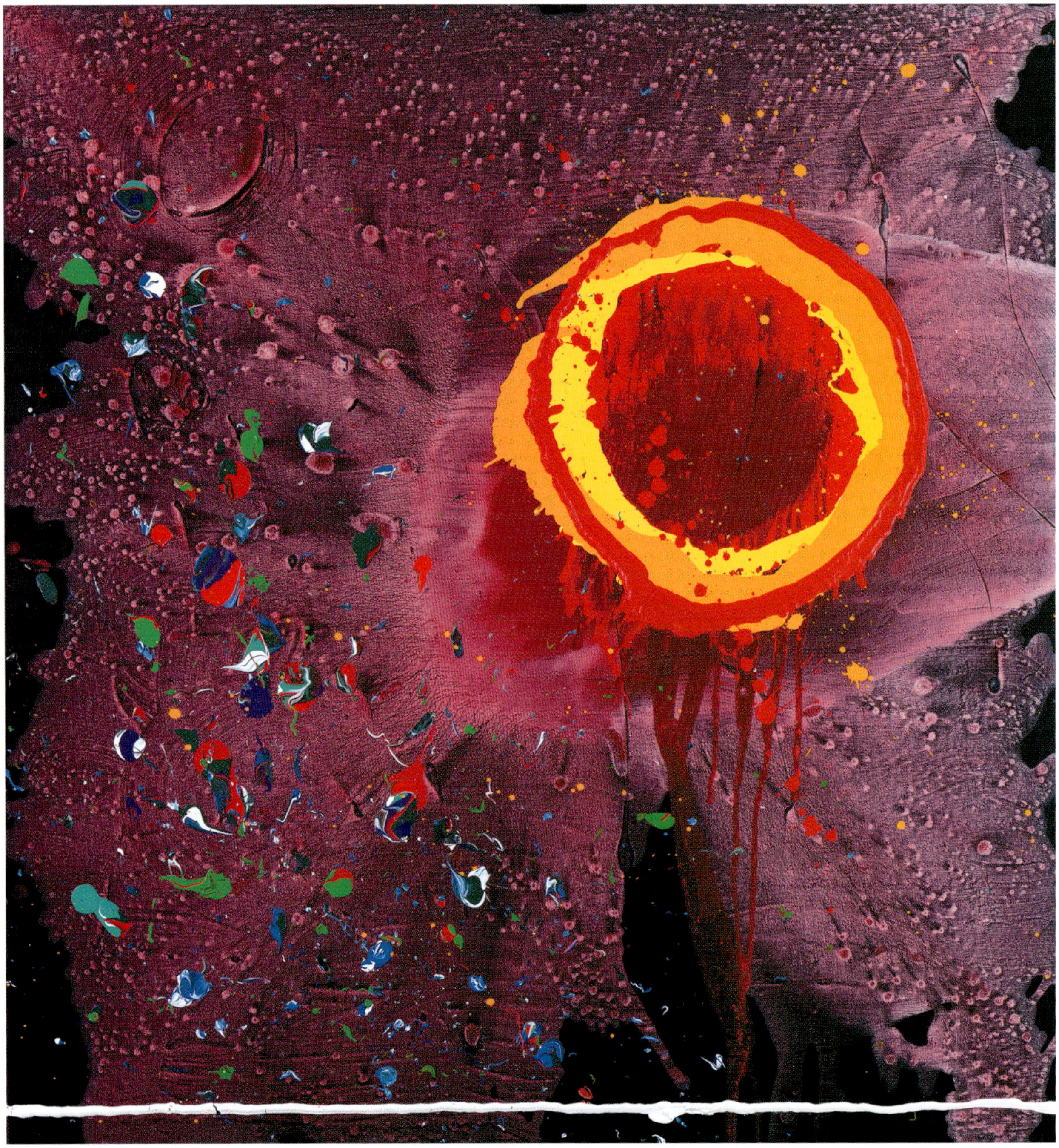

still optimistic in those days.' (Motherwell died in 1991.) In this unofficial series, *Goodbye* (23.3.08), shown on page 16, is a final lament, this time for Hoyland's friend and neighbour Clifford Pugh, a portrait draughtsman. For a change the canvas has been turned through 90 degrees to make a landscape format rather than Hoyland's preferred portrait. Note the powerful, thick, slightly drippy white line across the bottom of the canvas, like a heart-line or a life-line amid the nerve storms of Hoyland's form-composing.

Blood and Flowers, 20.11.07
Acrylic on cotton duck
152.5 × 140 cm (60 × 55 inches)

11

Hoyland and Creative Patronage

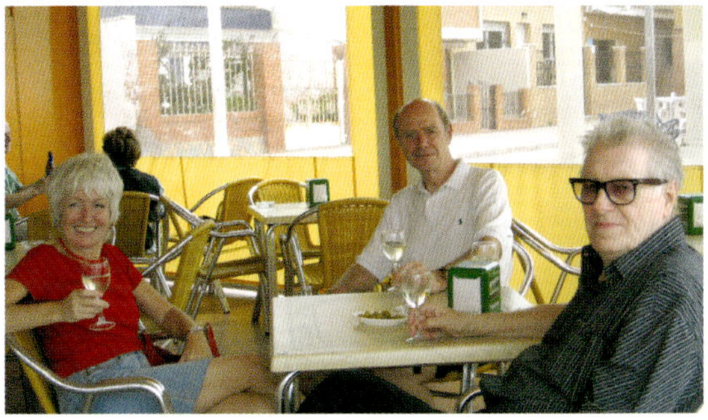

John Hoyland with the owners of The Don, Robyn and Robert Wilson, in Malaga, 2009

Hoyland is always ready to consider an interesting commission, and laments that they so infrequently come his way. To date, his most successful foray into interior design has been in the decoration of The Don, a restaurant in the City of London, owned by Robyn and Robert Wilson. The Wilsons have become great friends and patrons of Hoyland and have built up one of the largest private collections of his work in their Suffolk home.

Robyn Wilson writes: 'We met John in the late 1980s when he came into the Bleeding Heart Bistro for the first time. At that stage the Bistro was underground, fairly dim and very busy – a good place to be anonymous if you were with someone you shouldn't have been with. In John's case a young lady. Robert recognised him, got him a good table and later we started chatting. After that he became quite a regular customer, bringing both potential customers and a variety of attractive young ladies.

'The following year for Robert's birthday, I bought him a Hoyland print. We had always had modern art on our walls at home. The first one we bought in London in the late 1970s was a Moynihan, then a Terry Wilson, and then our first big spend, an artist's proof of Hockney's *Lilies*.

'In 1999, we took over the derelict City of London site that had for 200 years been the Sandeman Port Warehouse. While the basement still retained its wonderfully vaulted brick cellars, the ground floor had been gutted. We were left with seven large windows and a long white wall. We spoke to John about creating something and took him to see it. The following weekend, we all repaired to Oporto to visit the home of the Sandeman Don.

'George Sandeman took us on a tour of the Sandeman cellars on the banks of the River Douro and then a tasting of some nine different ports. While Robert, Beverley and I were swirling, sipping and spitting these highly fortified wines, John left not a drop in any of the nine glasses in his search for the true spirit of The Don.

'The week after our return John phoned to say he had produced something we might like – it was the seven paintings of the Don which now hang in the

Restaurant opposite the seven windows. He had a totally free hand – and we loved them. Once the paintings were in situ, the very high ceiling beckoned, so John created the template for the massive stainless steel sculpture that hangs above the room. Then the staircase needed some attention. Working with Didier, our glass producer, John created a series of etched glass panels for the banister, followed by etched glass lighting for the bar.

'In 2006, we extended the Restaurant, taking over a space that had been the Rothschilds' directors' dining room. There were two long white walls – one measuring just over 17 feet in length. John looked at it, and said, "I think I have something down in Wiltshire that might be the right size for that." We all went down to his Wiltshire studio and he was right – *Shooting Stars* was 15 ft 6 inches.

'The customers are all very positive about John's work – one, Mark Goodman, was so impressed that he has loaned us another of John's very large early works for the wall opposite.'

The interior of The Don restaurant which Hoyland has transformed with a steel ceiling sculpture and silkscreened blinds

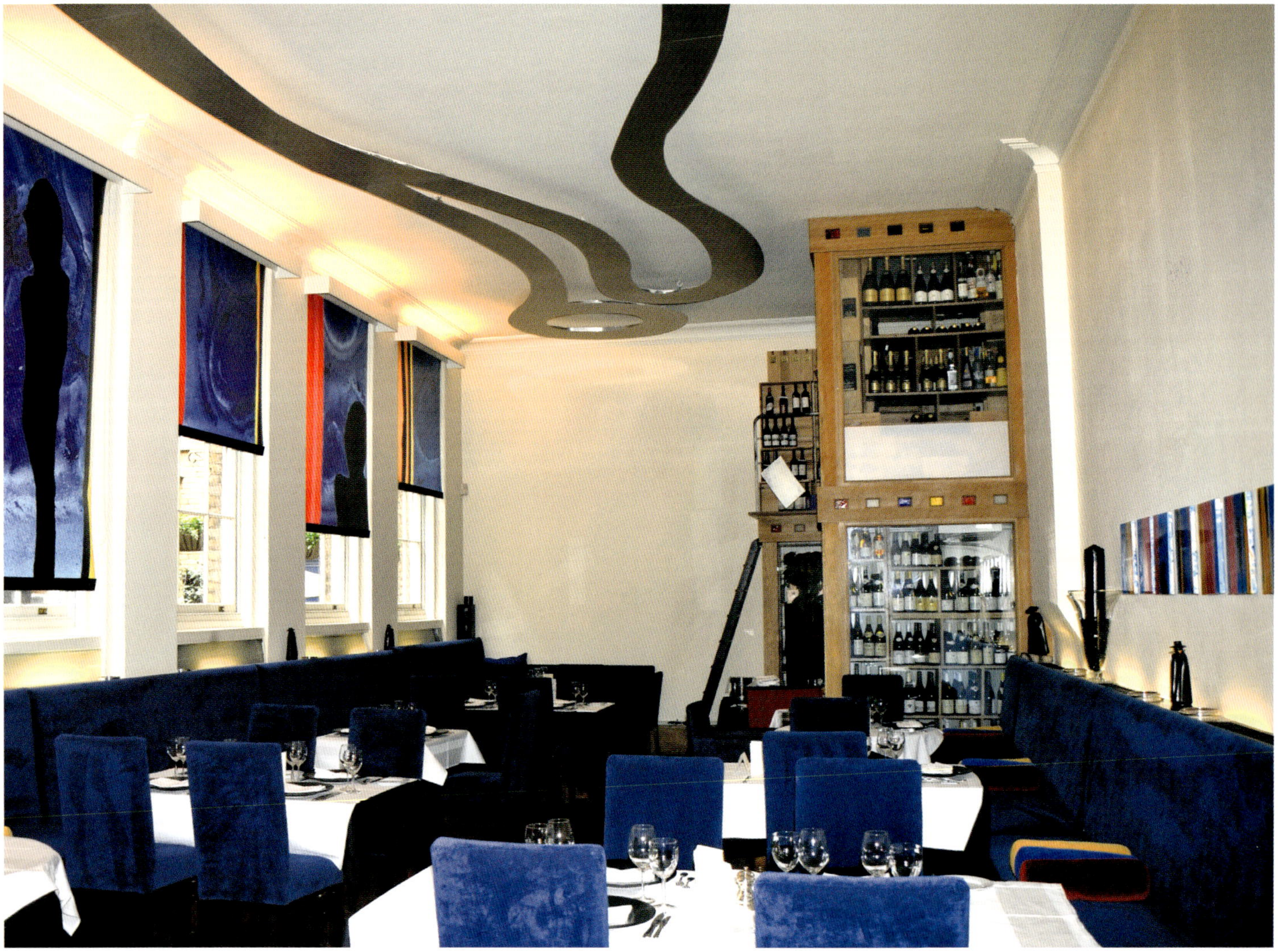

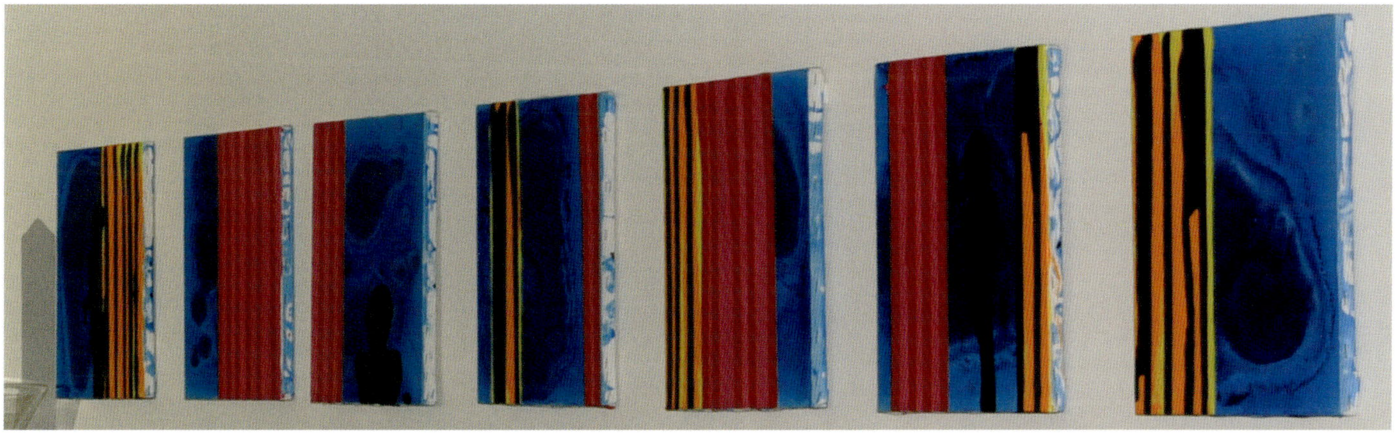

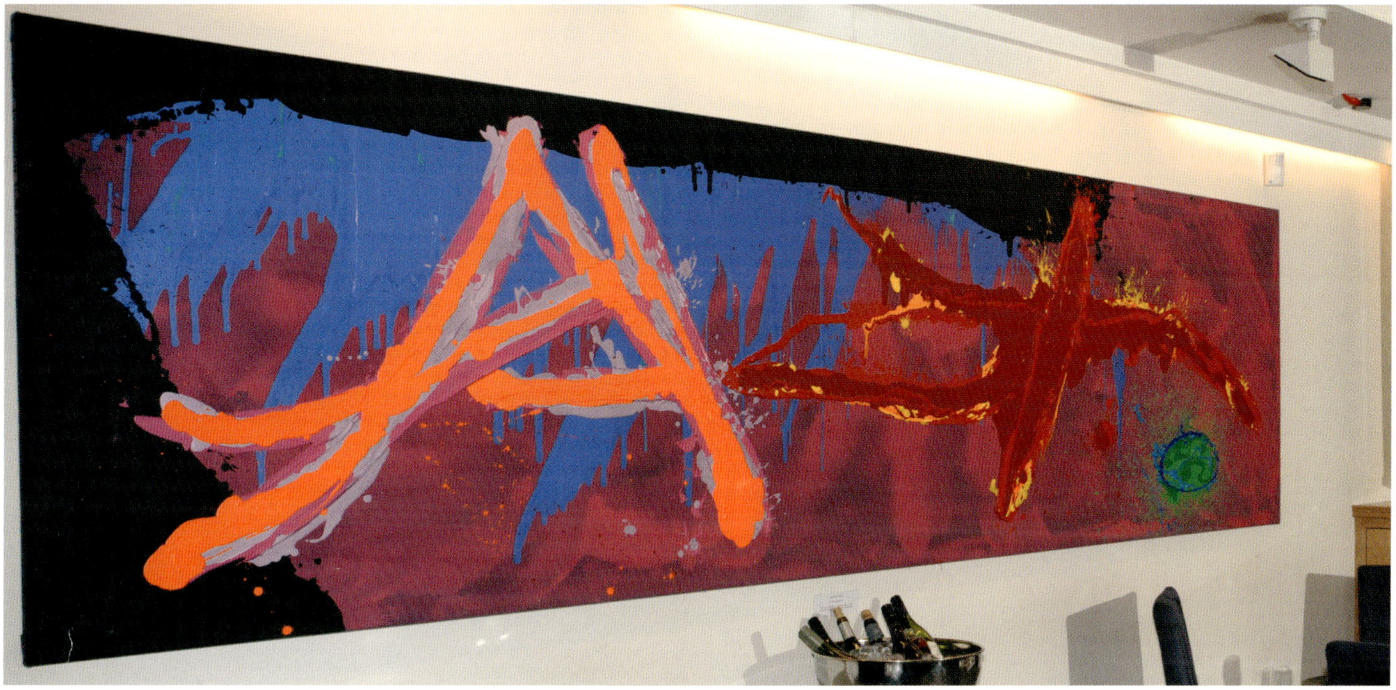

Hoyland's paintings for The Don; and *Shooting Stars* which runs the length of the new dining room

Hoyland enjoys eating surrounded by his art. The imagery of the seven small canvases has been copied and then digitally silkscreened onto a series of seven roller blinds on the windows opposite, which hang down to show off their designs. The cushions on the banquettes are covered in Hoyland's colours. The scheme evolved gradually, which enabled Hoyland to resolve each demand as it came up, rather than presenting him at once with a huge, off-putting project. This suited him. The design for the ceiling sculpture was arrived at through black brush drawings Hoyland perfected in the studio, and the same method was used for the etched glass. When it came to install the heavy stainless steel ceiling sculpture, Hoyland called on his old friend Anthony Caro, who lent his team of specialist technicians to help raise and fix it in place. The ensemble makes a highly original dining room, one of the most unusual settings in the City.

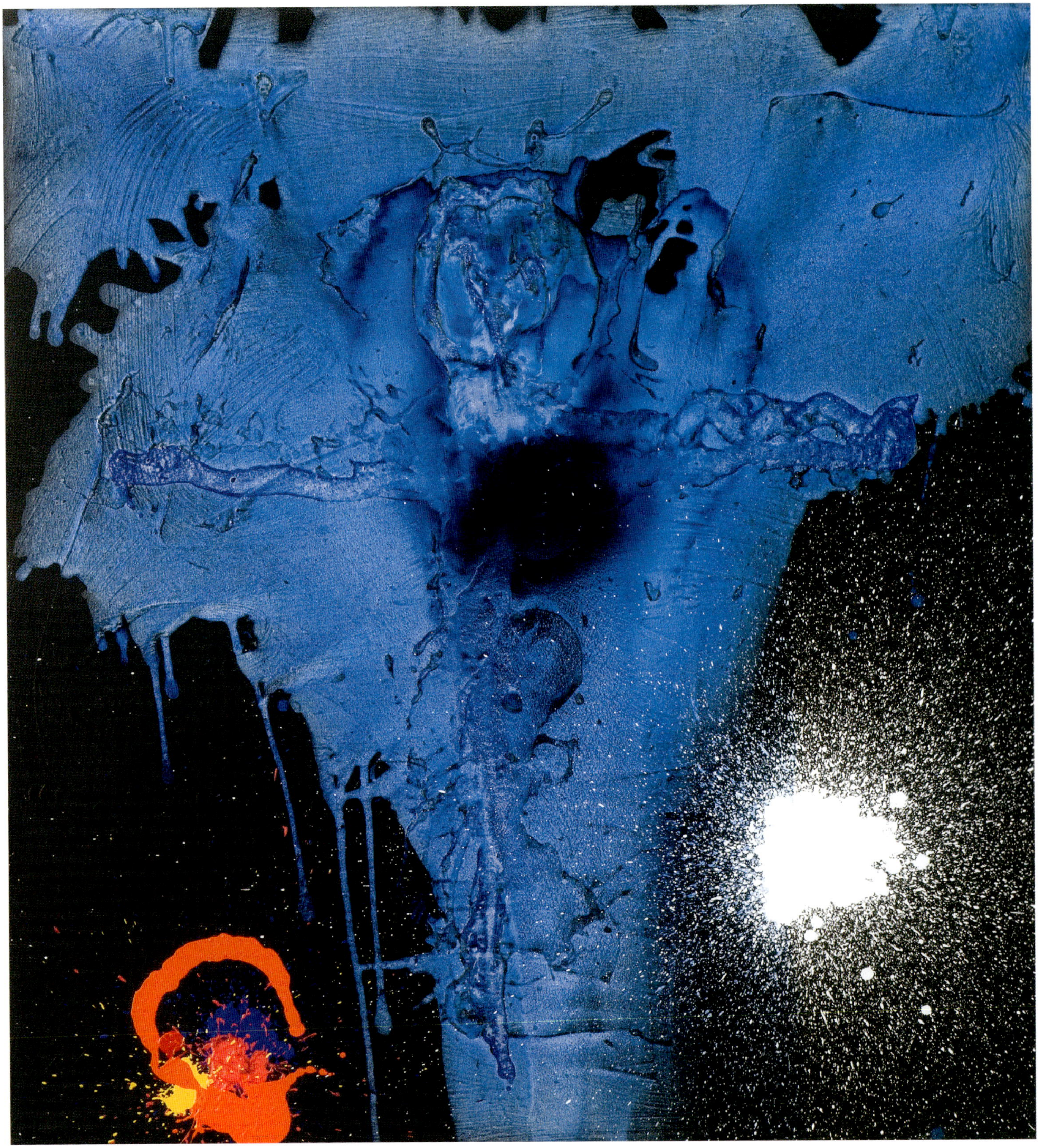

12

Snatches of Dialogue

When you paint a picture do you set out to convey a particular set of emotions?

No, I think that just comes along as the picture develops. But why you choose to start with a certain colour, or tone of a colour – whether it's dark or light – is not a conscious decision, but it is a choice. I would say a subconscious decision. Even ordering the canvas is a subconscious decision – you've made a decision about the size you're going to work on. But then of course you have to go partly where the picture leads you.

De Staël was the first exhibition you saw at the Whitechapel Gallery, in 1956. Why was de Staël so important to you?

Everybody at that time was struggling with how to make a figurative abstract painting, and he succeeded better than anybody else in making that synthesis. Plus the wonderful lightness of touch and the sensuality of his colour. His greys. And the way he applied paint – thick paint or thin paint. His paintings got thinner and thinner, and lighter and lighter, and more silvery – and then he killed himself! He was only in his 40s! He was a great painter. He's still a revelation to me. Of course the reason they never made a fuss of him in America is that he wasn't American.

What do you think about Surrealism?

I've never really got Surrealism in its more literary form. I like the Dada-ists. Occasionally I like Max Ernst, I've never really liked Dali, and Magritte would never be my first choice. Matta though was a formidable artist. My experience of Surrealism is really through Rothko.

What do you mean?

Surrealism had been a big thing in Europe and quite a lot of Abstract Expressionists had been influenced by it. Baziotes, even Barnett Newman. But also there was the terrible shadow of Constructivism hanging over them. Barney was well aware of it

Shroud, 6.4.05
Acrylic on cotton duck
127 × 114 cm (50 × 45 inches)

when he wrote about confronting geometry. In a way I think Rothko made paintings that came out of a marriage of Surrealism and Constructivism. Once he'd found that formula, he was free to express his emotions through that form because he didn't really have to concern himself with structure.

This is the problem I have. We were born under the shadow of this situation – Constructivism and Surrealism – and we had to find a way out. I thought the only way out was to go back to basics. To form and shape, illusion and colour. It was the end of the line what they did. We had to reinvent the language of art.

When I was living in New York I could see that the most potent part was grinding to a halt. I just felt intuitively, 'Go back to Europe where your friends and family are.' It was a lot to do with the richness and complexity of European culture. That was at the back of my head. I thought there's so much in Miró, Picasso, de Staël, Caro to plunder. This was rich pickings – stuff that they hadn't followed through with! Of course there was the danger that you'd be looking like an eclectic or a copyist, but I don't regret that I came back and tried to take them on, to see what I could do.

How do you respond to people thinking your paintings are spiritual?

I think they've become a little bit spooky in that way as I've got older. It's a lot about loss, about friends dying. The visceralness of my work – all the bloody shagging and stuff in the earlier works – is gradually fading away.

Why do you dislike the term abstraction?

It's just too abstract a word. It smacks always of geometry to me, of rational thought. There's no geometry, there's no rectangles in nature, no real straight lines. There's only the circle, the one really powerful form in nature I keep getting drawn back to.

Tell me about Rothko.

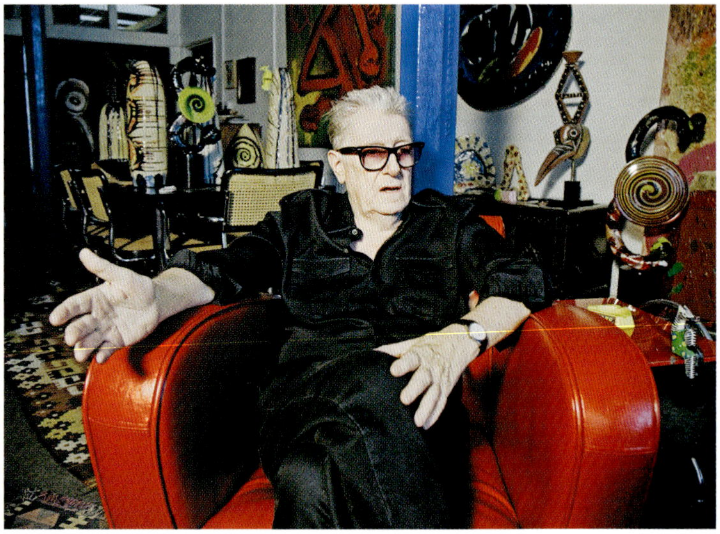

When I went to see Rothko I asked him what he thought of a de Kooning show that was on. It was a show of drawings of nudes in oil paint on paper. As Rothko remarked, they had that extraordinary feeling of female flesh.

Rothko said to me: 'What do you do in the afternoons? I don't know what to do in the afternoon. I'm all right in the morning: get the subway, run down here, full of energy and life, look at the painting until I get on the couch and fall asleep.' I thought, I know that feeling. Then he said: 'And in the evening we go out for dinner, we go to the theatre, we do this, we do that. But the afternoon? You get to thinking a lot about women's flesh. I guess *you* just go

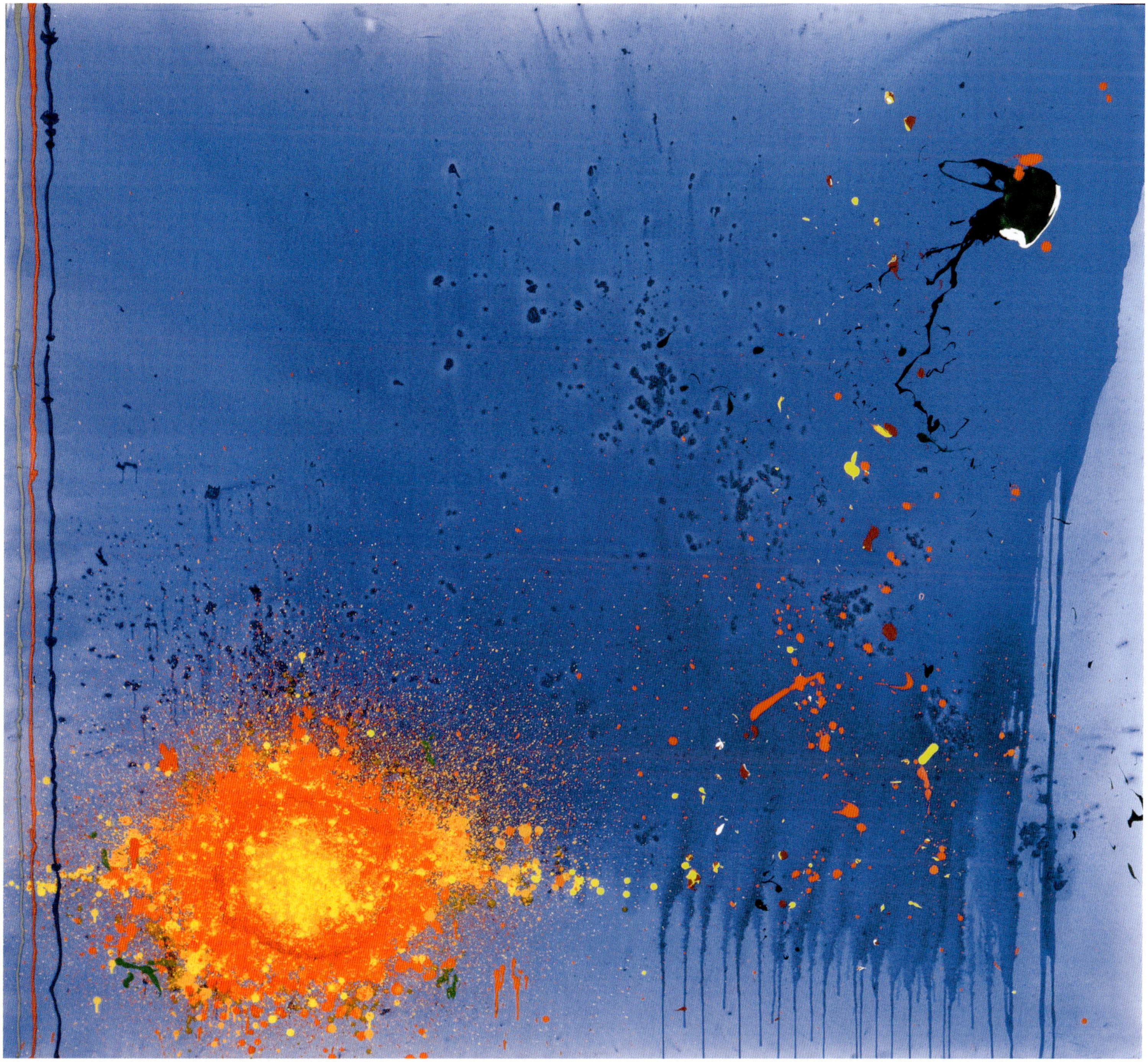

The Path of Love, 8.3.04
Acrylic on cotton duck
236 × 254 cm (93 × 100 inches)

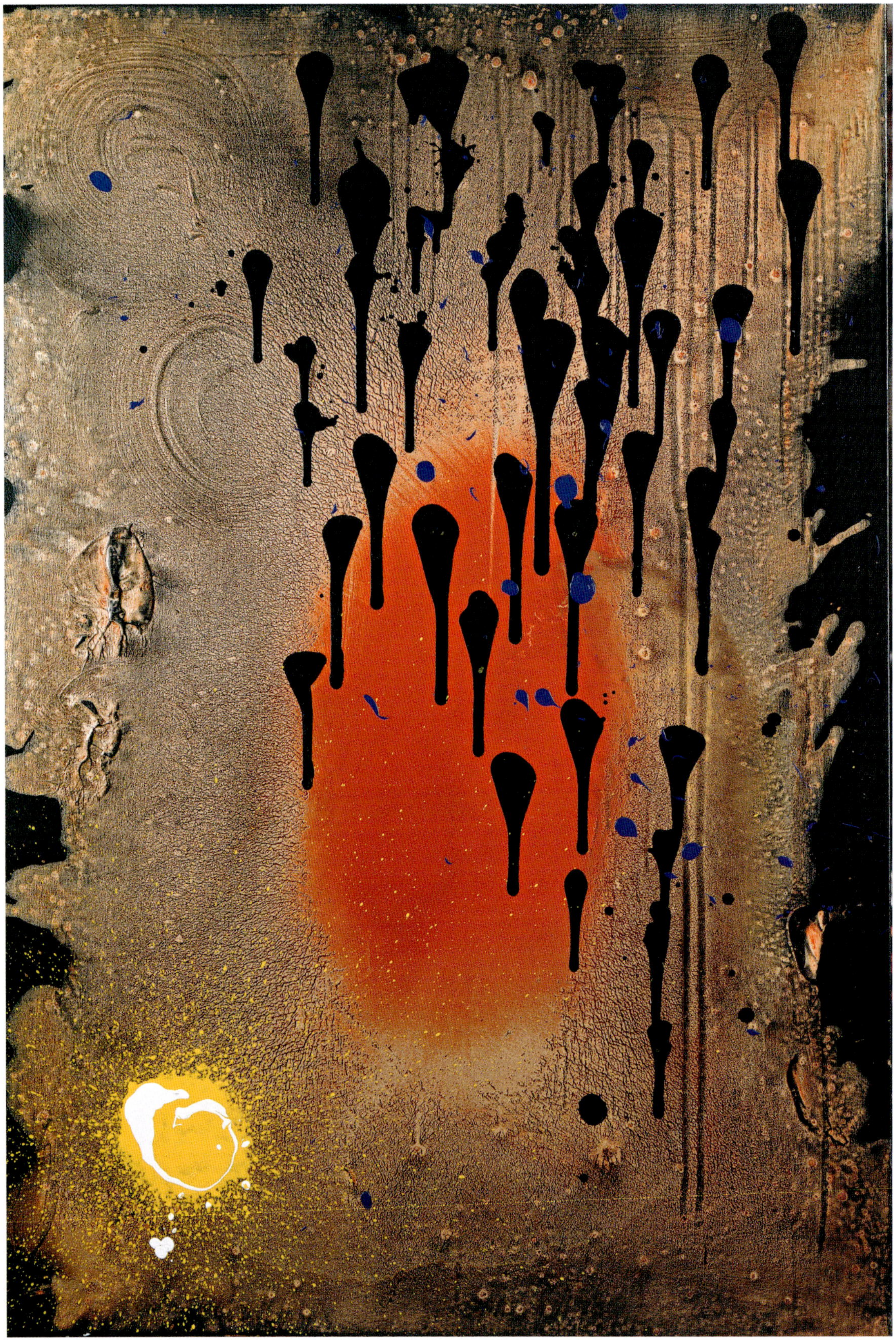

Beyond, 9.10.04
Acrylic on cotton duck
152.5 × 102 cm
(60 × 40 inches)

out and get it.' It's only now that I'm old that I realize what he meant. Now it's all come home to roost.

In England you were either abstract or figurative. You hated figurative art if you were abstract, and vice versa. You know, the way Hockney and Kitaj hated non-figurative painting and mounted huge attacks on it, which is partly a PR survival technique, of course; they didn't want to be overtaken. I said to Rothko I thought the de Kooning was fantastic. If you'd have said that in England you'd have got a very different response, but Rothko said, 'Wasn't it? Wasn't it just?' So I was never in one camp; never in the Pop camp or the Conceptual camp, but never in the Abstract versus Figurative camp, either. In a way it's not been a big issue for me.

The fact was that I didn't know how to let go of what I'd got into, which became known as Formalism. I didn't know how to get out of it without compromising structure. I didn't want to go back to German Expressionism or cartoon-like illustration, or a combination of those kind of things (Baselitz, Kokoschka, all of that). I didn't want to let go of the purity of the kind of painting I loved, but at the same time I knew I just couldn't keep painting from inside and not looking outside. Then Motherwell gave me that book on Miró and that confirmed that it was all right to look around you. But then how to do it? Where to go? Where to look? I gradually was able to go back to using line, colour and plane, and not just plane. That was a kind of hard-won freedom that I had eradicated early on.

And the metaphysical, if we can call it that?

That sort of quality that you find in some great paintings, it's either there or it's not there. It's when two and two make five. Things don't quite add up the way you think they will. It's the difference between Frans Hals and Rembrandt, nobody knows what that quality is or where it comes from, or how people can achieve it. I hope I will, but I really don't know. You can't build spirituality into a work, you can't set about it. But I think if you're not thinking about it, it won't happen either. You've got to be receptive to it.

Strangers, 8.2.05
Acrylic on cotton duck
46 × 36 cm (18 × 14 inches)

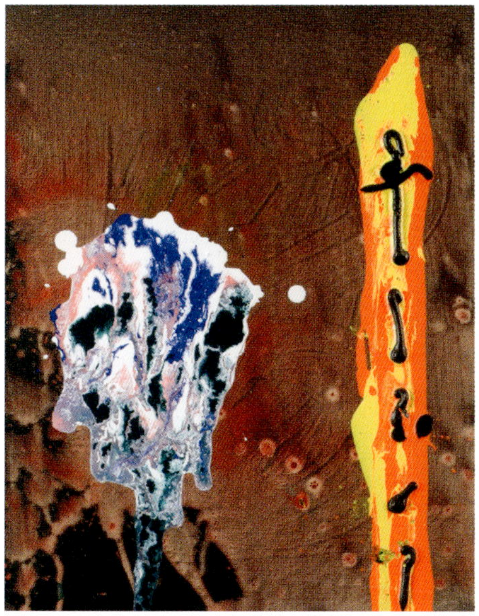

I slightly took issue with you about Roger Hilton. I thought he was a very good artist but he allowed himself to trivialize his own art through his ill-health and self-inflicted damage. I think I'm stronger in the sense of the intellectual and physical integrity of the work, and the responsibility of structuring a work somehow. I don't see how I can let that go easily, much as I would like to make my work even simpler than it is.

When you make complex work you risk a hell of a lot. You could say everything in a painting but you can't put everything in a painting. In a way, the less you put in, the better it is. It's a whole world. It's like a film or a great novel, it's scatological, it's very primitive, but it's still got to have as much in it as an encyclopaedia. Every painting has to have that. There is a danger of trying to put more in. I suffer from that weakness – I think a lot of people do. And a lot of other people do simple paintings and they're just bloody simple, just stupid! Painting has to be a synthesis of something complex made simple. It's not that easy to do. I'd rather risk being complex than being stupidly simple. I see a lot of stupidly simple paintings which are not potent with feeling through their simplicity. They're just stupid paintings.

Tell me about your attitude to Zen.

I don't know anything really about Buddhism or the stages of Zen but I think there are different levels and it's very hard to get from one level to the next. To become a master seems to take a long time. There are exceptions like Basquiat who had a lot of talent which he blew very quickly. In the end, it all boils down to character and will. We don't know why we are how we are.

You say you don't really know anything about it yet you often quote the blind Zen archer.

There's something about that Eastern mysticism, that kind of grasping and recognizing the moment which seems to have a relationship to painting. There's no explanation for it.

Miró said that the best art lesson he ever had was when his teacher told him to draw with his eyes closed. I've tried it, don't think I haven't tried it. It didn't work particularly for me. No, again, as Picasso said, it's the unlearning process, doing what you don't know.

You were very close to Motherwell. What was he like?

He was very well educated, probably the cleverest person I've ever met in my whole life. He could talk about what was going on in music in the 18th century, what was going on in wars, in art. He had that kind of lateral vision. You only spent five minutes with him and you learnt something. He said to me, "You could be the next Turner", but I didn't think much of it. He gave me this book on Turner in which he'd underlined all these things – for himself, not for me. Talking about space and colour and oblivion and whatever. Then he gave me the book on Miró. And that helped me more.

Was Barnett Newman important to you?

He was a fantastic guy. Barney came very late to painting but he really understood painterliness.

Out of the three, Newman, Rothko and Motherwell, which one was of more interest to you as an artist?

I think from the point of view of being moved by an individual work, I have to say Rothko. There's an emotional truth to his work that you just have to recognize. But

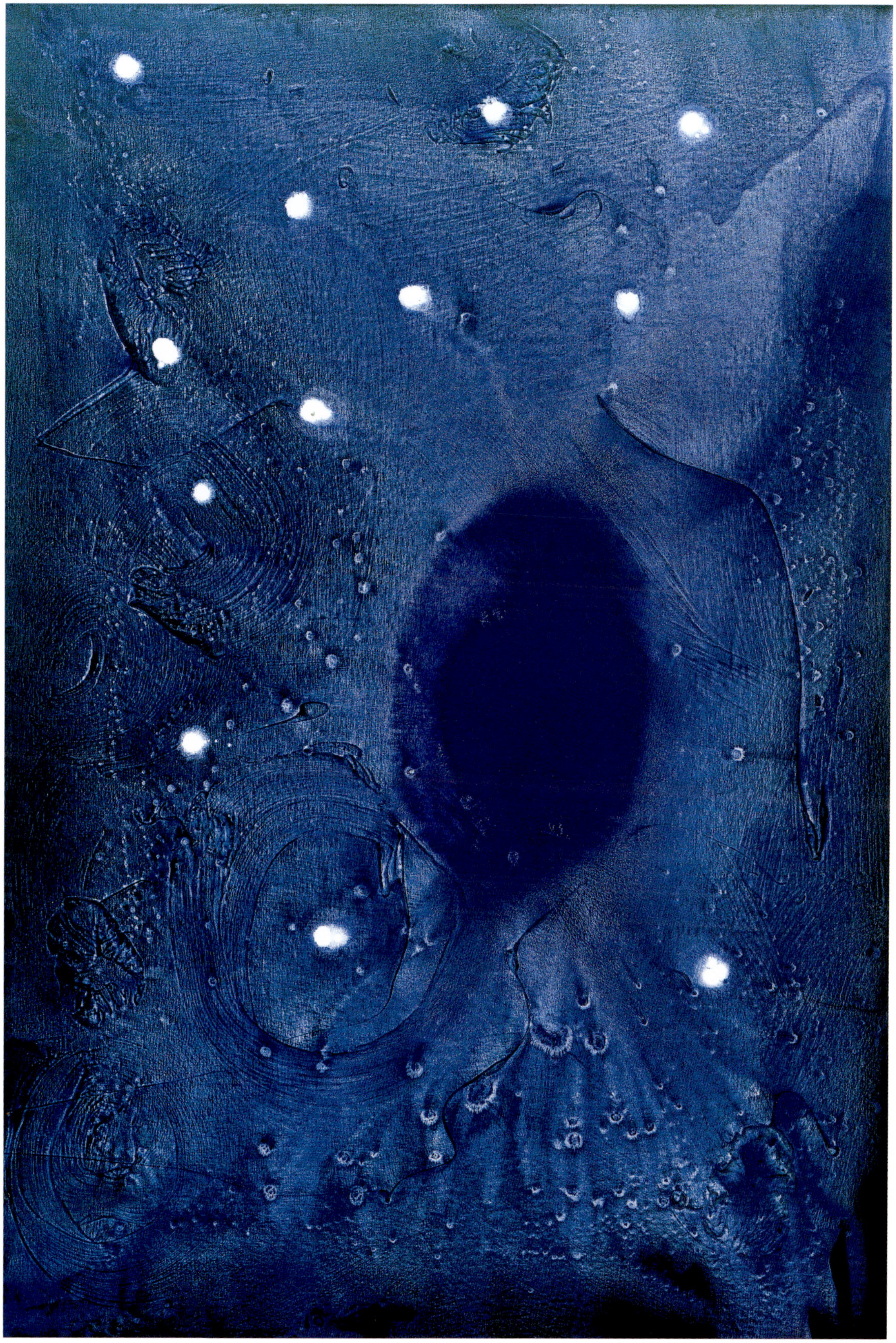

Night Sky, 10.1.05
Acrylic on cotton duck
152.5 × 102 cm
(60 × 40 inches)

as a kind of more complex and much more interesting genre, I have to say Motherwell. Because Motherwell was a bridge in the way that Hans Hofmann was a bridge between Europe and America. Of course what I was getting bored with in America was that people were churning out similar products, but Bob was desperate enough to try out different ideas. Rothko was in a trap, he knew he was in a cul-de-sac at the end of the day. That's what he bequeathed us.

Once you'd made the decision to use line again, did it feel dangerous or exhilarating to be drawing?

Kind of dangerous. As I've said before, I'm trying to be able to paint anything. And I'm not there yet. But I'm painting more things than I was able to do 20 or 30 years ago. So it's hoping to achieve a gradual liberation and a more potent synthesis. I want each painting to be like a person or a place. I don't know how specific you can be, but to have the presence of a living thing.

You've said that when you're painting you imagine certain forms and then when you travel subsequently you sometimes discover those same forms in nature.

I think that happens. I think you imagine things and then somehow they are justified in something you've seen. Maybe that's because you're looking for it.

You mean you're recognizing it? As if your mind has already been there and then you find that what you imagined is confirmed by nature?

Yeah, that's right.

When you work, are you ever in a state of trance?

I'm always very aware of what I'm doing but I'm also open to suggestion. I used to play very loud music to kind of hype myself up and try to paint an equivalent of the music. But now I think that's a kind of artificial stimulant, so I paint without any music at all.

Two Quotes

In conversation with David Sylvester in 1961 Motherwell said: *'The process of painting is a series of moral decisions about the aesthetic … .* I really think art is basically a moral enterprise. And that the artistry, if you want to put it that way, is the beauty and completeness with which a moral position is asserted. But the very nature of this beauty is dependent on the moral position.'

Rothko once said: 'Often, towards nightfall, there's a feeling in the air of mystery, threat, frustration – all of these at once. I would like my painting to have the quality of such moments.'

The Tiger Guard, 10.7.05
Acrylic on cotton duck
152.5 × 127 cm (60 × 50 inches)

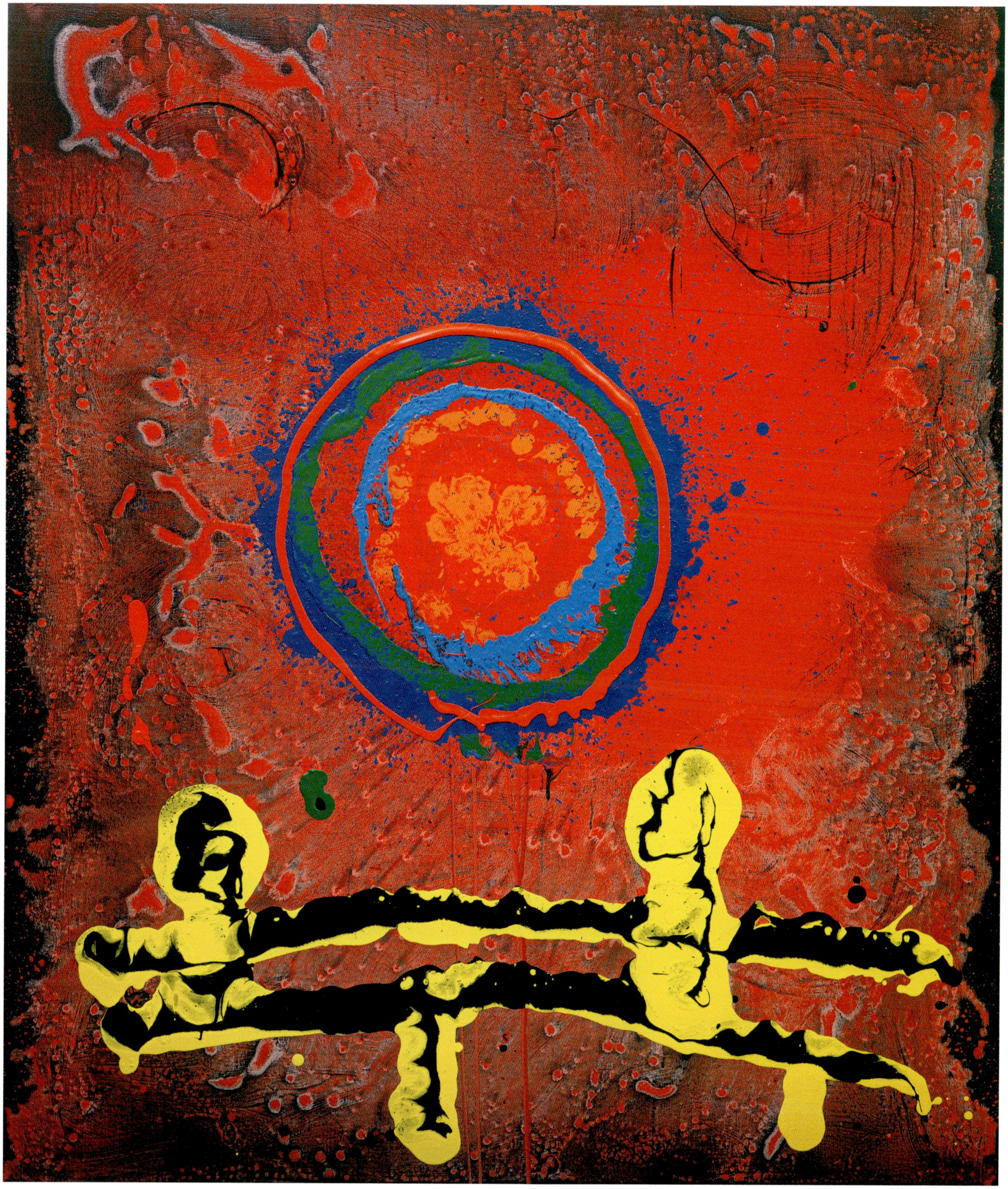

13

The Sketchbooks

When he was a child, drawing for Hoyland was a total preoccupation and delight. It was also a way of getting to stay up late, as his mother encouraged all signs of the budding artist. But when he got to art school, Hoyland began to hate the drudgery of drawing, whether anatomy, still-life, from the antique or in the life room, and he had to endure plenty of it. (He was at art school for a total of 15 years, 1945–1960, from junior Sheffield to the RA.)

After a break of many years, Hoyland is drawing again. He is more involved these days in calligraphy and the ideograph, with line that is declarative rather than nervy, yet that is also sensitive in its intermissions and excursions. He says that drawing is the rational intellectual side of what he does, and is mostly about structures. 'Colour's more like love. Colour comes over you and you respond to it.'

Drawing has led to a retrieval of figuration in Hoyland's work, as he reinterprets the look of the external world in his personal language of sign and gesture. If the great thrust of Modernism was towards formal abstraction, there was always a strand of even the most revolutionary experimentation which questioned abstraction as a final goal. Even the Russian Constructivists had their doubts. As Liubov Popova said in 1921: 'I don't think that non-objective form is the final form: it is the revolutionary condition of form.' And revolution is only, of course, a temporary phase. As mentioned earlier, Victor Pasmore was another artist who recognized that figuration was no longer off-limits to the experimental avant-garde artist.

Hoyland makes schematic diagrams rather than descriptive drawings. He keeps a series of sketchbooks in which he uses water-based Stabilo lay-out marker pens in a wide range of colours, and achieves with these some of the chromatic richness and startling optical juxtapositions of his paintings. He makes notations from his surroundings, as he might take photographs, to isolate a potentially useful detail that may develop into a painting back in the studio. His painting practice involves using drawings, photographs or even postcards to trigger further creativity: stimulus and reaction, then further response. The painting emerges through the process of

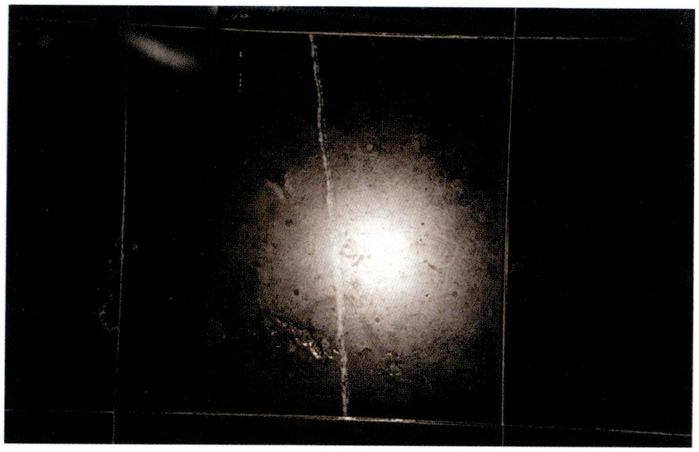

Inspiration from the bathroom floor taken during a trip to Malaga

its making, it is not thought-out beforehand. Hoyland does not make preliminary drawings which he then transfers to canvas. As he says, drawings are more likely to be ideas for compositions: 'Sometimes a very simple outline of where I think the positioning of something ought to be.'

At the time of writing, in spring 2009, Hoyland had just returned from a brief trip to Malaga to visit the Picasso Museum. Back in the studio we looked at photos he'd taken of the patterns in marble slabs on the plazas of Malaga. In one he sees a Turner landscape by the sea. 'This is the sort of thing that could kick me off. This one is part of the starry night series – the bathroom floor. Black marble with flash. You know the line I've been doing? This would be a way of breaking it down even more. Tiles. I don't know if any of this will feed in. I'll nick anything.' He also shows me beautiful photos of leaves in Jamaica, elegantly distributed on the pavement by the wind, other photos of the patterns of tree bark. None of these have yet been used and may not be. There is a large degree of natural wastage in Hoyland's research material.

Photos of fallen leaves and foliage in Jamaica

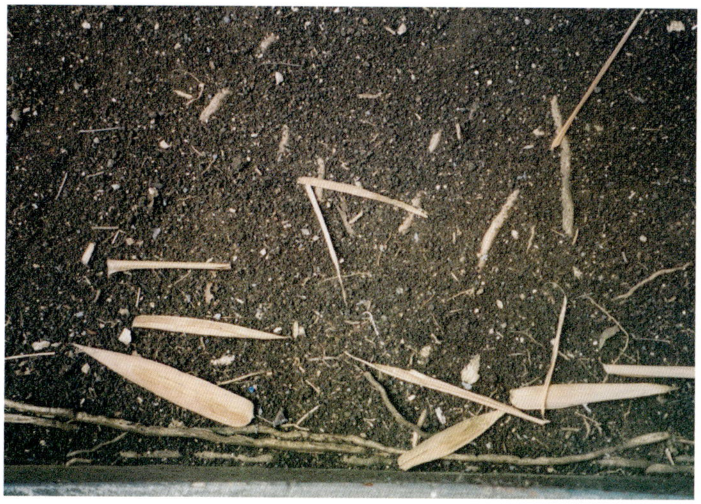

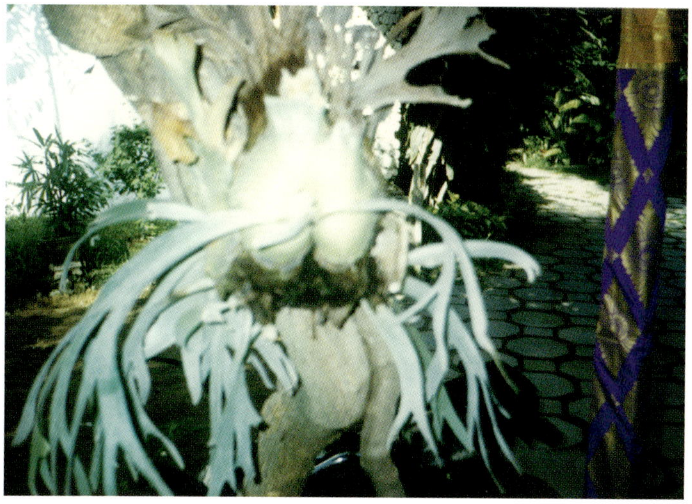

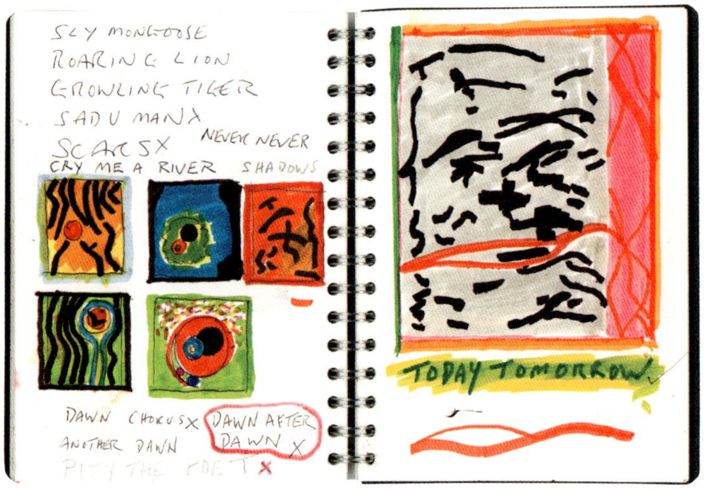

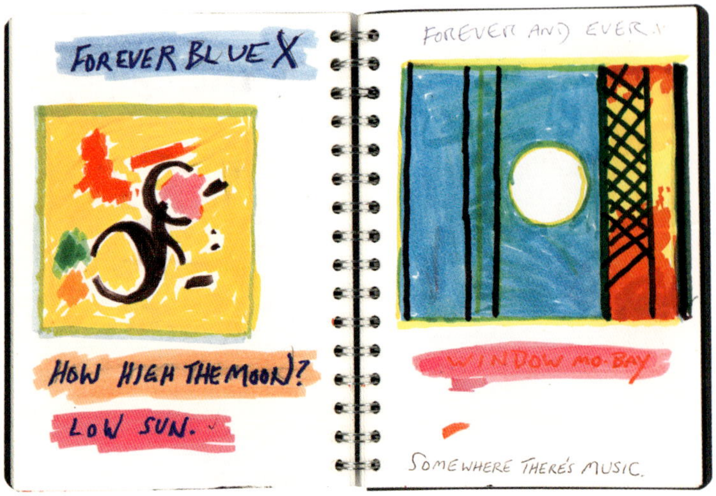

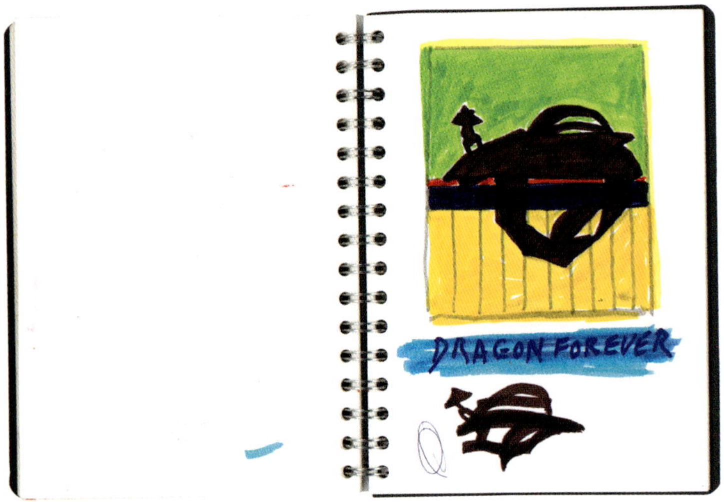

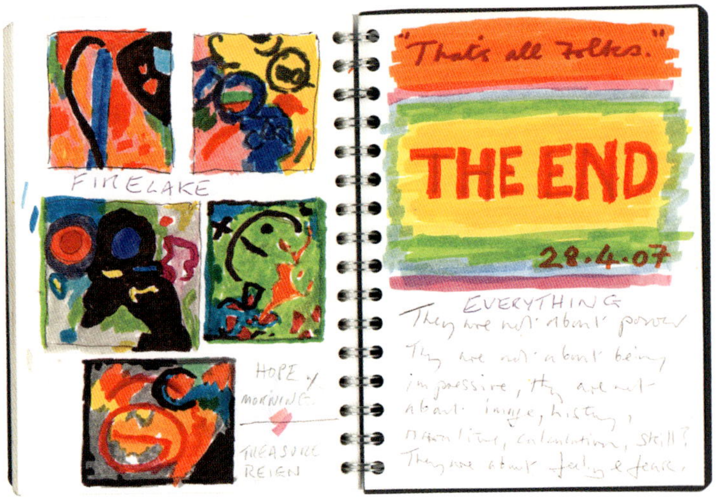

He often makes written colour notes for pictures beside the drawings. Sometimes there will be as many as six or eight small, intensely-coloured diagrams on a page. These small sketches each contain the seed of a painting, though not all are realized. Many form the miniature blueprints of much larger paintings. These first sketches can be remarkably detailed in their disposition of forms and colours, and although Hoyland does not slavishly follow their dictates, the finished paintings can betray an intimate relationship with these first ideas.

The renewed interest in drawing in sketchbooks has extended to his paint application. Is Hoyland's current linearity a long-delayed response to the inspired trickling and liquid scrawling of Jackson Pollock, whose work he first properly studied at the Whitechapel in 1958? But Pollock goes for an all-over mesh of interwoven lines, a pulsing network which holds the space of the picture as much as it dominates its surface. Hoyland uses line sparingly in comparison, as just one method of applying paint in a large vocabulary of gestures. His line is less a

The sketchbooks contain ideas for titles, general observations and philosophical thoughts alongside actual drawings

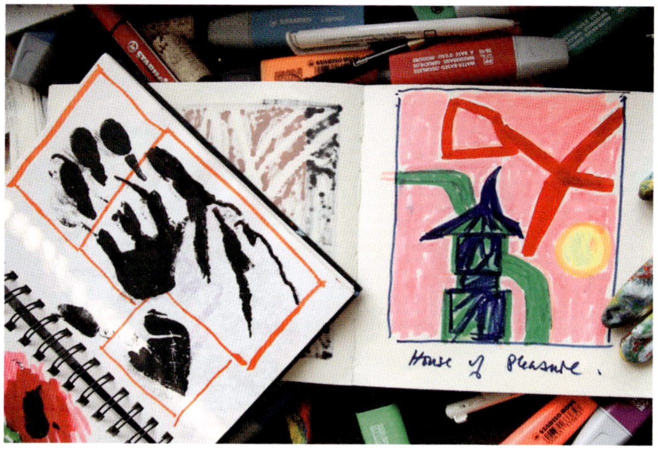

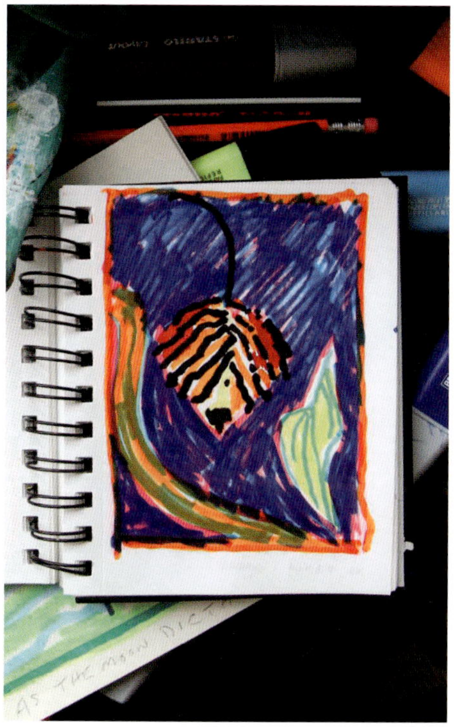

tracery than a calligraphic sign or arabesque, more like an oriental statement but with a far richer, more enrobed or embedded, context.

The sketchbooks alternate drawing with writing. Hoyland has made drawings after cave paintings and children's drawings. He has also made drawings of cuts in tree bark, an idea involved with a memory of time which he admits he has never quite worked out how to deal with. His notebooks also contain long lists of possible titles for paintings. (He quips: 'It looks like I have more ideas for titles than paintings.')

These lists can read like poems. For instance:

WAVE PICTURE
CAN THIS BE REAL?
PARADISE LIKE THAT,
LOSING REALITY
LIVING THE DREAM
LIVING A DREAM

(This from a sketchbook begun in Jamaica in November 2004.)

Hoyland's gnomic comments can read like a series of rules for studio practice or the rough drafts for a philosophy of life. Such as: 'gratitude for light and life'; 'cataclysmic forces of nature. Power of the trees'; 'fulfilling spiritual goals as an artist'; or 'mingling of menacing or melancholy elements with effects of ravishing beauty.'

He likes to make lists of workpoints:

1) Intense industry and intense passion.
2) Reveal with greater clarity the poetry of the elemental.
3) Vivid and miraculous.
4) Poetry in the elemental, as though it had been painted by the elements that it depicts.
5) Everything must resonate.

A quote from Nabokov crops up: 'The spiral is a spiritual circle, a circle set free.'

Longer observations include such typical ruminations as this: 'When one is young and has experienced a good deal of rejection, you want to show everyone how tough you are. Later you want to show how clever you are. Later still you want to see how far you can push yourself. And finally you don't give a fuck about anything, you just want to howl at the moon.' (2.4.06)

The sketchbooks also contain quotes from what Hoyland has been reading. In a 2007 sketchbook he quotes from Delacroix's *Journal*: 'What moves men of genius, or rather, what inspires their work, is not new ideas, but their obsession with the idea that what has already been said is still not enough.'

There are also quotations here from Shelley, including this one: 'Crisis can join the buried self for certain moments to our trivial daily minds'. And personal observations such as: 'I choose the sky over buildings any day.' Or: 'What I mind most in this country is being force-fed mediocrity.'

From the same sketchbook comes the following: 'If you can't use colour emotionally you are limited, but if you can't deal with structure you are equally tied. Motherwell's colour was limited; Rothko equally with structure. De Kooning couldn't escape the "old ways" but he did try. I think he made it a few times.'

More sources of inspiration: photos of graffiti and cracked pavements from Hoyland's scrapbooks

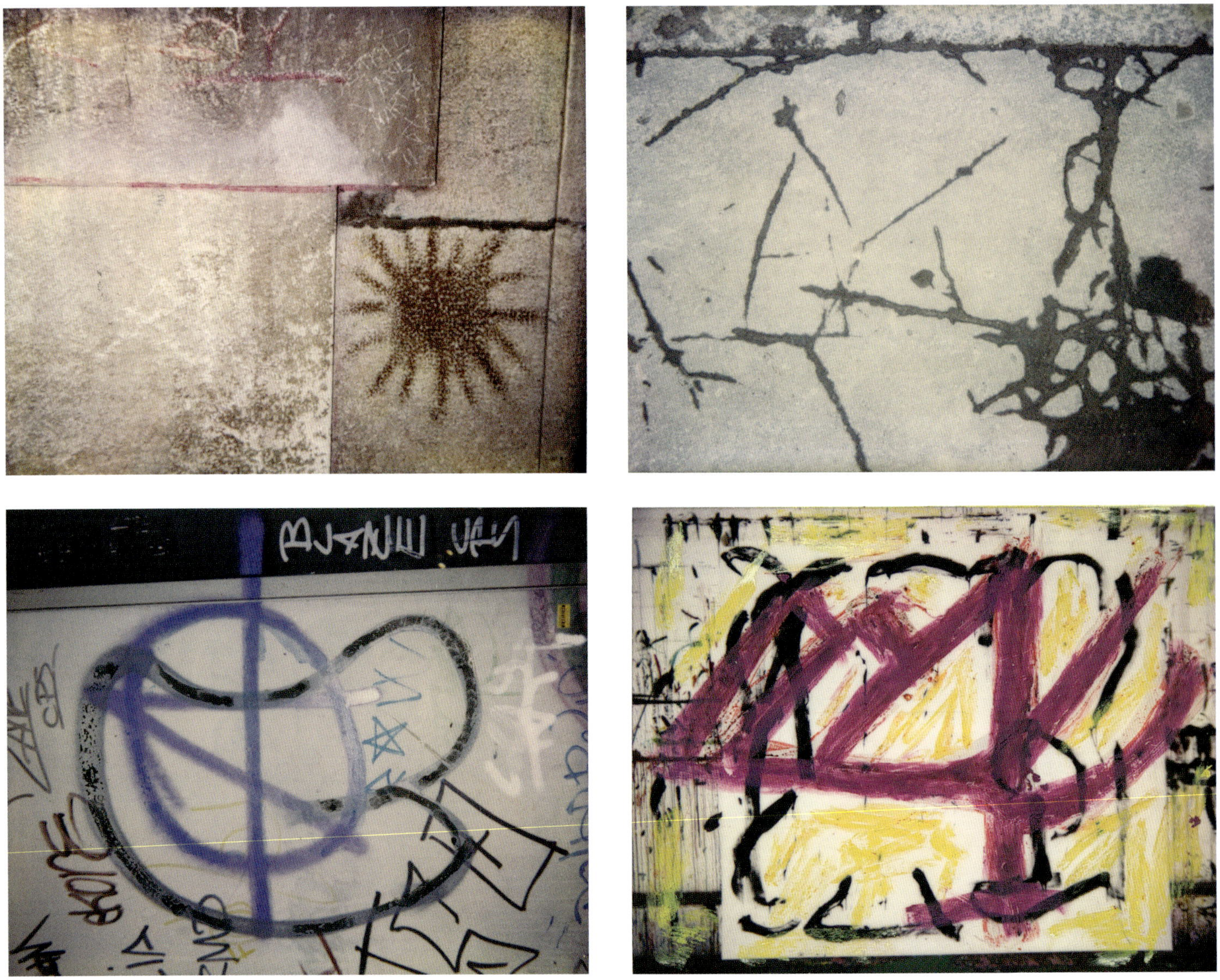

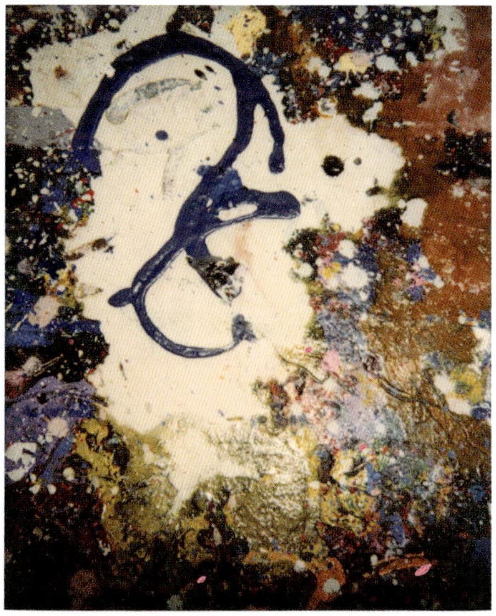

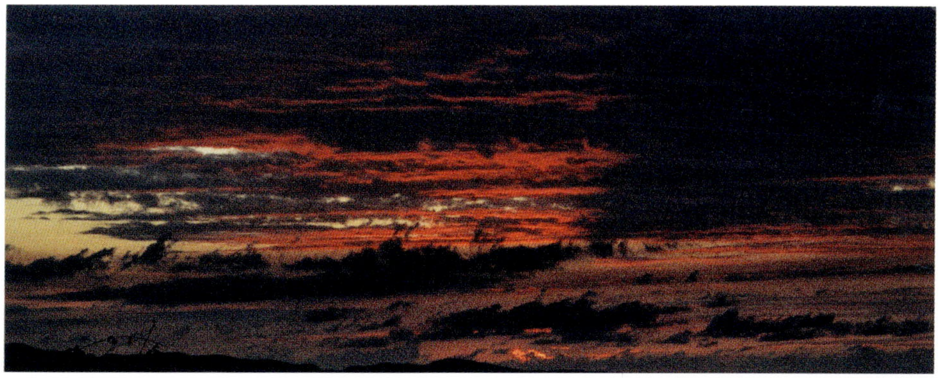

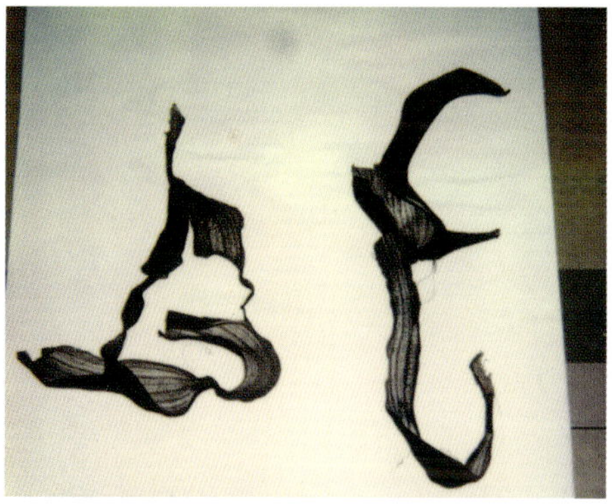

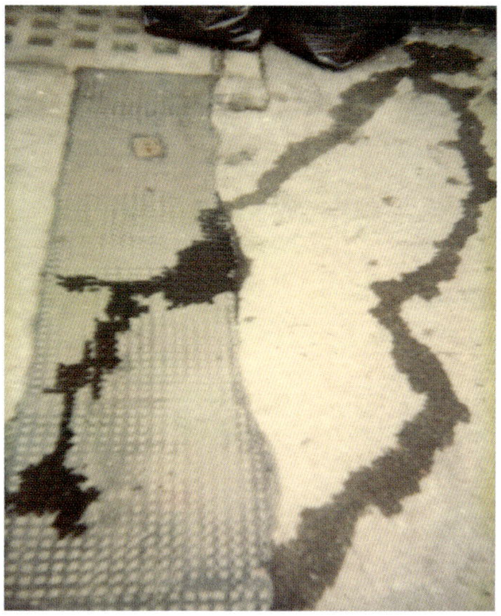

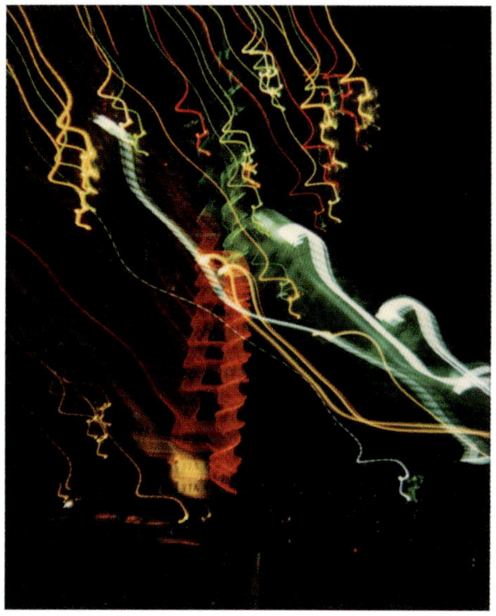

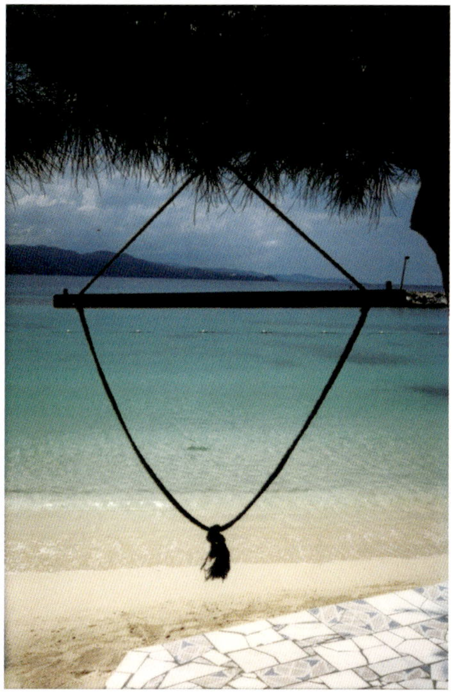

A selection of Hoyland's photos: (clockwise from top left) his studio floor, a Jamaican sunset, a distorted image of a waiter serving beer in a Bali bar, pavement stains, blackened banana skins, and a beach-side swing

In addition to the sketchbooks, Hoyland keeps a series of cheap scrapbooks which he fills with images: polaroids, postcards, newspaper and magazine photos, colour drawings done on loose sheets of paper, photocopies. The newsprint or photocopied images might be worked over in coloured inks or paint as the original image summoned forth a response in Hoyland who wanted to intensify the experience and make it his own.

Over the years, Hoyland has taken hundreds of photographs and polaroids, both in England and abroad. As he says, he likes bad photographs – he doesn't want anything too good. Sometimes he translates a polaroid into a drawing to give himself 'a kick off. I always have to start with a structure but whether it ends up that way is another matter' (from a 2005 interview).

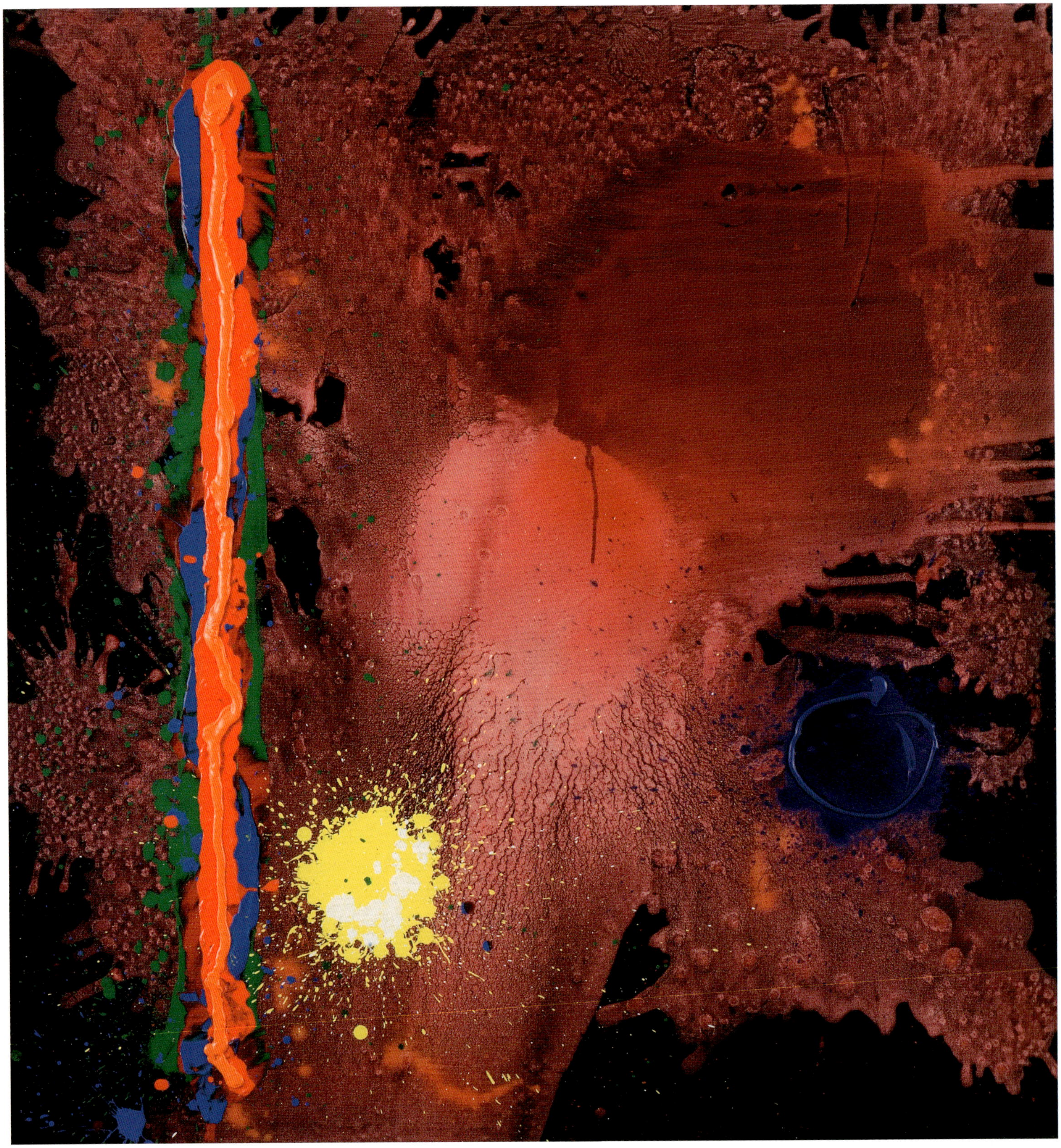

14

Important Themes

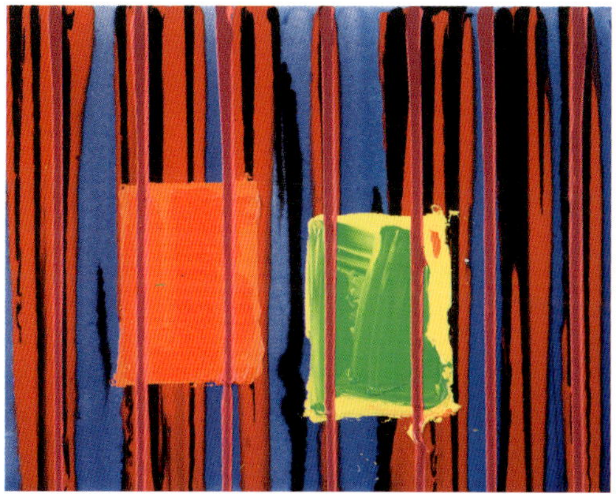

Homeward Thoughts, 31.8.00
Acrylic on cotton duck
61 × 76 cm (24 × 30 inches)

The One, 28.8.08
Acrylic on cotton duck
152.5 × 140 cm (60 × 55 inches)

H E Bates, a novelist and short-story writer with a particular penchant for the exotic, seems on occasion to be describing a Hoyland painting. Take his short story *The White Wind*. It begins like this: 'The lagoon had the hot brilliance of a stretch of celluloid constantly ignited by sunlight into white running flame. From far beyond it the Pacific galloped ceaselessly, charging, white-maned, against the coral reef. At each point of the gap, where the swell poured in, flew great conical flags of splendid spume.'

Bates writes evocatively of this unnamed South Sea island. 'The sun had gone down in a startling agony of carmine, purple-black and flame. A few pinkish clouds, like high birds, were flying far overhead, delicate broken-feathered.' Or again: 'A long serrated cockscomb of green and violet seemed to float out of the horizon under a scalding sun.' The similarity with Hoyland's imagery is unmistakeable.

In *Riverman* (15.7.99), overleaf, the central motif like a tall skinny figure bent at the knee is based closely upon an African wooden sculpture Hoyland recently bought. It is a grave-marker, a long body with no arms, in this respect like one of Craigie Aitchison's crucified Christs. Here we see how an artefact can directly influence the conception and execution of a painting. This happens occasionally in Hoyland's work, but is by no means a regular occurrence.

Traveller (20.7.99), on page 12, features a figure peering out from behind a waterfall of cerulean and orange. Note the luscious after-image of purple on the blue and orange, subtle but daring. And the molten, fleshy horizontal passage near the top. The juxtaposition of these separate richnesses is visually provocative and inventive.

Homeward Thoughts (31.8.00) offers a reprise of earlier concerns, echoing Hoyland's 1960s' paintings in a strongly geometric composition which explores the interweaving of rectangles and stripes, the vertical and the horizontal axes, flatness and depth. (What John McEwen calls the 'measured bars of poured paint', intermitted with oblongs, like envelopes stuck in a lattice.) It has all the pep of a later work, combined with the formal concerns of 'pure' abstraction. Hoyland revisits earlier interests because they still occupy his attention – though in a less

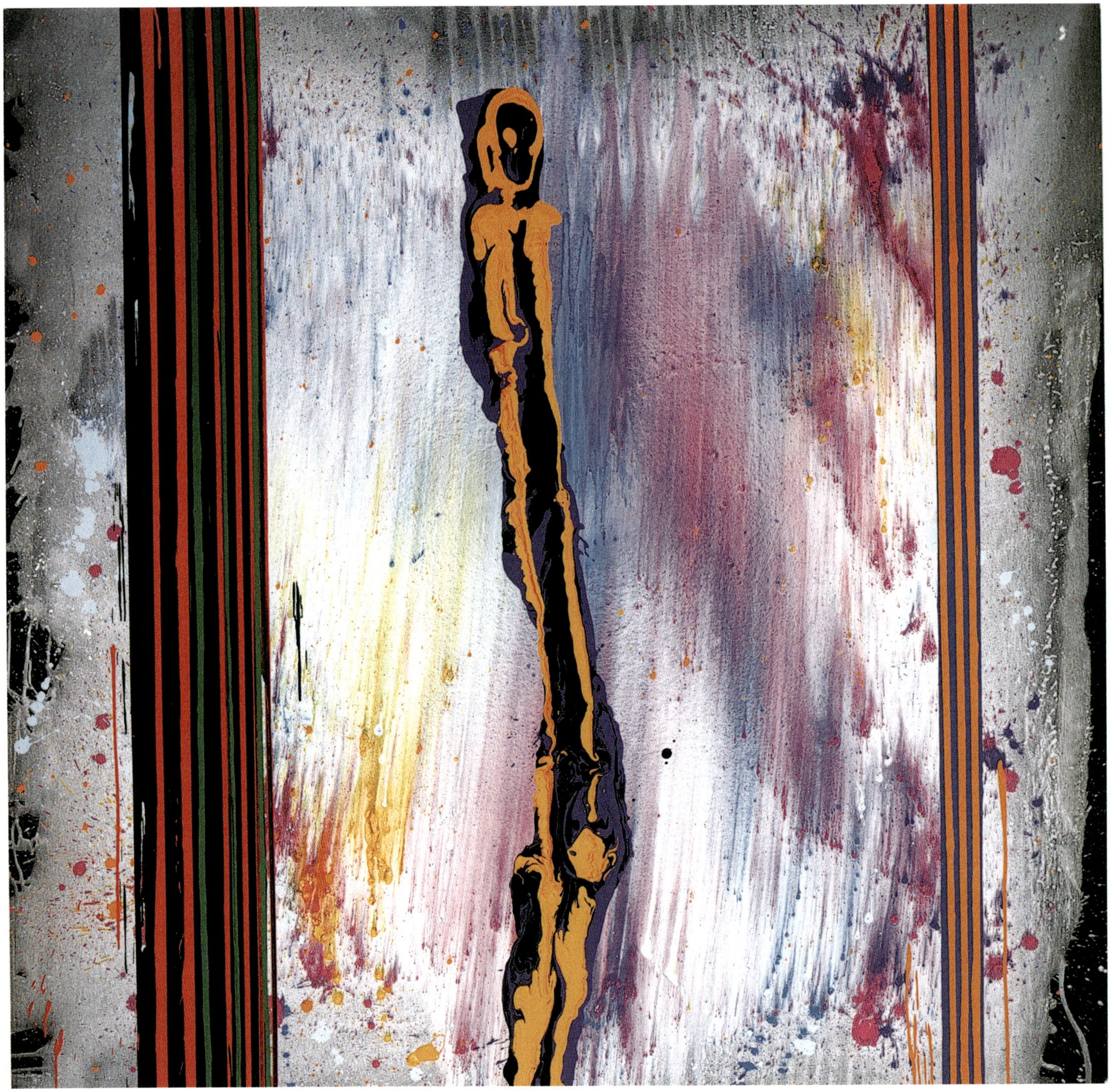

Riverman, 15.7.99
Acrylic on cotton duck
254 × 236 cm (100 × 93 inches)

intense way – and because his new-found freedom allows him to interpret earlier preoccupations in a much more inventive and satisfactory way. Also because he likes to raid his own back-catalogue as much as steal visual ideas from wherever he finds them.

In *1000 Fires* (28.12.00), the vertical shuttering of the painting's landscape format, with its poured stripes of colour against blue lake-like reflections and a top

1000 Fires, 28.12.00
Acrylic on cotton duck
160 × 201 cm (63 × 79 inches)

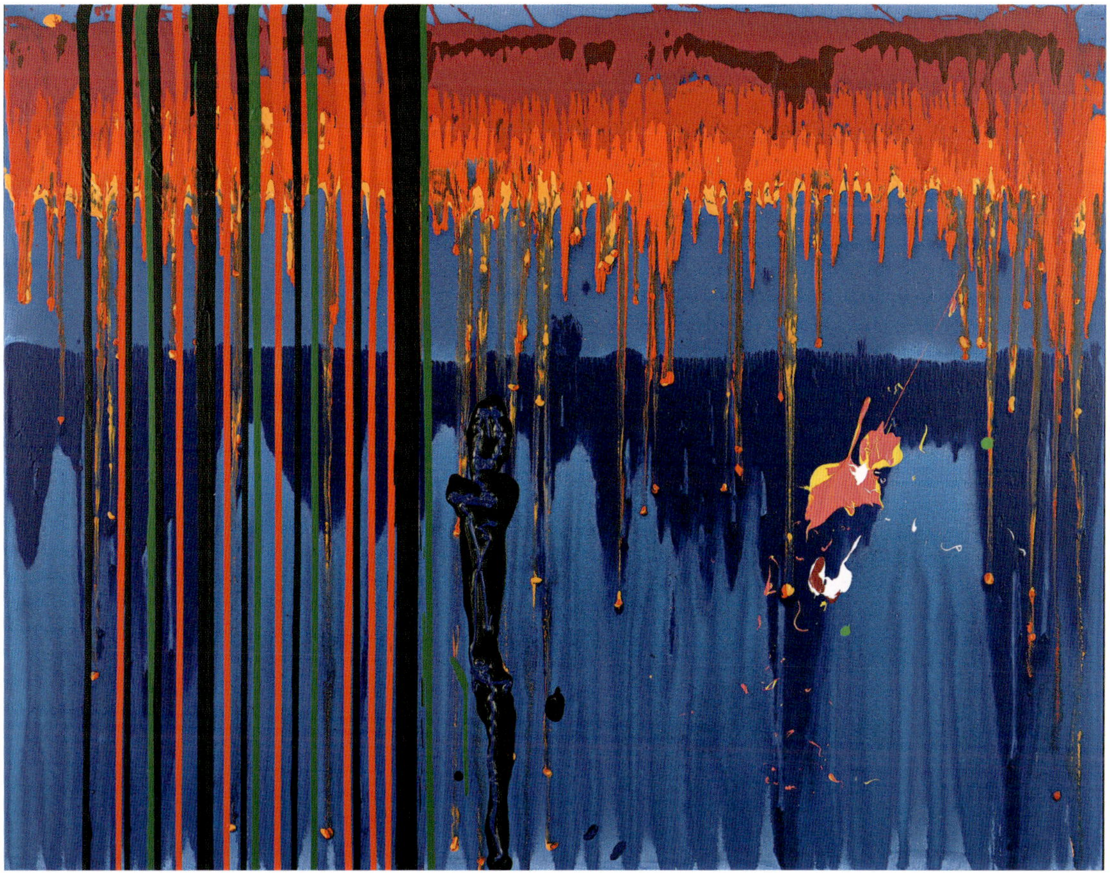

horizon of fire, allows for a corresponding sideways development of incident. Hoyland paints a central figure in dark outline, like a puppet on a stick, and near it an explosion of pink and yellow, as if some other life-form is melting in the heat. The stripes again suggest an earlier more rigorously geometric approach, here surpassed in emotional resonance and colouristic bravado.

Falls (28.3.01), overleaf, is a painting directly inspired by an observed event. Hoyland saw a figure jumping off the cliffs into the sea at Negril in Jamaica, when he was sitting at Rick's Café watching the world go by. It's a common enough occurrence, people diving from a height into the water, but something about the particular combination of events (mood, weather, light, movement and so on) stayed in his mind and later demanded expression in a painting. Here the figure in vividly complementary green and red is half-twisting, half-sitting on the way down, backed by giant falls of paint: tall pours and luscious tongues of red and yellow, punctuated by thinner verticals in black and blue and puce. The thin black verticals cut the painting into panels, and the figure lies beneath one of these divides, like a prisoner behind bars. It's an unsettling image about power and powerlessness, free-flow and entrapment. It's also a marvellous waterfall of pigment, a *coup de main* of great virtuosity.

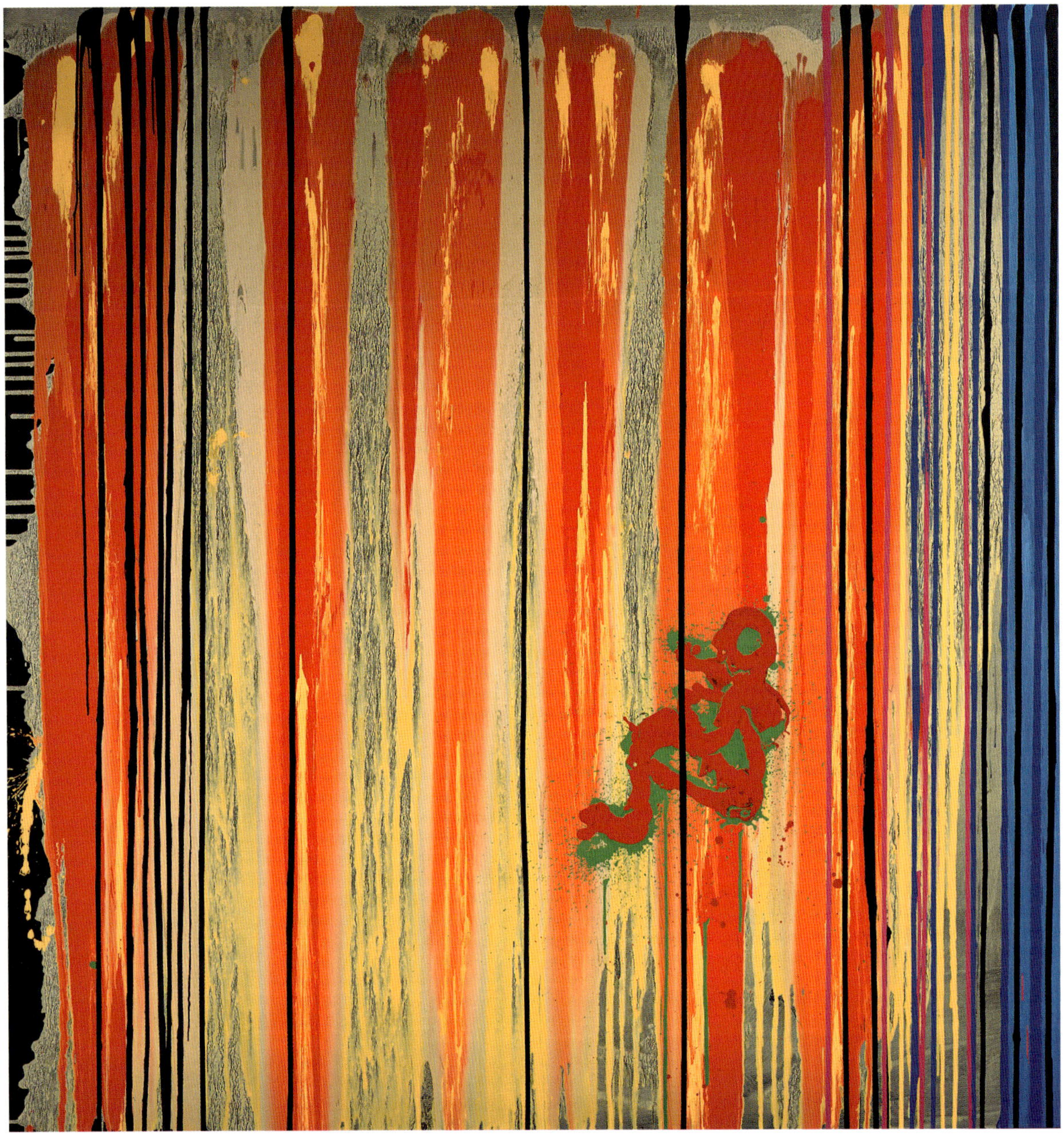

Falls, 28.3.01
Acrylic on cotton duck
254 × 236 cm (100 × 93 inches)

Elsewhere (3.4.01), a very Caribbean picture as the artist calls it, works around a great diagonal of black which gathers the energies at top left (an egg of fire) and carries them down to bottom right, to an ember cavern and green grate. The red and pink spider at bottom left might be a reference to lobster pots, just the sort of little detail observed by Hoyland on his Caribbean forays. He notes appraisingly: 'It's got a lot of depth but you always get pulled back to the surface.'

In so many of these paintings there are echoes of bodies, either in the direct reference of outline figures or in the indirect fleshy curves and undulations of thighs or buttocks, the weighted roundness of a breast. There has always been a sense of

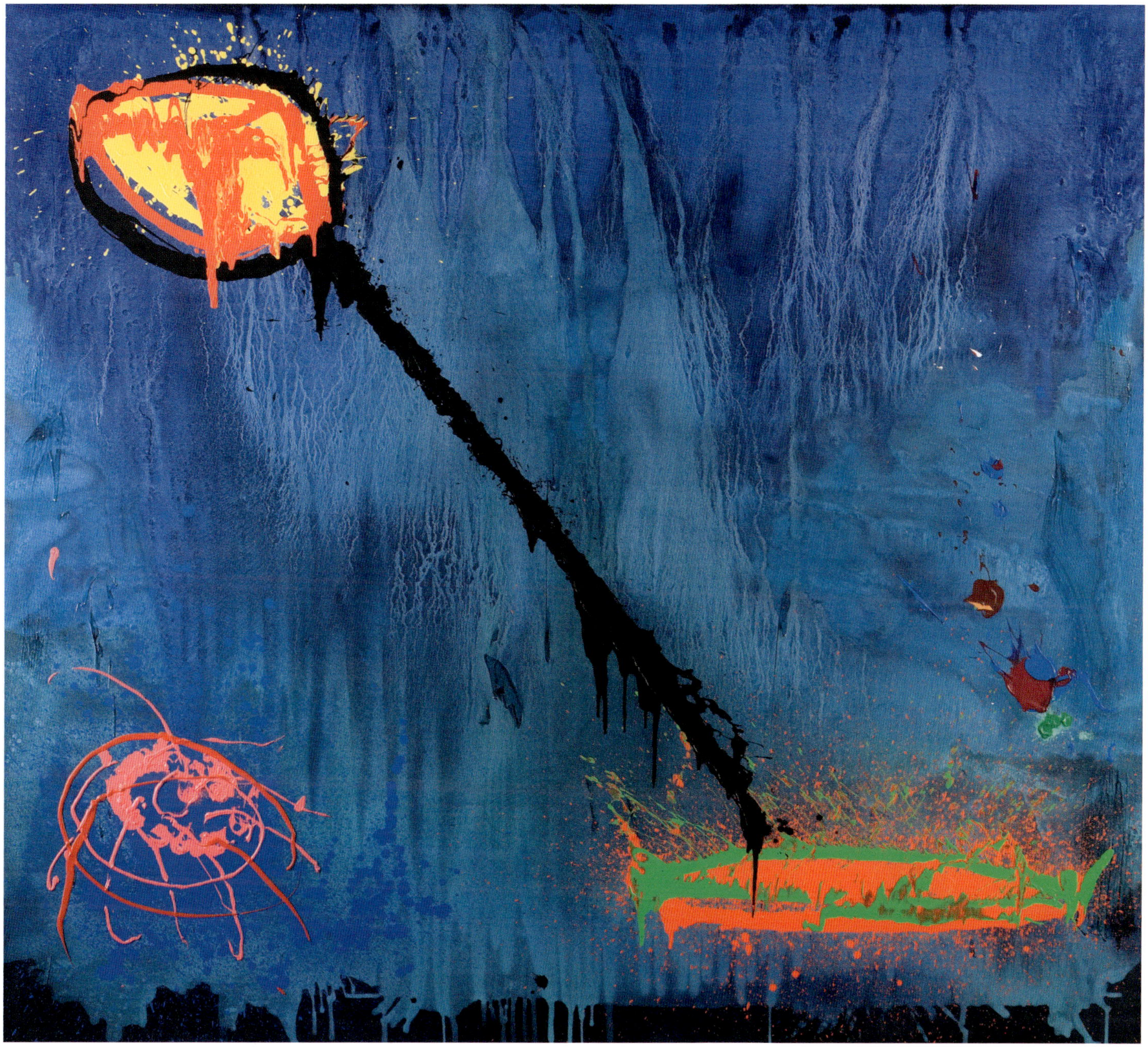

Elsewhere, 3.4.01
Acrylic on cotton duck
236 × 254 cm (93 × 100 inches)

the body in Hoyland's paintings, however ostensibly abstract his imagery. The figure is an unstated presence, whether standing, leaning or lying. This quality has become more apparent in recent years.

Hoyland's predilection for a dark ground often results in an effect in the overpainting resembling holes in leaves (like the distinctive apertures in a cheese plant). When he paints on a paler ground, the effect can be of light coming through foliage, a tree in full regalia against a bright summer sky; against a black ground, it becomes leaves against a night sky.

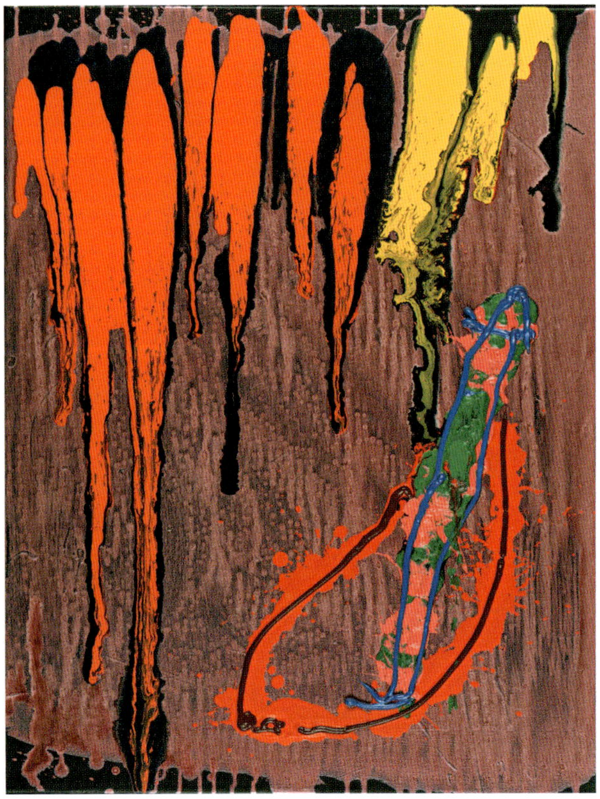

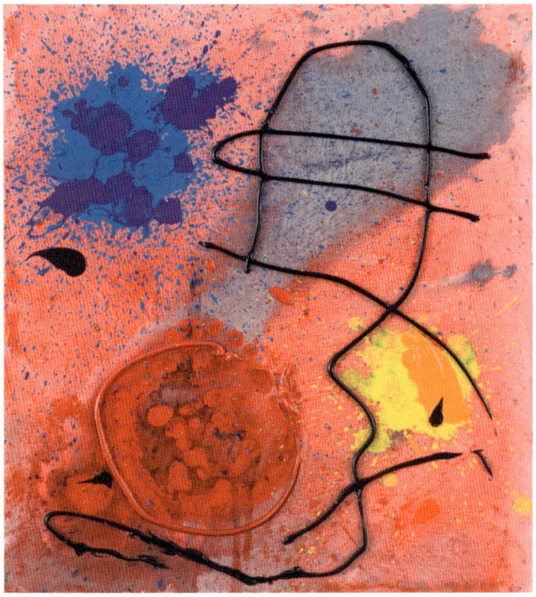

Dandy Man, 19.7.07
Acrylic on cotton duck
61 × 51 cm
(24 × 20 inches)

LEFT
The Boatman, 18.4.01
Acrylic on cotton duck
80 × 61 cm (31.5 × 24 inches)

The Boatman (18.4.01) features – as might be expected – a man in a boat. His long thin blue outline is distinctly penile, leaning against a very sketchily enclosing shape (the female?), which is presumably the boat. The rest of this memorable image is dominated by a series of flares along the top of the canvas, a couple of which extend down the whole surface: eight in a wilfully difficult orange (seen against a magenta pink ground), and three in bright yellow, all with an insulating edge of dark purple. The pervasive verticality of this very masculine image is defused with humour in the way the impudent boatman and his wonderfully primitive boat are drawn. It takes great panache to make this kind of hybrid imagery work, and Hoyland achieves it triumphantly. He himself likes this painting and calls it 'the nearest I got to figuration'.

Sometimes he has doubted his return to representational imagery. In 2005 he abruptly dismissed the figures in his work as 'no good'. Thankfully, this dark mood soon passed. Hoyland is very aware of the riskiness of what he is attempting. He is usually prevented from falling into complacency by the ravages of self-doubt. The activity of making art doesn't get any easier, and can indeed grow more difficult the more knowledge and experience you accumulate. The element of combat always remains. As he says: 'Painting is a killer sport … . Painting is really dangerous.'

Spirals and circles continue to feature regularly in the paintings, but other elements also intrude. In *Ride the Sky* (20.7.02), the central black motif looks like a

Ride the Sky, 20.7.02
Acrylic on cotton duck
254 × 236 cm (100 × 93 inches)

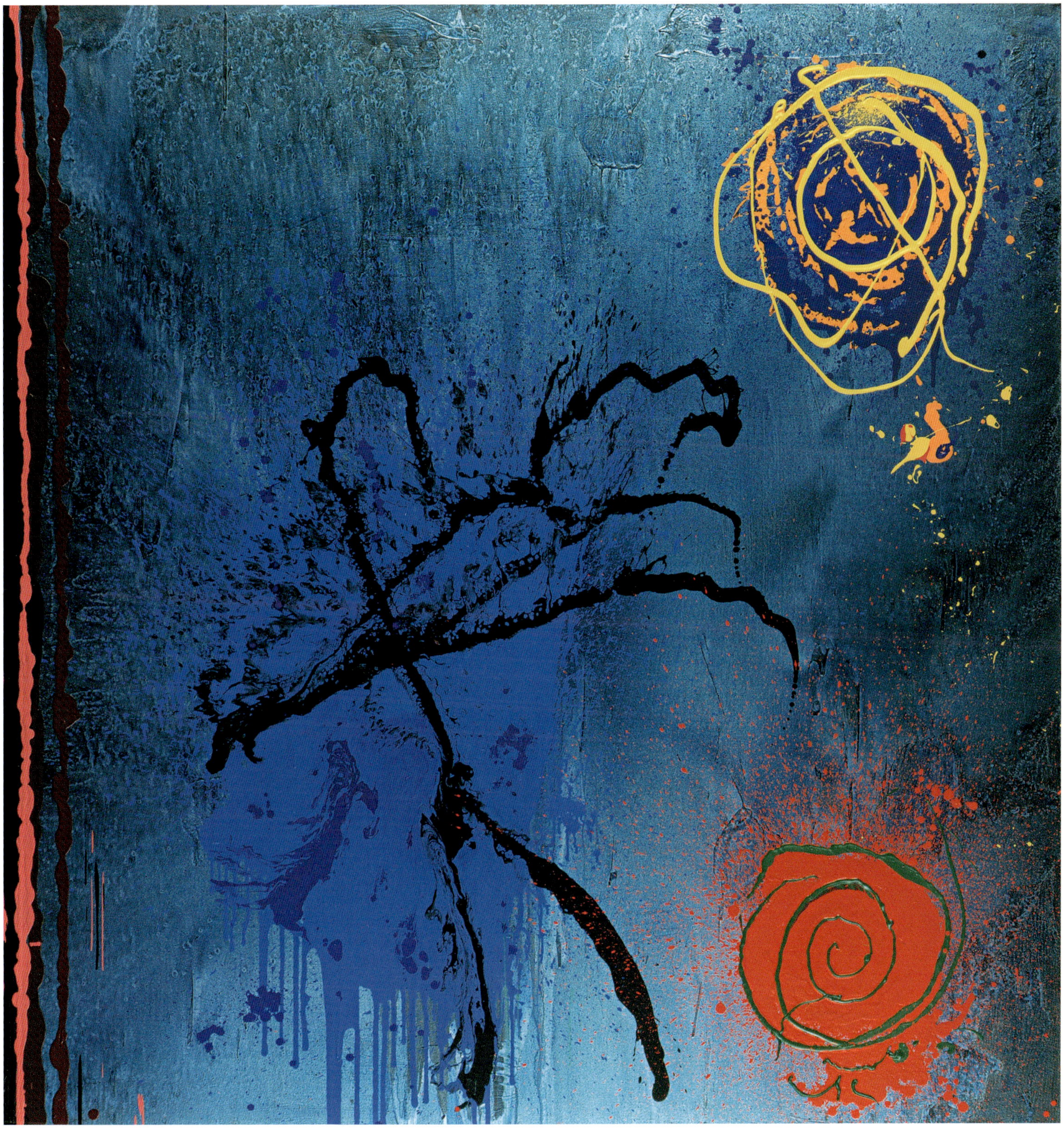

combination of a walking figure and a galloping or leaping horse, and is reminiscent of the horse-and-rider combination that Kandinsky made a trademark in the paintings of his transitional period between figuration and abstraction. Here Hoyland is returning the other way, and allowing himself a similar preferentiality, for a similar reason – to encourage the viewer to see deeper into a painting and more closely ally their personal concerns with the visual imagery. Hoyland's horse and human have some of the vigour and economy of cave painting, but they do not dominate the picture. Again, the figurative echoes are only one aspect of this passage in the painting, which works equally (if not more) effectively as mark-making.

In *The Birds' Path* (8.2.03), the motif in black on the left of the painting looks like a triple wing, perhaps of some insect. Instead of making signs to represent

OPPOSITE LEFT
New Journey, 26.1.04
Acrylic on cotton duck
127 × 76 cm (50 × 30 inches)

OPPOSITE RIGHT
Secret Summer, 11.7.05
Acrylic on cotton duck
127 × 102 cm (50 × 40 inches)

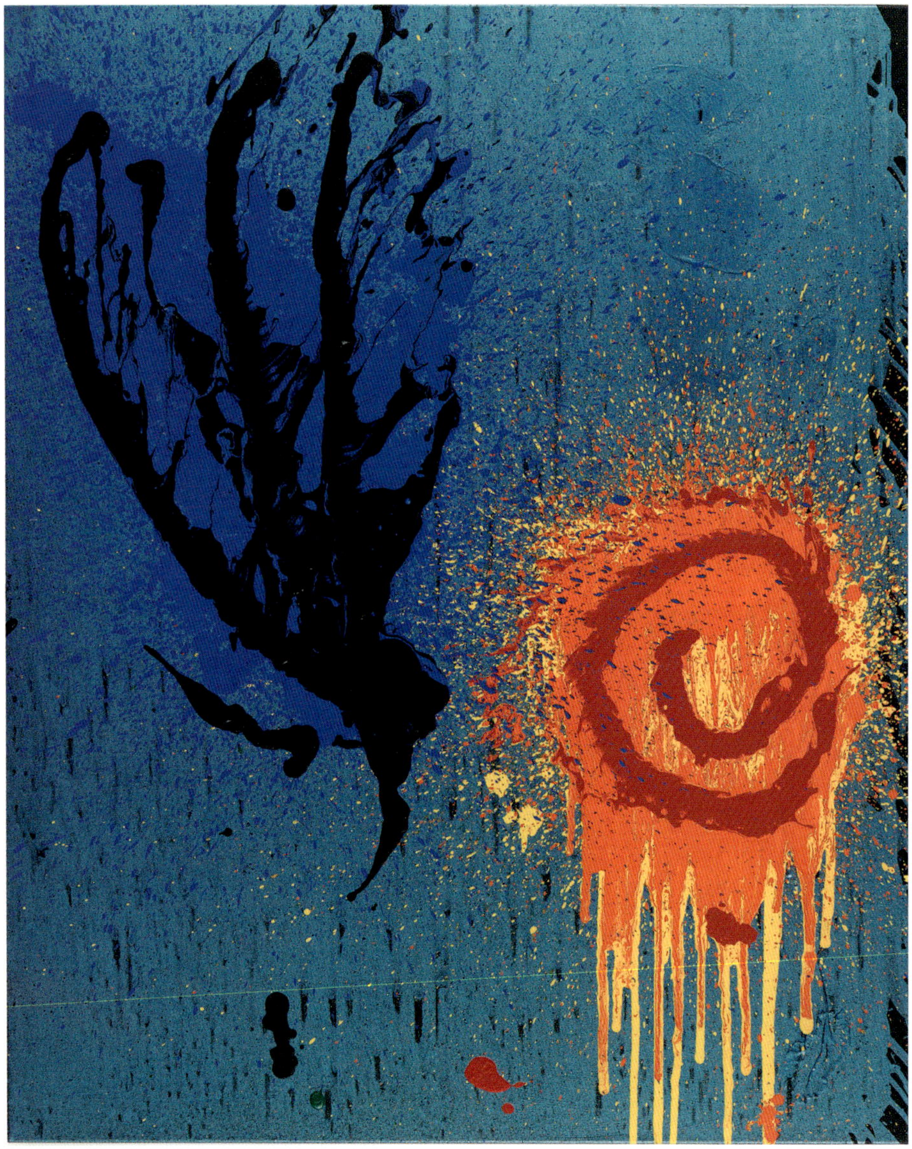

The Birds' Path, 8.2.03
Acrylic on cotton duck
127 × 102 cm (50 × 40 inches)

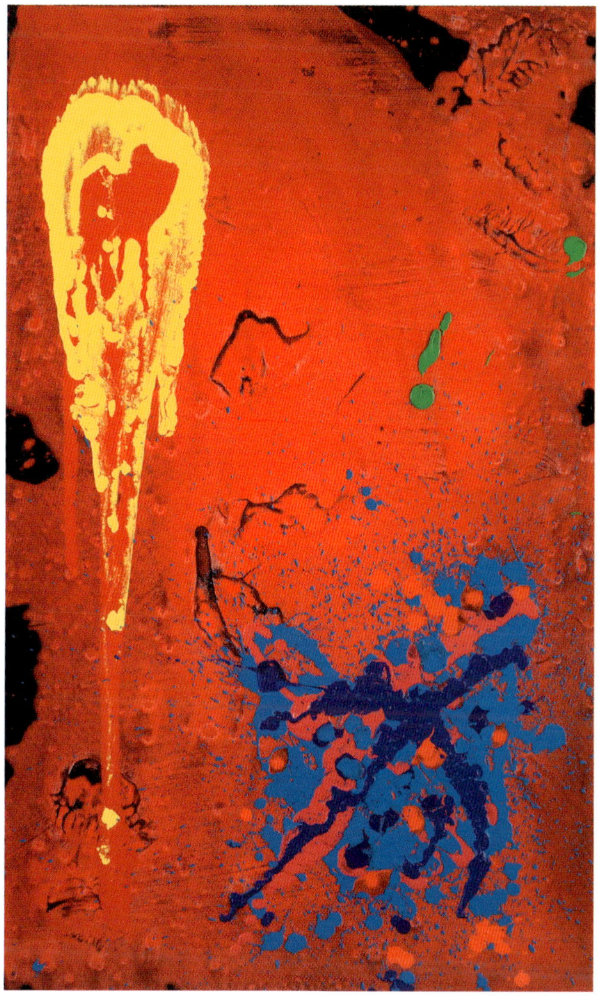

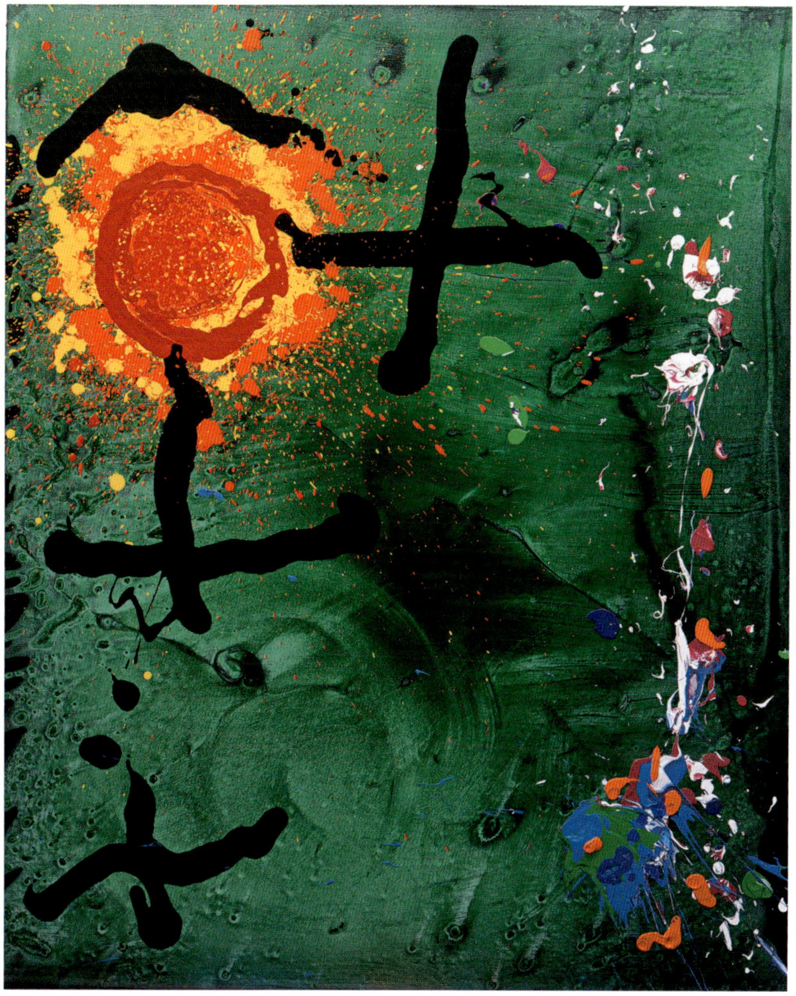

birds, like the animated cruciform pictograms he often uses, Hoyland has concentrated here on the idea of flight, while also bringing together an archetypal combination in his painting – wings and sun. The immediate reference, whether intended or not, is to the myth of Icarus, whose father Daedalus (the archetypal craftsman) made him a pair of wings to escape captivity. Despite his father's warnings, Icarus flew too near the sun – whether from simple hubris or some other more complex emotion – the wax holding his wings together melted and he fell to his death. All this is contained within a magical meeting of colours – fiery red-oranges and a range of blues that make most other colourists look pedestrian.

New Journey (26.1.04) is another bird image composed of electric blues over red – a favourite Hoyland combination. A narrow upright, it is a less familiar format and emphasizes further the sense of movement implicit in the title. The ball of yellow deliquesces and pours down the left side of the painting: the tangle of blue rises up from the right-hand bottom. Various splots and splashes of green and black add to its incarnadine splendour.

In Mauritius in April 2004, Hoyland jotted down his recipe for what he calls 'The Cuisine of Art':

Learning your instrument
Choosing your favourite song
Acquiring the skills you need
Listening to others in a discerning way.

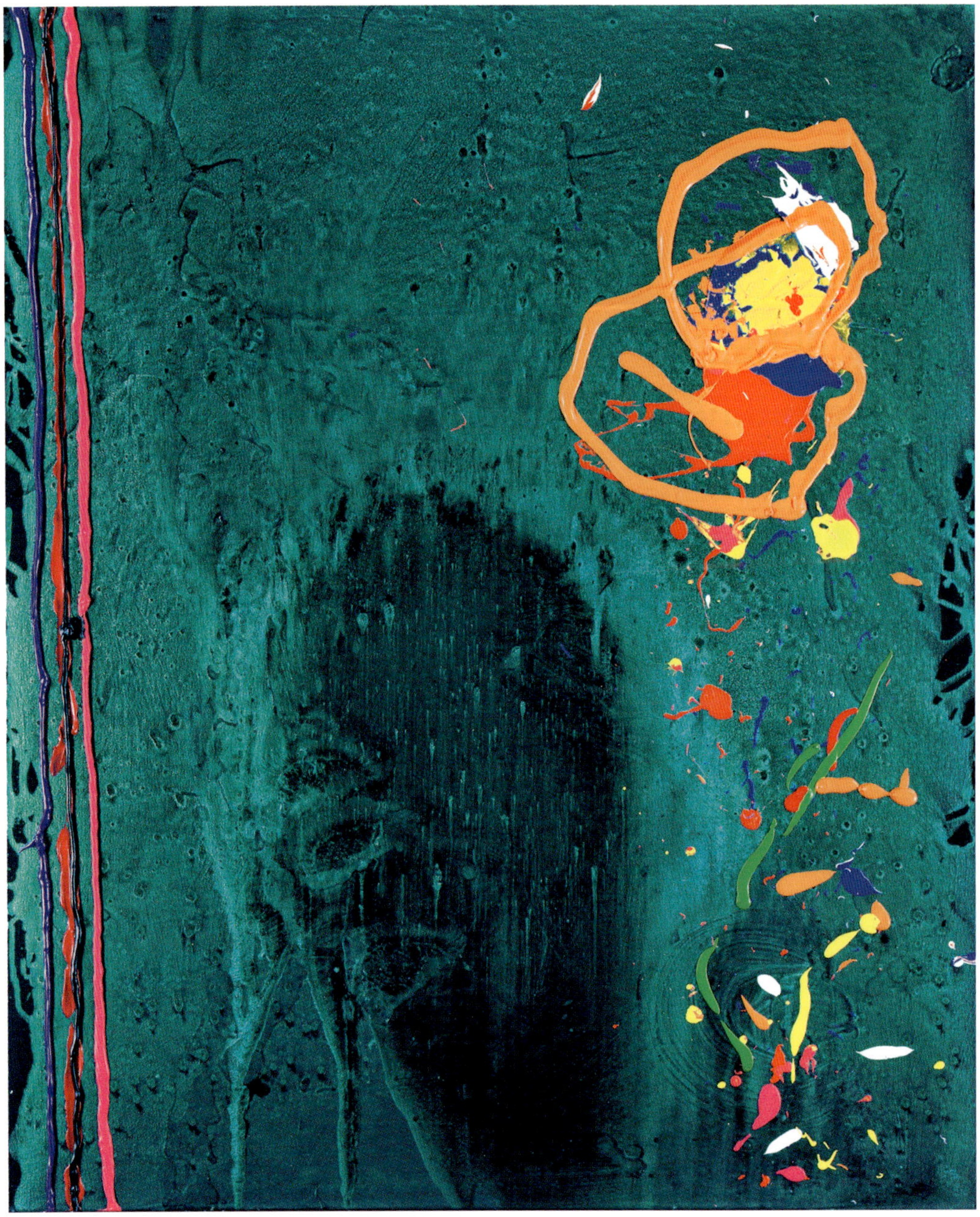

Rio Crystal, 18.7.05
Acrylic on cotton duck
127 × 102 cm (50 × 40 inches)

Rio Crystal (18.7.05) takes the palette of the elegy paintings, with their distinctive blue-green glazes over black, and hikes it up a notch. Serenity has fled, and a slightly frenetic activity replaces the melancholy calm. The descent into deep distance has become a veiled cave-mouth and the fluidly-drawn surface activity has the abandon of a drugged dance. To the left of the cave-entrance are three shadowy shapes like eyes or mouths, yet they are only suggested in the rich marine mystery of green over black.

In *Spirit Lake* (20.3.06), there is much re-working of the ground, leading to a degree of impasto and texture that vivifies the picture plane and adds incident like

Spirit Lake, 20.3.06
Acrylic on cotton duck
152.5 × 140 cm (60 × 55 inches)

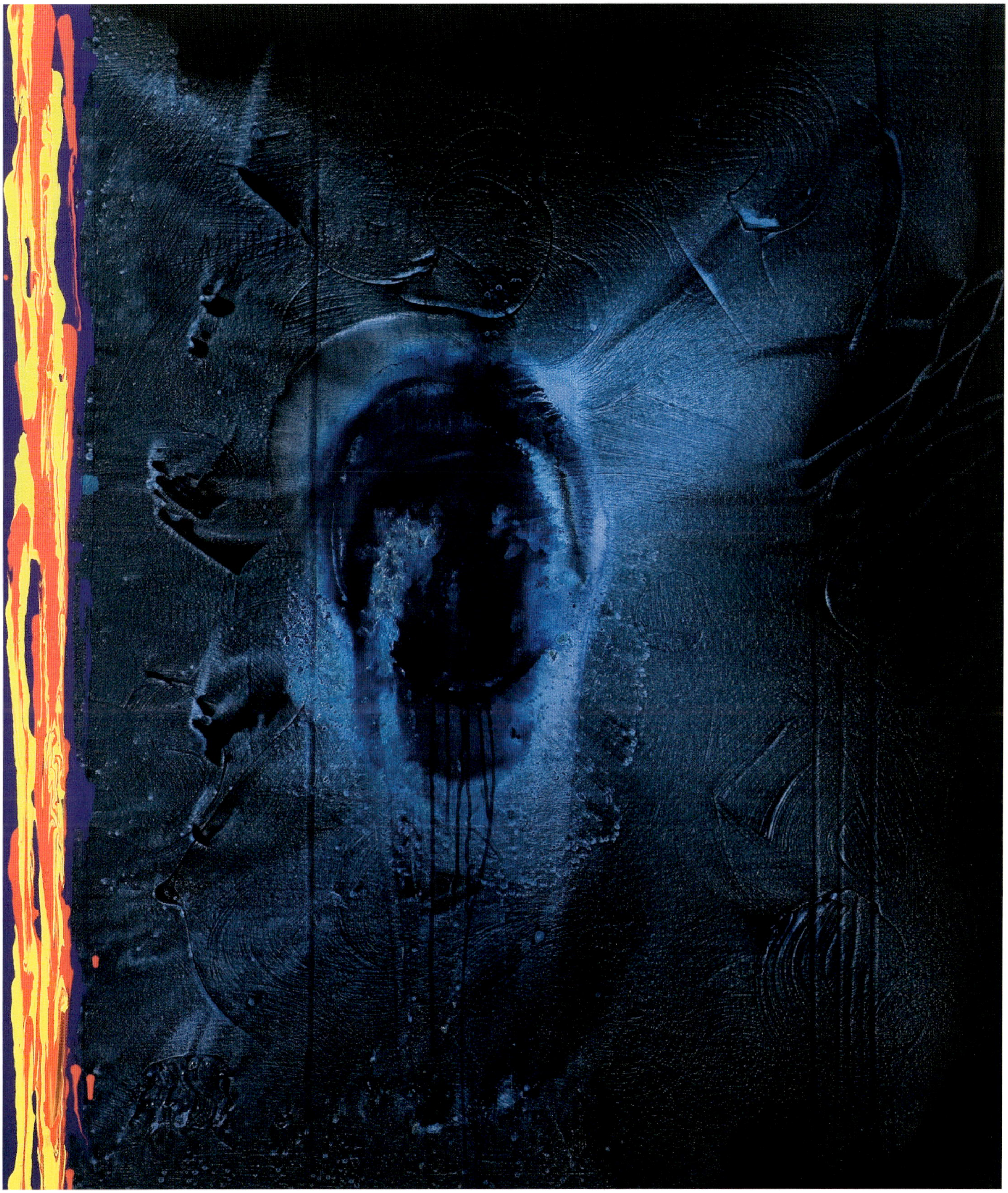

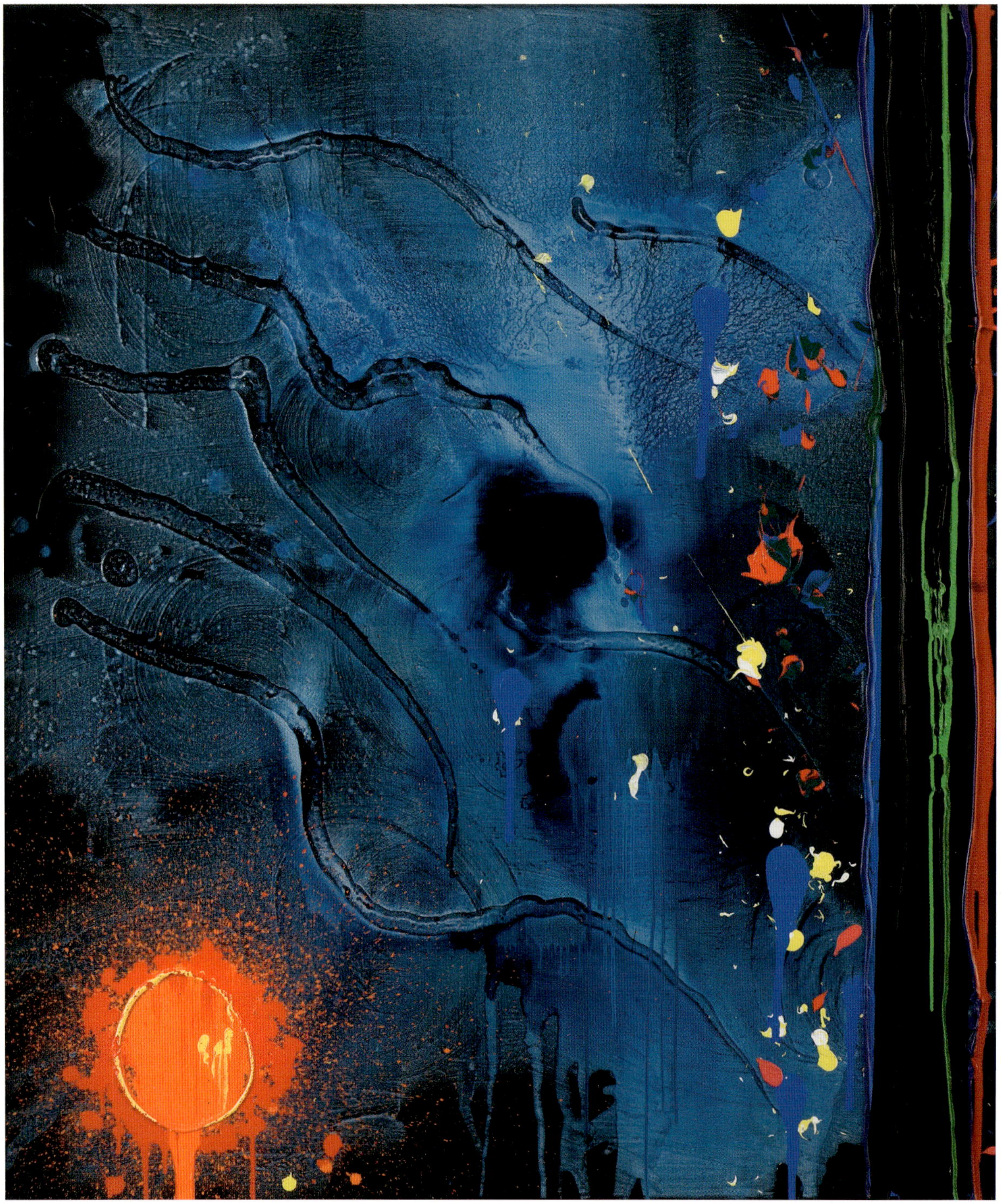

Snake River, 4.2.07
Acrylic on cotton duck
152.5 × 127 cm
(60 × 50 inches)

the shadows of hilly terrain on a plateau. It's a dark blue painting, similar to its fellows *Sky Mirror 2* (on page 49) and *Snake River*, its looming depths redeemed by a brilliant vertical edging of yellow and pink on the extreme left.

In a 2006 notebook Hoyland wrote: 'Sometimes I feel like an old Zen monk, thinking about everything and doing nothing.'

Also: 'I hope that my work can go beyond verbal communication, that's what painting is.'

And: 'In the tropics Nature is stronger.'

And: 'In Nature all conceivable forms already exist.'

Blue Wheel (22.10.06) has something of the look of an apoplectic face beneath an Afro shock-wig, the energy of the blue wheel driving the spark that makes everything stand on end. There is here a profusion of references: to the circular motifs that dominated Hoyland's own paintings in the mid-1980s, to the mechanistic Dada of Picabia's *Voilà la fille née sans mère* (1916–17), to the molten ore in the heart of a furnace or to the green fuse of nature put under a microscope. All is bursting energy, and creative rather than destructive. Sap rivers and outbreaks

Blue Wheel, 22.10.06
Acrylic on cotton duck
152.5 × 127 cm (60 × 50 inches)

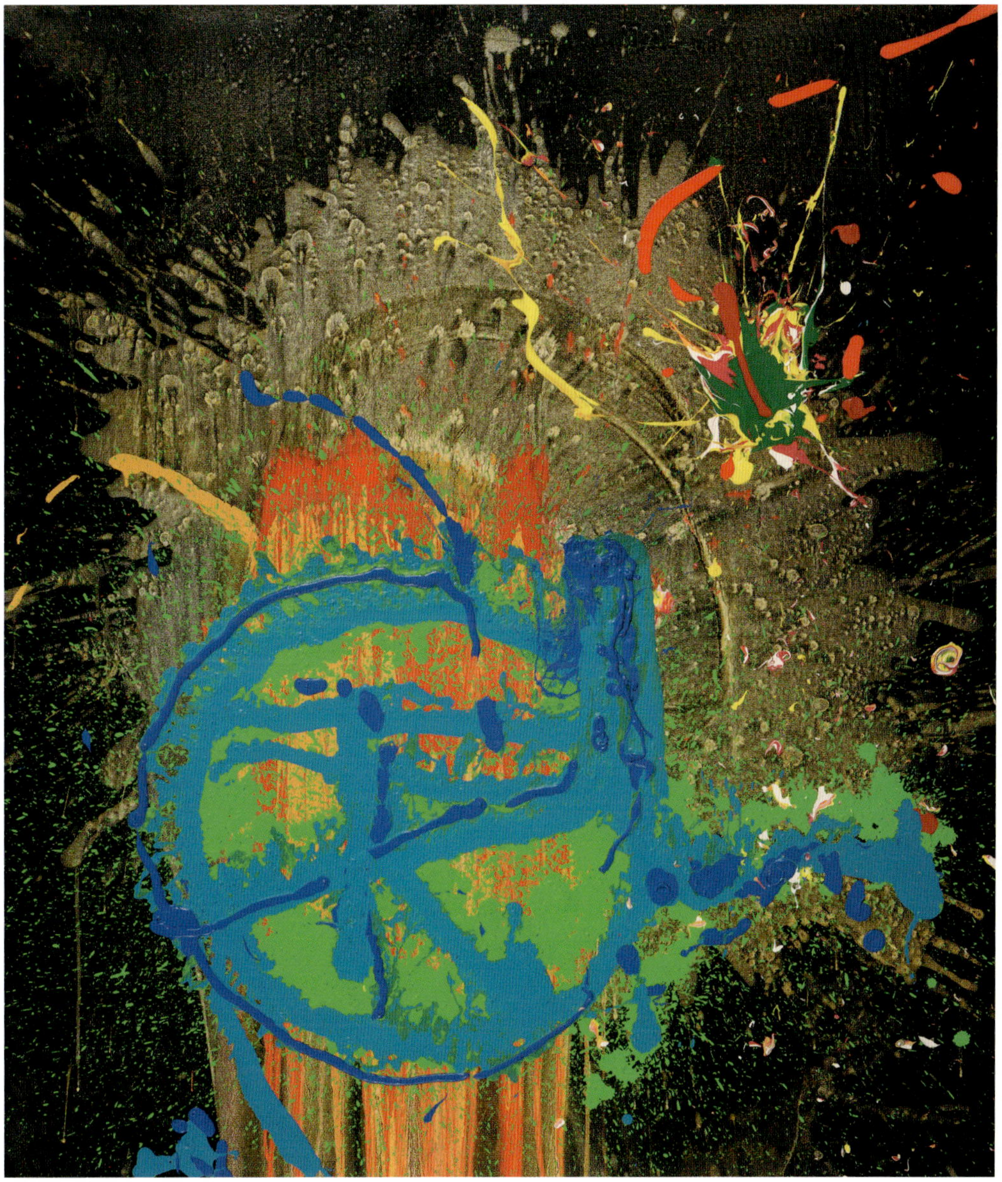

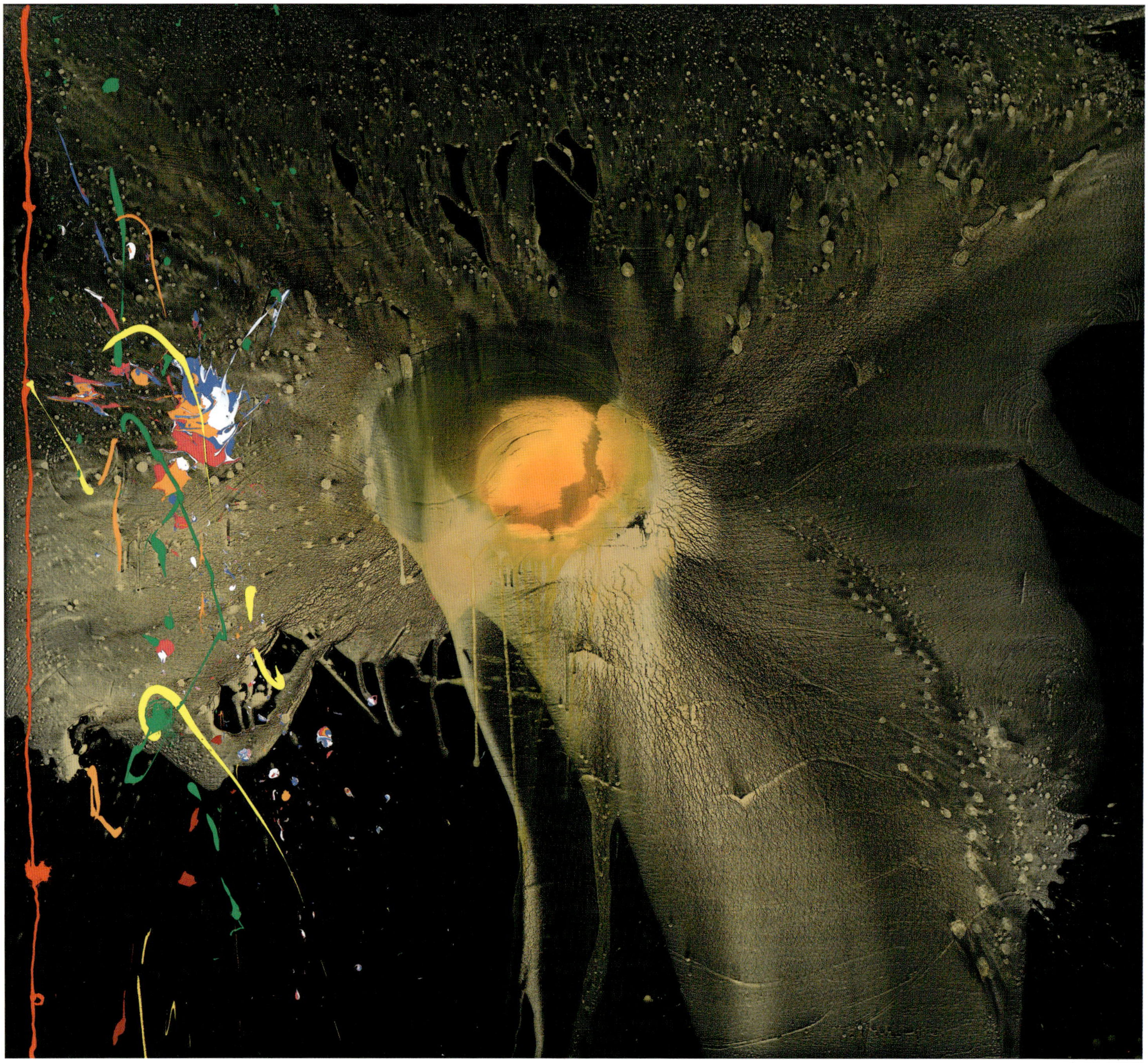

Winter Tiger, 2.2.07
Acrylic on cotton duck
236 × 254 cm (93 × 100 inches)

of pollen. The explosion of background colour and texture is firmly controlled by the geometric overpainting ('Oh, how the wheel becomes it!'), which is yet also Spenser's 'ever-whirling wheel of change'. That particular combination of order and chaos is absolutely quintessential Hoyland.

Winter Tiger (2.2.07) has a tiger's eye as the central focus. This painting has a wonderful and unexpected serenity to it, a great golden mane of light and warmth, an imposing beauty in its rhythms and cascading inevitability. By contrast,

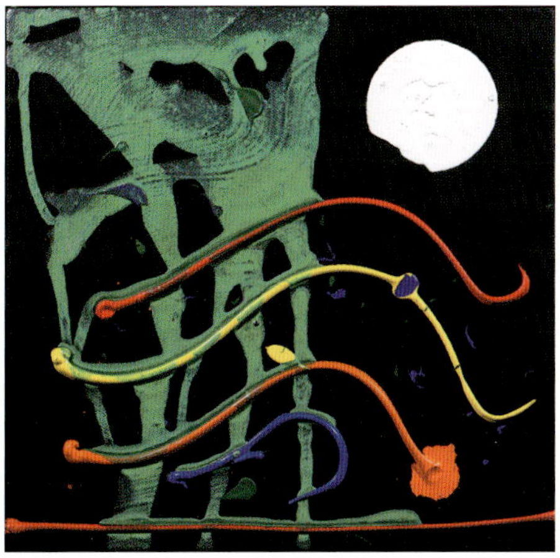

Eclipse, 17.1.07
Acrylic on cotton duck
30.5 × 30.5 cm (12 × 12 inches)

Eclipse (17.1.07) is one of Hoyland's most effective small paintings, delivering a brilliantly successful combination of balance and attack, the kind of resolved statement Hoyland usually finds it easier to achieve in a bigger painting. Notice the virtuosity in the triple echo of whiplash lines (red, yellow, orange) above the blue fish-hook which anchors the whole composition. And the green mid-ground, like a chemical forest, beneath a crunkle-faced, bad-tempered moon. Nothing jars, nothing is out of place, nothing lacking: a perfectly contained image with a wider reference.

Dawn after Dawn (15.4.07) adopts a folded vertical presence like a mountain range seen from the air, delicately done in watered crimson. The ridges across the picture look like the striations left in sand by a retreating tide. At bottom left there's a variation on the spiral: a blue circle winged with green, with black and yellow beneath. The universe, Edgar Allan Poe wrote, is 'a shadowy and fluctuating

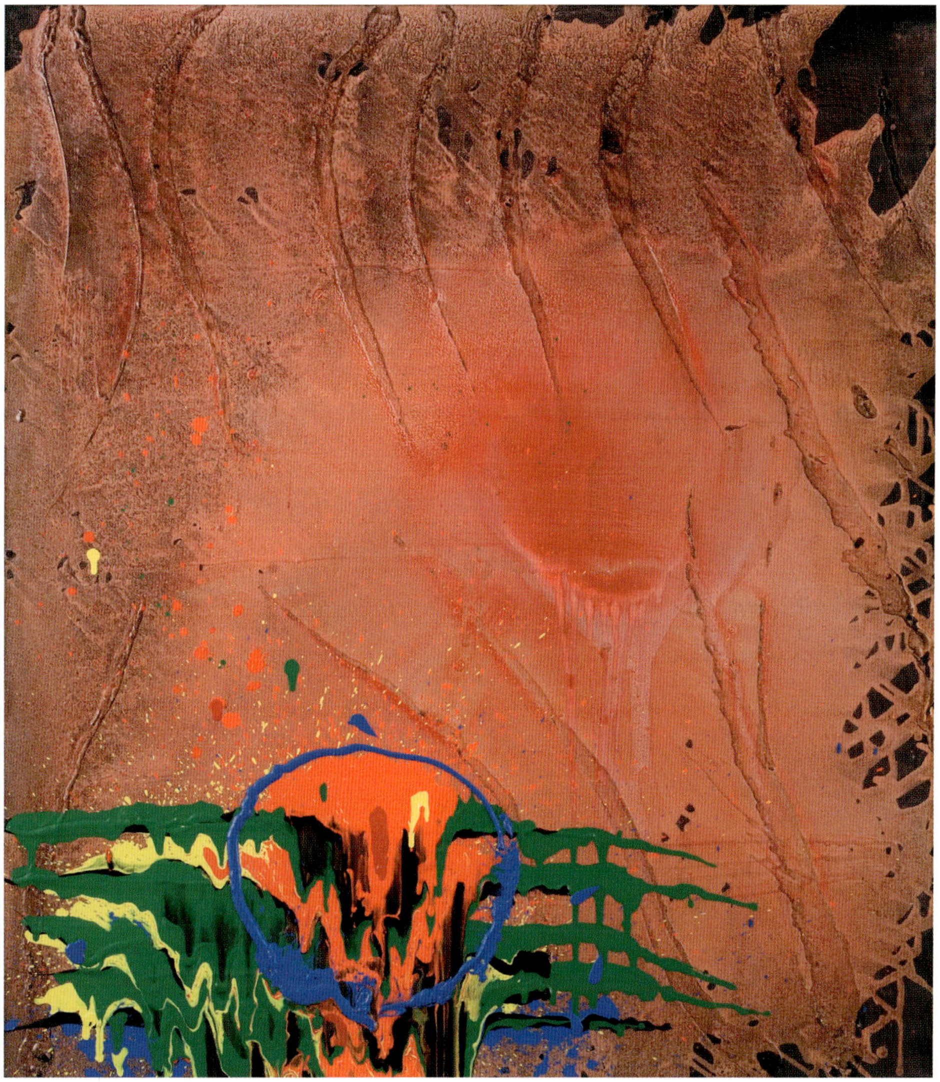

Dawn after Dawn, 15.4.07
Acrylic on cotton duck
152.5 × 127 cm (60 × 50 inches)

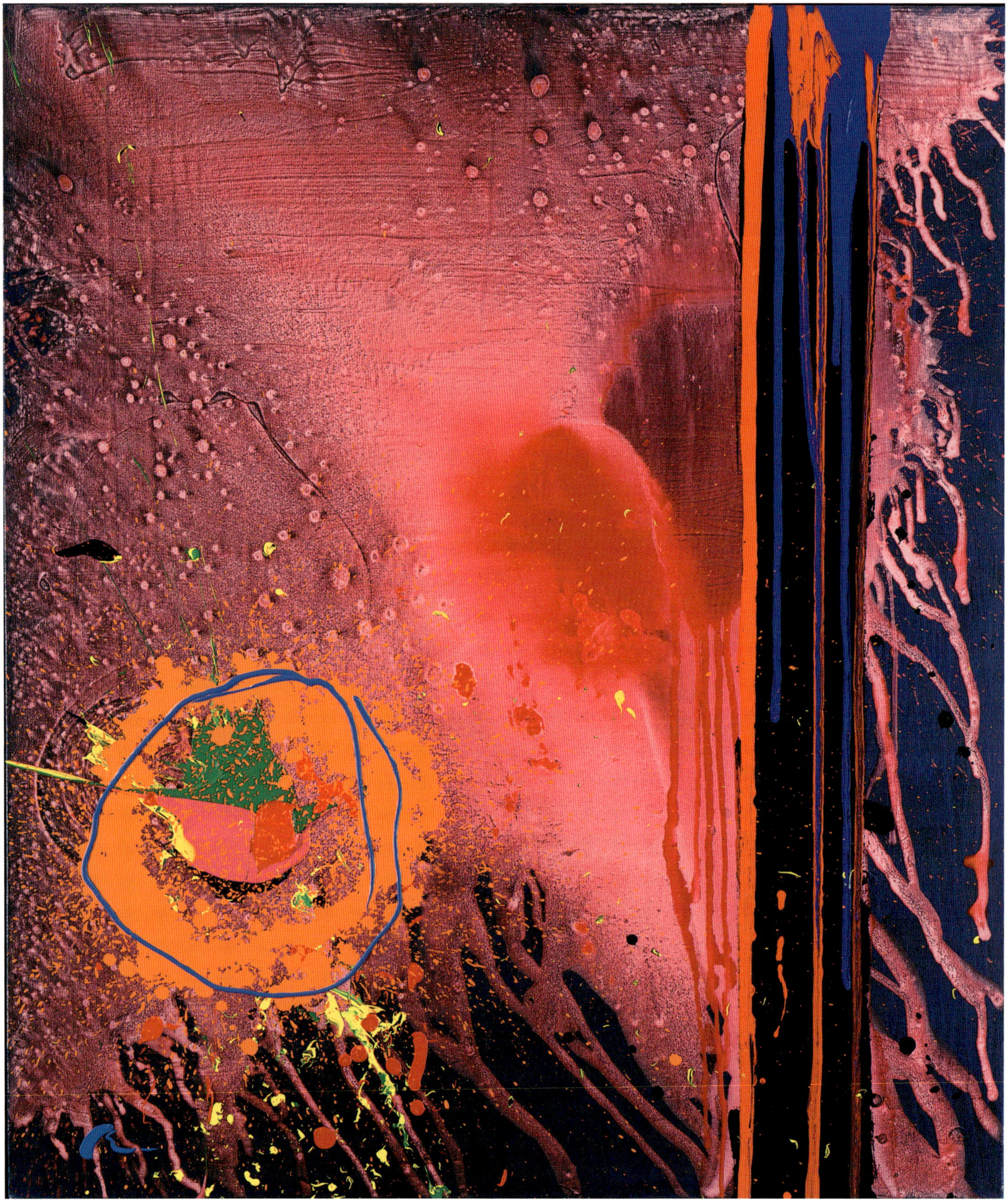

OPPOSITE
Greetings of Love, 14.6.07
Acrylic on cotton duck
152.5 × 127 cm (60 × 50 inches)

domain, now shrinking, now swelling, in accordance with the vacillating energies of the imagination.' Hoyland's paintings, with their enduring anarchy and variegated saliencies, their subtle glazes and imperious ligatures of paint, convey just that sense of becoming.

Greetings of Love (14.6.07) has a bold and unequivocal sexuality to it, an erotic impulse that is all-embracing, extending from deep within to the very nerve-endings,

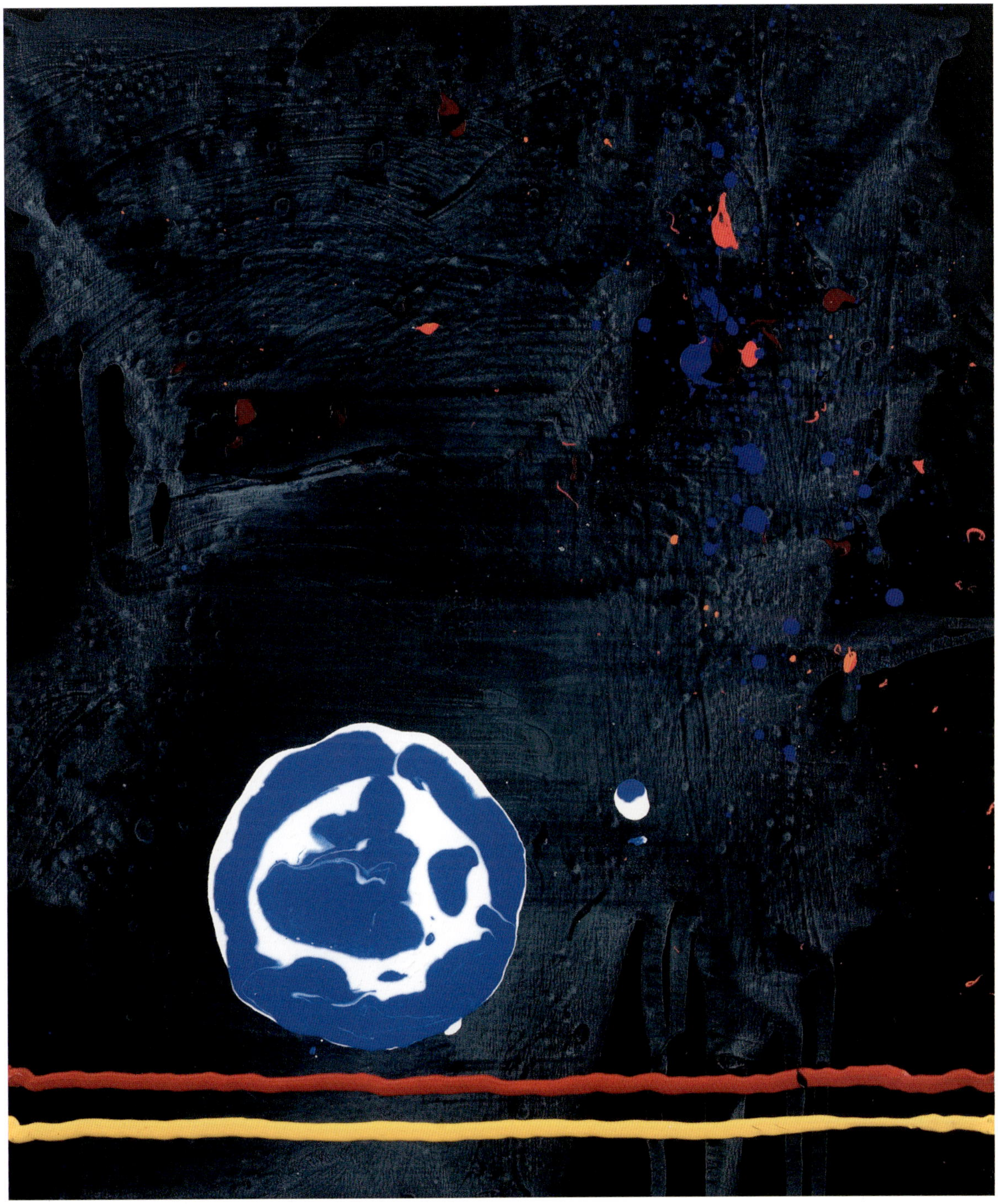

The Night, 15.7.07
Acrylic on cotton duck
91.5 × 76 cm
(36 × 30 inches)

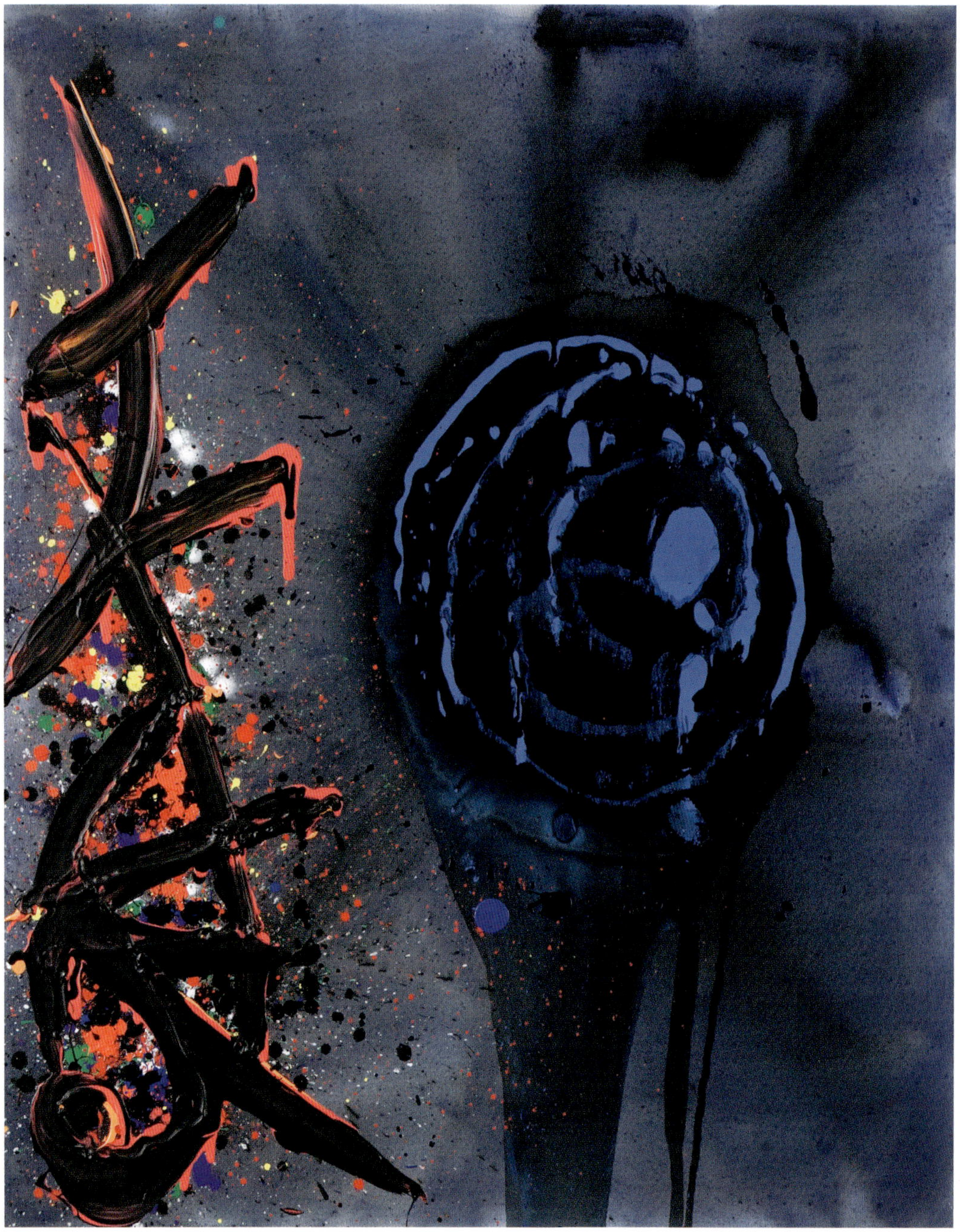

Bitch Goddess, 23.7.07
Acrylic on cotton duck
152.5 × 127 cm (60 × 50 inches)

in a sumptuous interplay of colour and mark. The runs and splatters of paint have a febrile urgency that is only matched (and possibly held in check) by the column of orange, blue and black, offering a vertical brake two-thirds of the way across the canvas. This and the scrawled blue circle, like a necromancer's spell, hold the surface against the molten depths. A deeply passionate painting, and one of a series of late Hoyland masterpieces.

Hoyland sees *Bitch Goddess* (23.7.07) as a response to de Kooning's famous paintings of women from the 1950s, memorably described by Robert Hughes as 'those shark-grinning popsies before whose dumpy and threatening torsoes so much critical rhapsody has been laid'. The bitch goddess is success, at least according to the psychologist and philosopher William James, brother of Henry James, writing in a letter to HG Wells in 1906: 'The moral flabbiness of the bitch-goddess SUCCESS. That – with the squalid cash interpretation put on the word success – is our national disease.' Strong stuff, and a fitting accompaniment to the crossed swords or switchblades that form a stack down the left side of Hoyland's painting. These crosses look a little like his habitual ideograph for birds, a pun perhaps on de Kooning's women. They also look like the remains after the sharks have had their fill: all that's left is the grins.

'I want to make them as different as portraits, as heads are', says Hoyland. *Golden Life* couldn't be more different in mood. A blazing yellow sunsplash down the left side, heightened with pink, emphasizes the sensual appetite on display here

Golden Life, 9.12.08
Acrylic on cotton duck
152.5 × 140 cm (60 × 55 inches)

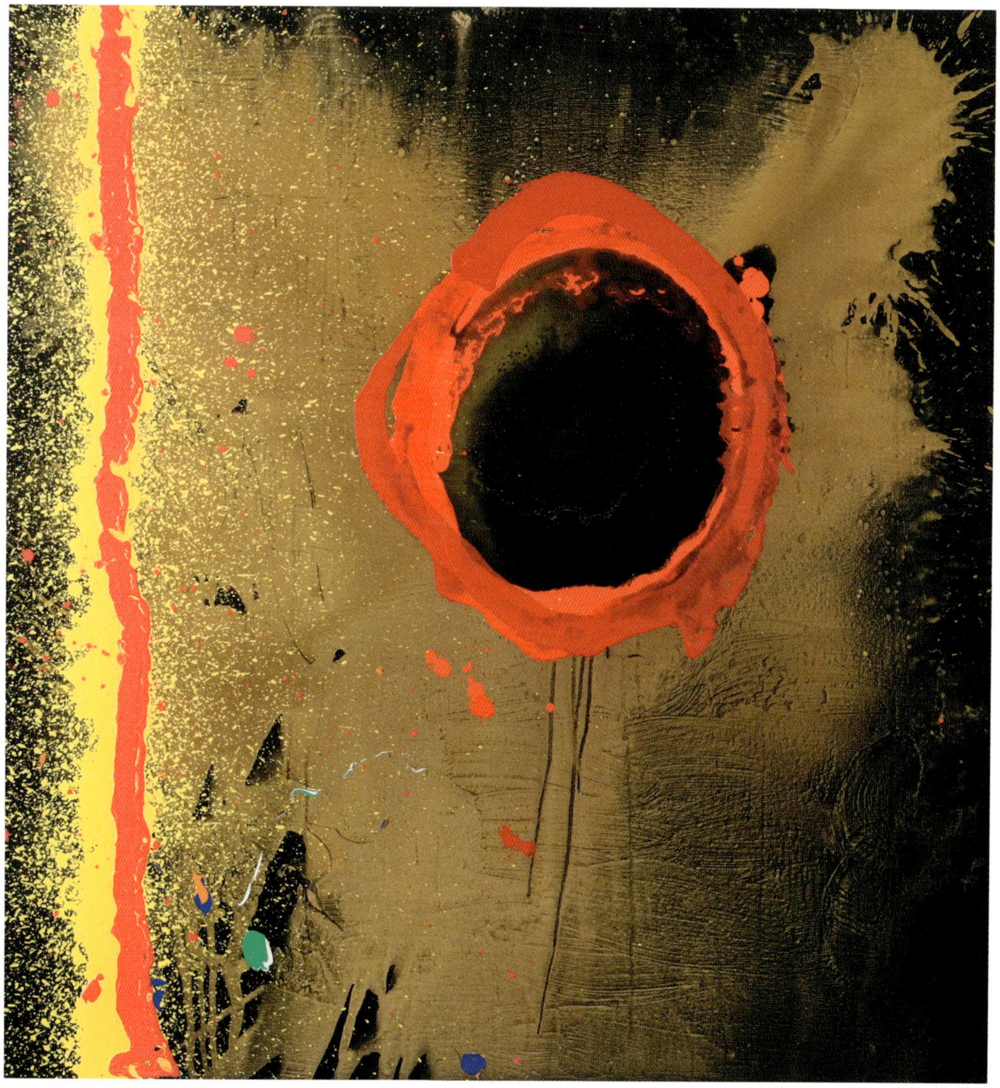

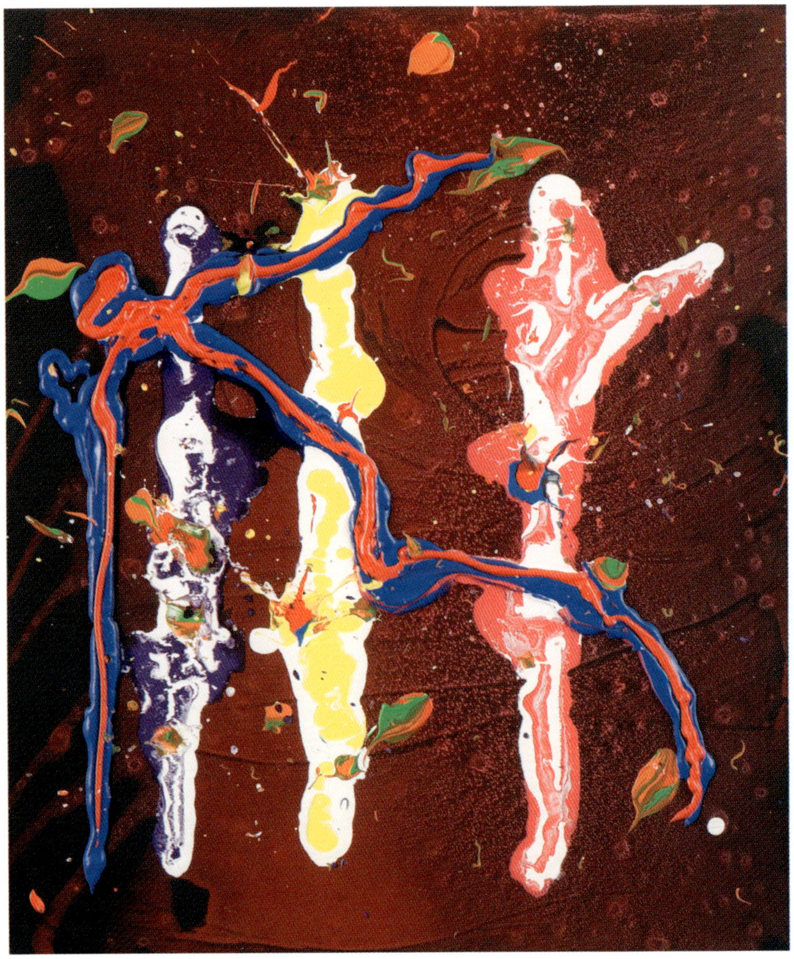

The Dancers, 23.10.07
Acrylic on cotton duck
61 × 51 cm (24 × 20 inches)

in the yawning red orifice dominating the canvas. An iridescent golden ground adds a hieratic air to the composition: voracity tempered by ritual.

The Dancers (23.10.07) is Hoyland's riposte to a famous work by Picasso. His painting of 1925, known as *The Three Dancers*, started life as a balletic version of *The Three Graces*, which Picasso re-painted and darkened in mood, parodying the original and turning it into something halfway between a crucifixion and a demonic Charleston. Based now upon a triangular love affair, it is also concerned with Picasso's misery at the death of an old friend. The dance has become one of love, sex and death, a Dionysian frenzy, with the maenad on the left deriving from the primitive expressiveness of African sculpture. Hoyland's response to Picasso's heavily burdened painting is lightly parodic; a glissade of red over blue scissors across the other vertical motifs, at once uniting the figures and controlling them (if not incapacitating them). Hoyland's line is swiftly but lingeringly balletic.

Hoyland himself is distinctly Dionysian. Dionysus was not only the god of wine and inspirer of ritual madness and ecstasy, but also a god of the dead and immortality. Not a bad combination. His faithful companion Silenus had the gift of prophecy from drinking wine. And maenads, the frenziedly passionate female followers of Dionysus, have frequently pursued Hoyland.

As Hoyland in his forthright way maintains: 'Blushing is a charming trait. No one does it any more, they're all tattooed tarts.' His painting in celebration of this quality, *Blush* (21.3.08), is a deeply suffused pink, centrally looped with green, and trailing away in slender trickles of paint against a dark ground. It's less about a sense of embarrassment or shame and more about modesty, whether outraged or not. And modestly Hoyland says of this painting: 'I don't know how it came out so good.'

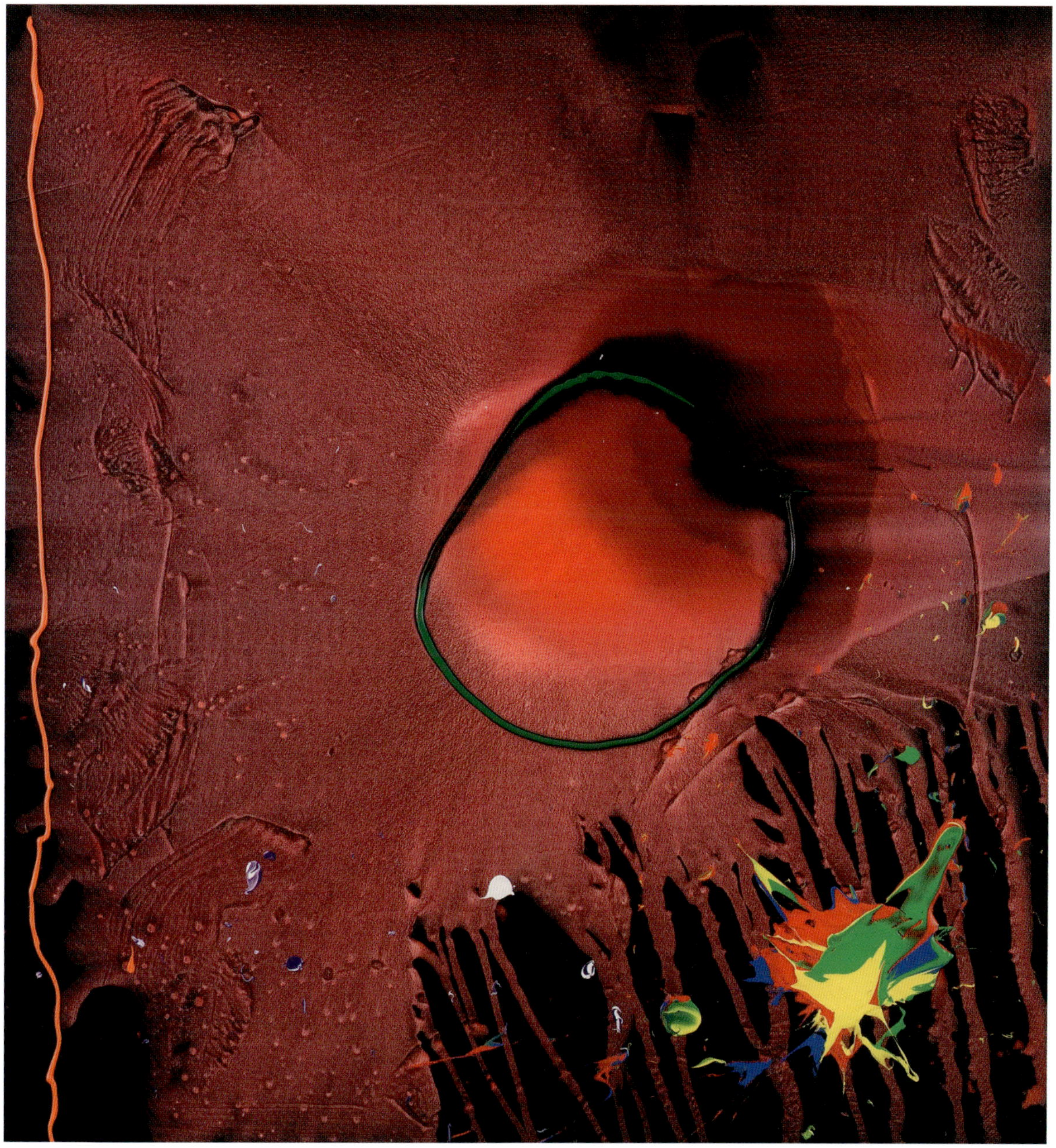

Blush, 21.3.08
Acrylic on cotton duck
152.5 × 140 cm
(60 × 55 inches)

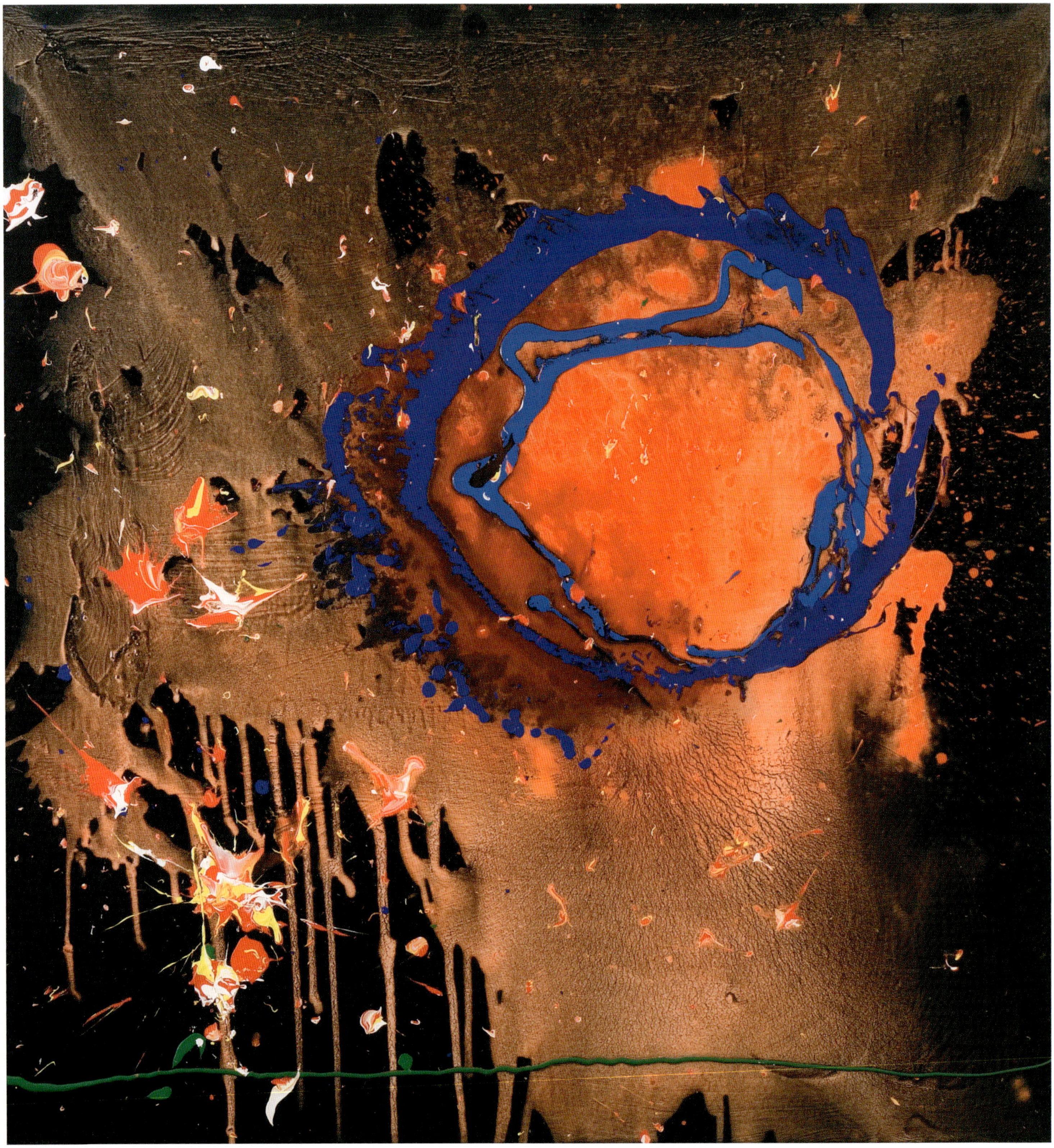

Some Fly, Some Die, 17.4.08
Acrylic on cotton duck
152.5 × 140 cm (60 × 55 inches)

Although the title *Some Fly, Some Die* (17.4.08) might with hindsight be read autobiographically to indicate some foreknowledge of Hoyland's own life-threatening and imminent illness, it actually refers to organic life, and the multitudes of tiny organisms that swarm through the world, and even to larger and more decorative ones such as moths and fireflies, the blips on the radar screen of our attention.

In May 2008, Hoyland underwent emergency surgery for a serious heart condition. While in hospital he decided to regularize his long-standing liaison with Beverley Heath, who comes originally from Montego Bay in Jamaica, a popular holiday destination Hoyland had discovered quite independently some years before he met her. They were married on 28 June, in hospital, in the boardroom of St Olaf House, in London Bridge Hospital.

Blood Summer (25.7.08), overleaf, was the first painting Hoyland did after coming out of hospital. The white vertical on the left is like the scar bequeathed by his operation, a Barnett Newman-like zip that will reappear in subsequent paintings. The 'blood' is painted with Cadmium red light. (Hoyland favours Cadmium red and its variants, light, medium and deep.) Another response to his recent hospitalization is *Heart Song* (2.8.08), on page 143. Even Hoyland admits that this one is 'a bit on the visceral side', whereas the recent tendency in his paintings has been towards the more lyrical and reflective.

Hoyland describes *Azure Wind* (21.8.08), on page 144, as 'flying a kite on a nice day', and allows that it's 'almost a landscape'. It is, in fact, nothing like as literal as he suggests, with its typical vortex composition, and the splatters and clusters of thrown paint moving centripetally or centrifugally in a complex abstract dance. Barnett Newman seems to have been on Hoyland's mind at this time.

Hoyland and his wife Beverley in the sitting room of his flat, 2009

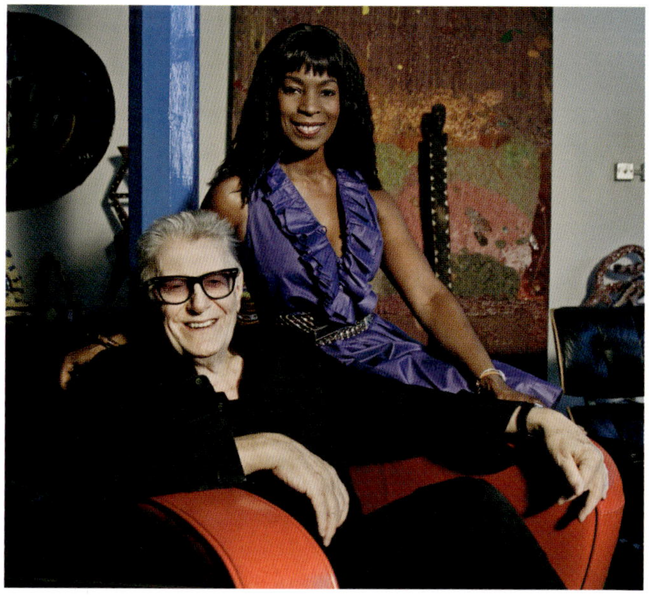

The One (28.8.08), shown on page 118, is a take on Newman's *Onement* series, with its multi-coloured vertical cicatrice recalling the scar Hoyland had himself sustained. The refulgent golden pinks and spatial complexities of this energetic painting belie Hoyland's convalescent state, and are hugely optimistic.

Water Theatre (2.9.08), page 145, is another dramatic image, and a particularly fine one, its quality of spectacle alluded to in its title. Red and green are juggled down the left side in spirited reprise of his early palette, with a shadowing of golden-yellow. Over this a white skeletal line weaves. The right side of the picture is dominated by dispersed blues shooting out of a circle, fleeing a dark vortex.

Zenist (23.9.08), page 146, is simpler in its effects, but no less luxurious in colour. A deep purple painting, it has another thin white line articulating its right flank, enhaloed in burning yellow.

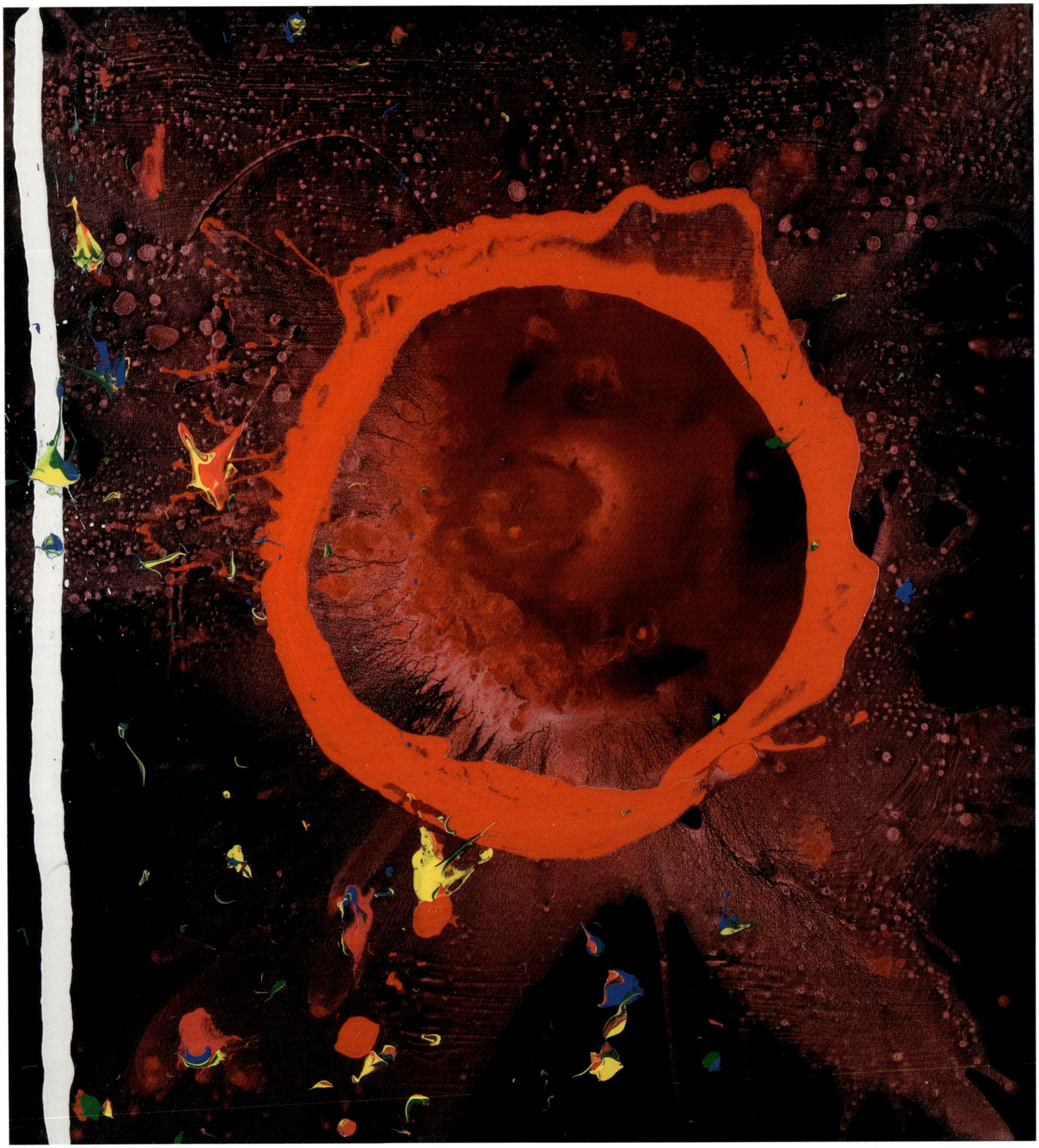

Blood Summer, 25.7.08
Acrylic on cotton duck
127 × 114 cm (50 × 45 inches)

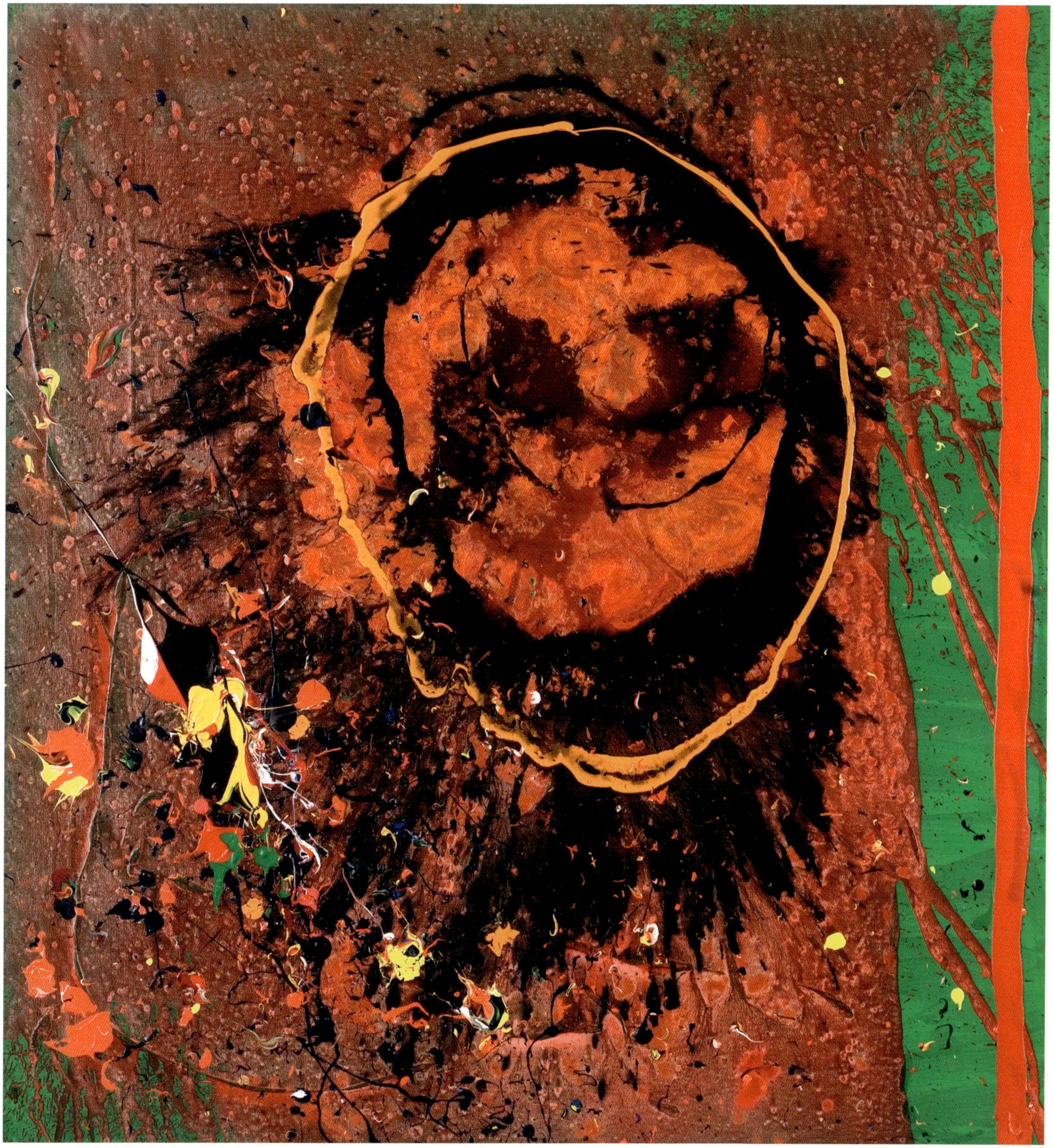

Heart Song, 2.8.08
Acrylic on cotton duck
152.5 × 140 cm (60 × 55 inches)

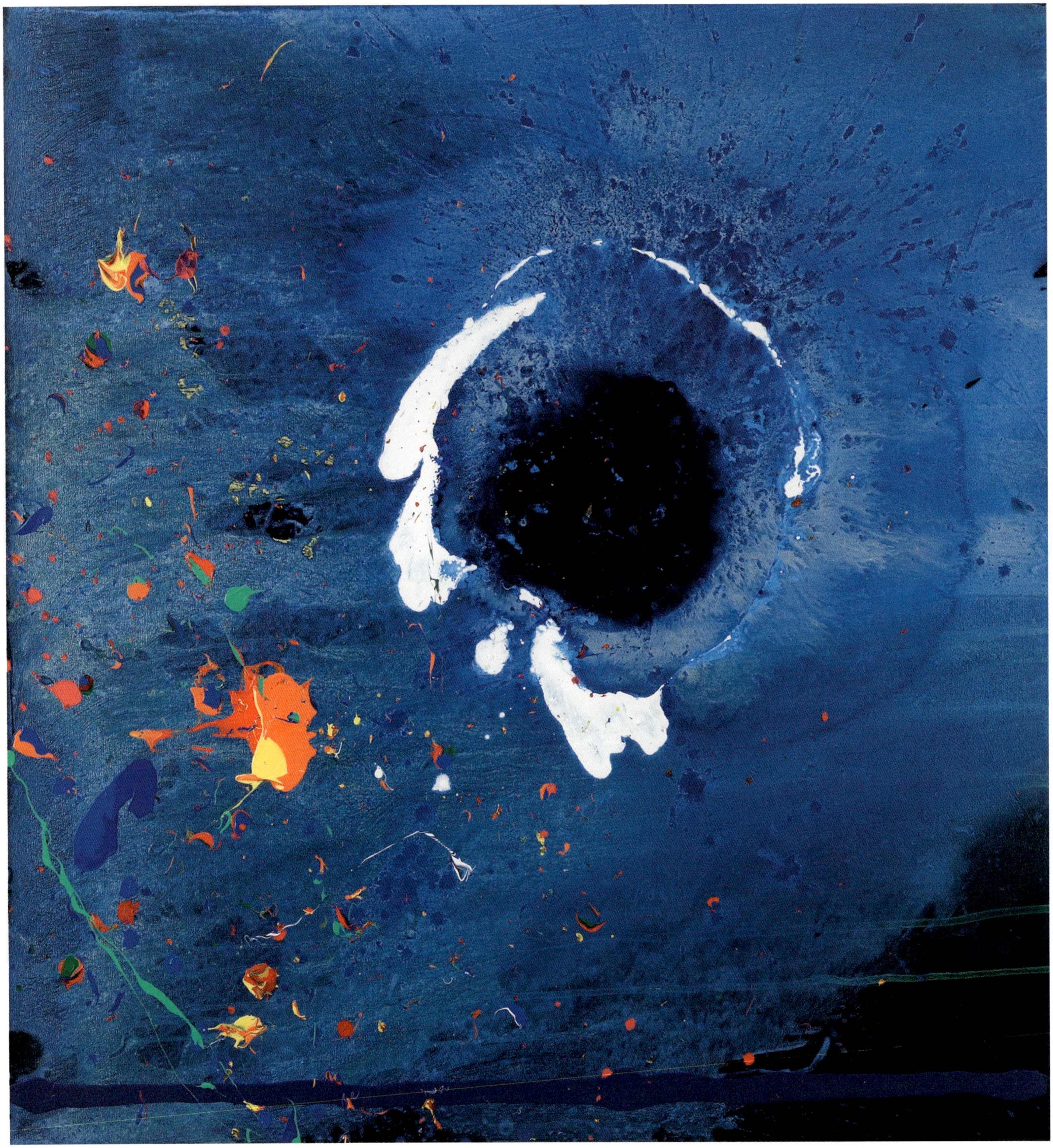

Azure Wind, 21.8.08
Acrylic on cotton duck
152.5 × 140 cm (60 × 55 inches)

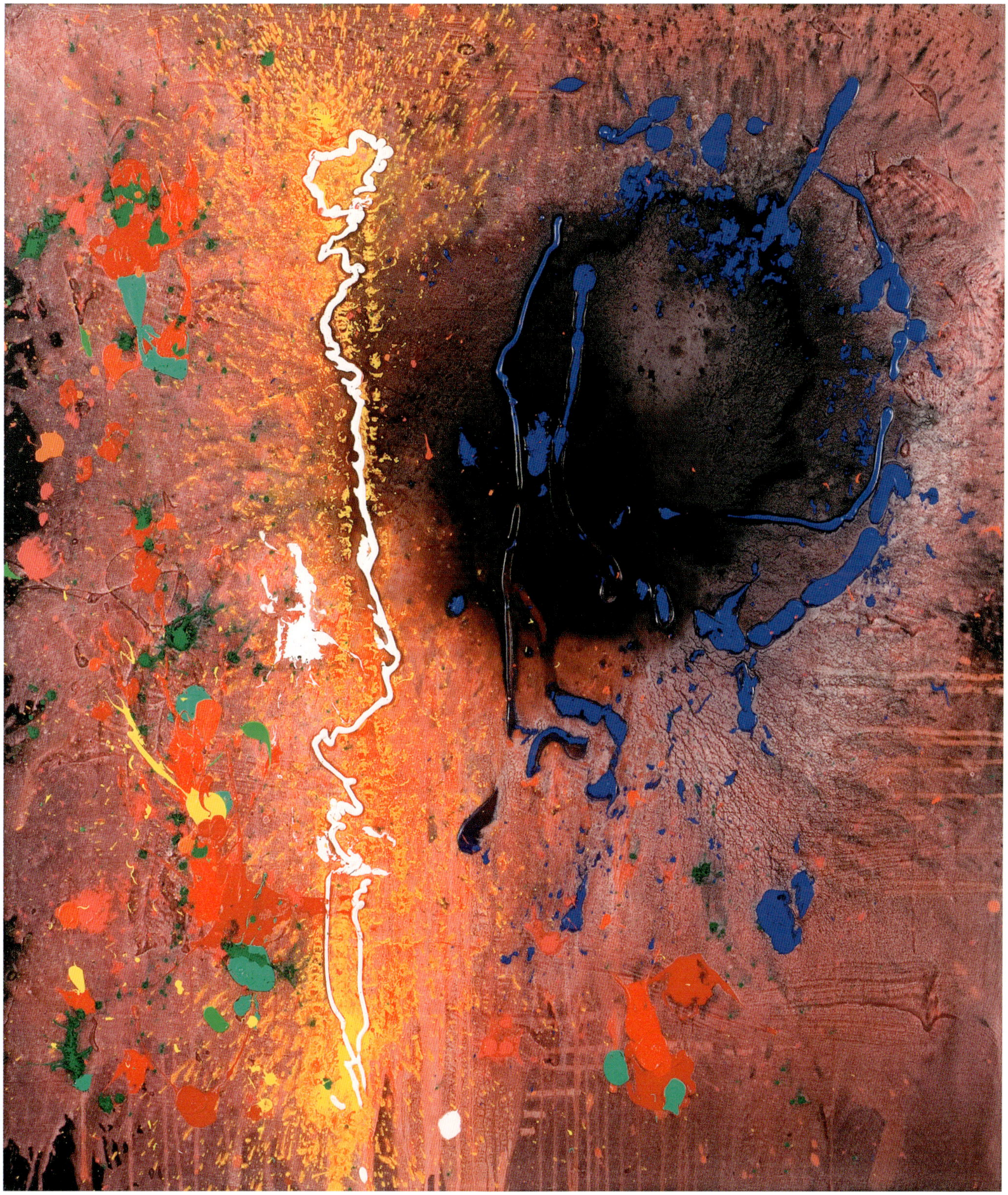

Water Theatre, 2.9.08
Acrylic on cotton duck
152.5 × 140 cm (60 × 55 inches)

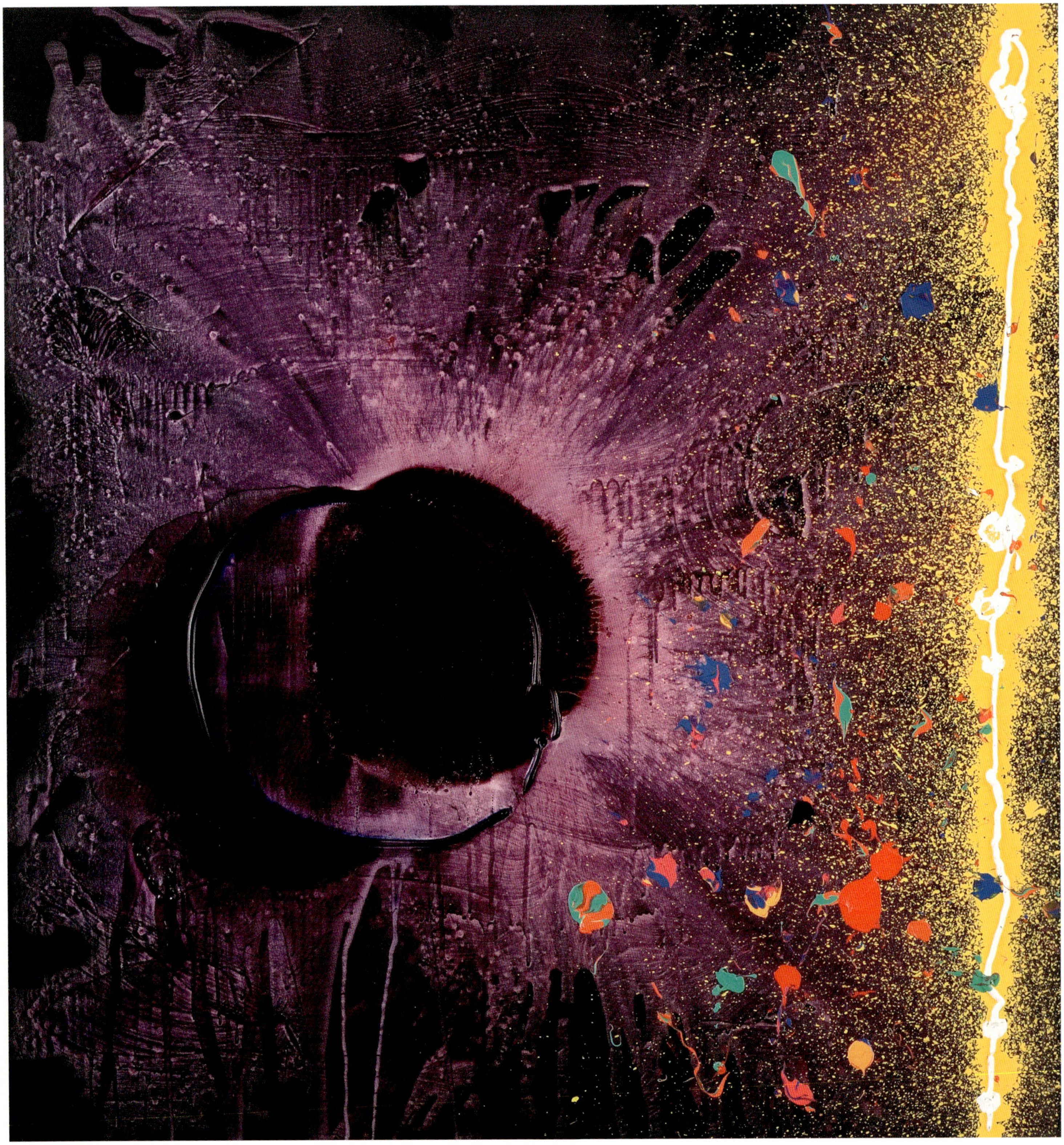

Zenist, 23.9.08
Acrylic on cotton duck
152.5 × 140 cm (60 × 55 inches)

First Man, 29.8.08
Acrylic on cotton duck
152.5 × 140 cm
(60 × 55 inches)

First Man (29.8.08) continues the train of thought, with a red vertical cicatrice reading either as a man or a cut. This degree of qualified autobiography is unusual in Hoyland's work, but the severe illness he suffered, along with the changes it wrought on his body, has needed to be registered. His scar is thus a frequent

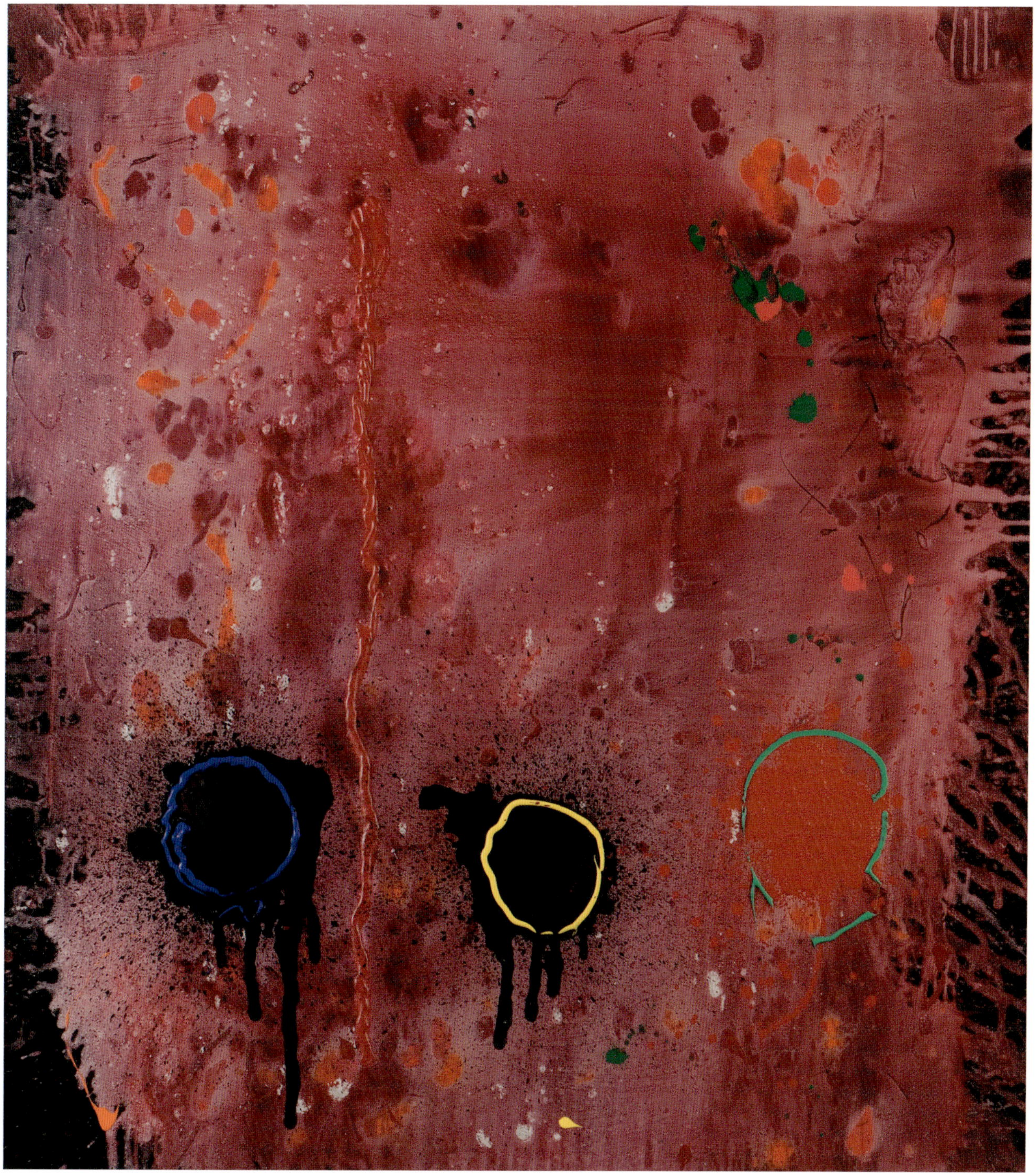

visitor to recent paintings. As he is fond of saying: 'Art is a seismograph of the human being.'

The more-or-less-central circle does dominate the work of recent years (see *Halo*), and harks back to the distinctive circular paintings Hoyland was making in the 1980s. But now the accent is on the linear, and the changing scale of the marks ensures a very different emotional complexion to the work. The line is exploratory as well as declarative, Hoyland's precipices and whirlpools of paint seeking out the primal creative forces behind his own work, as well as those behind the drive of the universe. *Everyworld* (8.1.09) continues to explore this idea, with three circles at the base of three scars, though the scars are less obvious and the colour increasingly vibrant. Of his recent painting *After Jamaica* (9.3.09), page 50, Hoyland comments: 'This is something that Patrick Heron never understood – making a discord with adjacent colours. The pink should be darker but when it isn't it makes a buzz on the edge.' Against the green it fizzes hypnotically, a luminary, offering light and inspiration like so many of the presences in Hoyland's latest paintings.

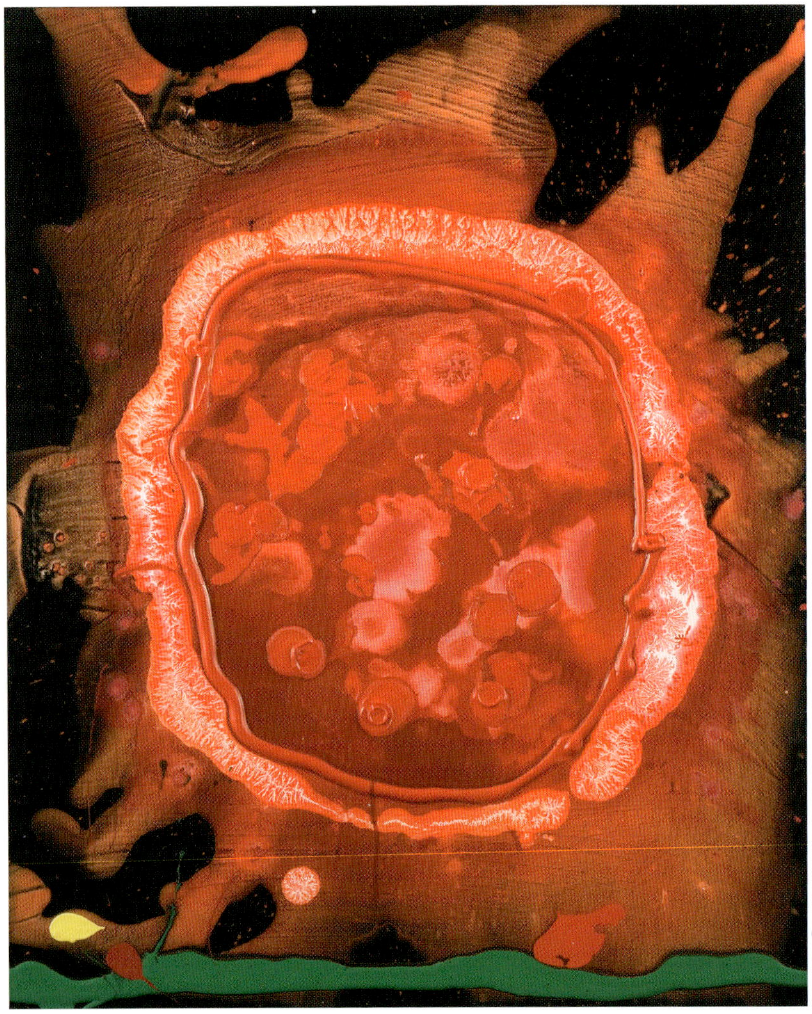

Halo, 13.9.08
Acrylic on cotton duck
76 × 61 cm (30 × 24 inches)

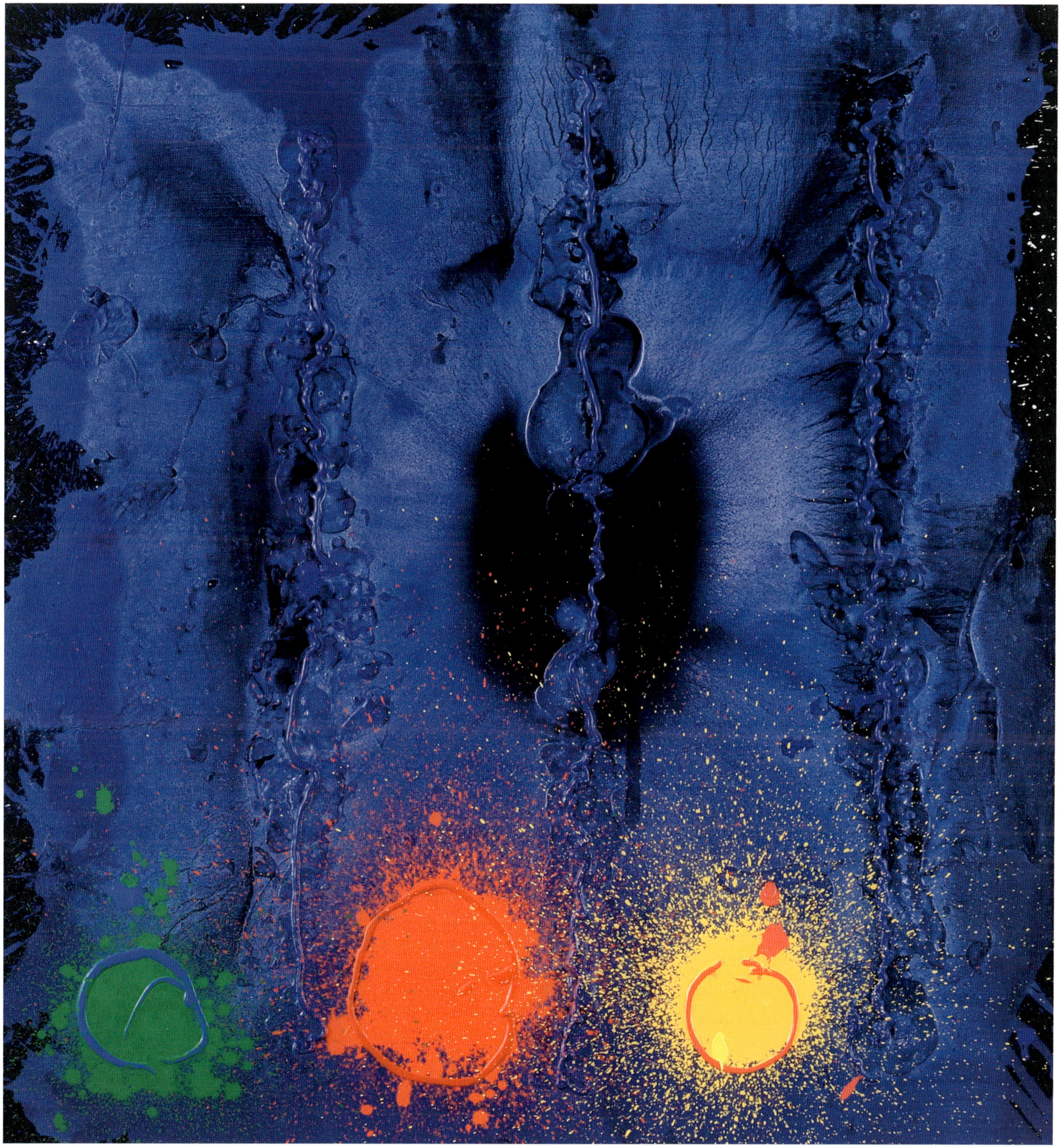

Everyworld, 8.1.09
Acrylic on cotton duck
152.5 × 140 cm (60 × 55 inches)

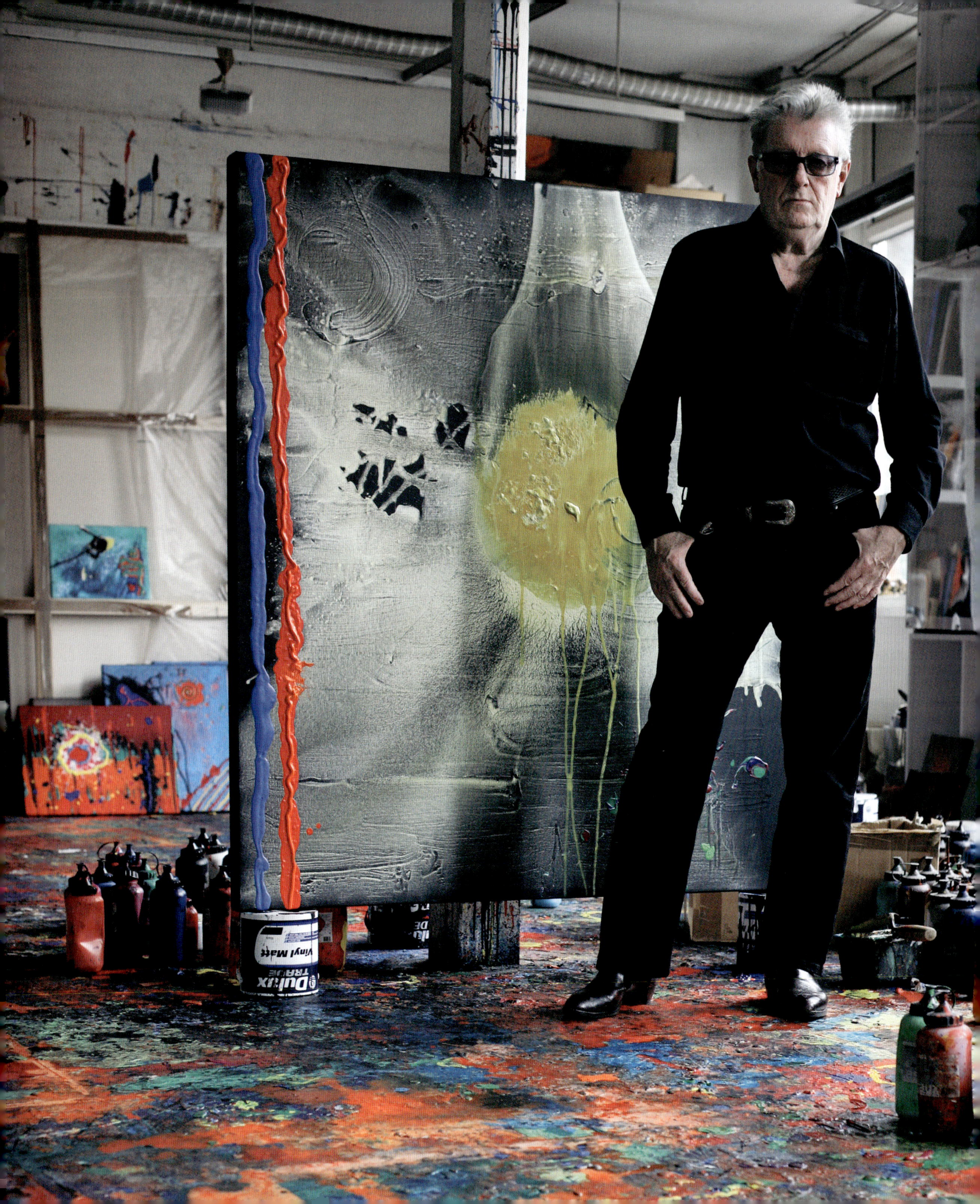
Dulux TRADE
Vinyl Matt

15

Conclusion

In Hoyland's recent work, he has gone all-out for formal and imaginative freedom. In this breaking down of barriers he is like Beethoven in the late string quartets, which have been described as moving 'from prayer-like tranquillity to profanity, from sweetly melodious song to jagged debate.' Not everyone understood or approved of what Beethoven was doing. Even the young Franz Schubert complained of what he thought was the master's tendency to confuse 'the tragic with the comic, the agreeable with the repulsive, heroism with howlings and the holiest with harlequinades.' And yet today Beethoven's late quartets are spoken of with awe, and are considered the apogee of his stupendous achievement.

Late Titian also comes to mind, characterized as it is by open brushwork and a looser, more fluid and informal style, allied with a complex system of glazes. Titian intended to convey the spontaneity of the sketch through the format of the finished painting, be it portrait or allegory, and Hoyland's torrential cataracts of paint and gyrating, leaping electric colours attempt to do the same. His re-appropriation of figurative imagery finds an interesting parallel in Anthony Caro's late work. The doyen of abstract sculptors, high priest of girders and welded sheet metal, has in recent years also essayed a number of distinctly figurative subjects, several inspired by Old Master paintings. Caro and Hoyland have remained good friends and keep aware of developments in each other's work. This parallel enlargement of subject matter is evidently an emanation of the zeitgeist, a coming-to-terms with contemporary pluralism.

Artists (by which I mean poets, painters, musicians) are there to bring back reports, sightings and soundings, of the great unknown glories of our universe. One of their purposes is to reveal what has not been articulated before, and to convey the experience of such encounters. Does Hoyland refer to the beginning of things, or their end? Do his great vortices of paint, his maelstroms of colour, suggest the bourne from which no traveller returns, or the molten magma about to become a birth pond? Whichever, they do not suggest *nothingness*. All here is potential. They

John Hoyland in his London studio, 2007

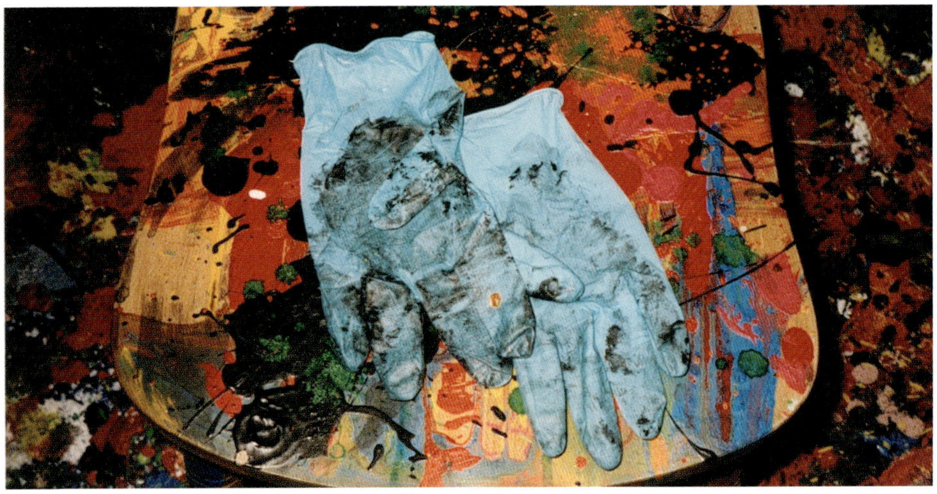

suggest going beyond – the endless possibilities of other states. As he would be the first to admit: 'You have to have ideas outside and beyond yourself.' In fact, his paintings are notable for the remarkable absence of self that they project.

Hoyland wrote recently: 'Imagination is the creative force; art as an idea of this world, but not in logical terms – a world of deeper meanings and mysteries, excluding forms of outer knowledge. Imagination creates a new reality and when rightness of form can be achieved the work will not be "understood" but will be recognized.'

Adrian Berg, a Hoyland sparring partner of long standing, has said of his own work: 'My subject is what man has made of nature.' Hoyland's subject, by contrast, might be said to be what nature makes of man – man reduced in importance to the speck of insignificance he really is in the general scheme of things, and in the context of the vast cosmic forces which govern this world. It's not so strange a proposition. After all, Victor Willing, an astute critic as well as a notable painter, long ago decided that Hoyland was a metaphysical painter. Which is to say, he paints mysteries.

Glyn Hughes cogently observes:

We know about as much of what's truly going on as someone
who, looking out to sea, catches sight of a fin.

Yet we can still recognize splendour; and if we have a responsibility to enjoy life to the full, John Hoyland can never be accused of shirking his duty. His greatness as an artist lies in his ability to give back his relish of the world and its imaginative potential through the transcendent visions of his paintings.

Bibliography

Mel Gooding is the leading expert on John Hoyland's work, and his two books have been invaluable for my researches. But others have written perceptive and inspiring essays on different aspects of Hoyland's output, and I should like to mention here Paul Moorhouse and especially John McEwen, whose recent catalogue essays have effortlessly captured the Hoyland spirit. I have quoted Hoyland's own words at such length because, although ostensibly talking about someone else (Terry Frost or Matthew Smith, for instance), they reveal so much about Hoyland himself.

Cockrill, Maurice: 'Delving into Chaos' (interview) in *RA Magazine*, Autumn 1999

Gooding, Mel: *John Hoyland*, 1990

Gooding, Mel: *John Hoyland*, 2006

Greenberg, Clement: *Art and Culture*, 1972

Haire, Susan: studio interview with Hoyland (typescript in the artist's possession), conducted 21.12.05

Miró, Joan: *Selected Writings and Interviews*, ed. Margit Rowell, 1987

Newton, Eric: *British Painting*, 1945

Robertson, Bryan: *'45–99: a personal view of British painting and sculpture*, 1999

Rosenblum, Robert: *Modern Painting and the Northern Romantic Tradition: Friedrich to Rothko*, 1975

Sylvester, David: *Interview with American Artists*, 2001

Von Joel, Mike: 'Hoyland at Home' (interview) in *Art Line*, No 4, February 1983

Yeats, W B: *Ideas of Good and Evil*, 1903

Biography

1934
Born Sheffield, October 12

1946–51
Attends Sheffield School of Art & Crafts (Junior Art Department) instead of following grammar school education

1951–56
Studies fine art at Sheffield College of Art, where emphasis is on figurative painting – no awareness of abstract art. Taught academic draughtsmanship but given no sense of possibilities of drawing; teachers uninspired with exception of the excellent Eric Jones. Reads Auden, Eliot, etc. Affected by Turner watercolours in Graves Art Gallery and Paul Nash's monochromatic *Winter Sea* with its abstract horizontal planes

***c.*1953**
Visits St Cyr in South of France, near de Staël's Cassis. Makes many topographical paintings

1956–60
(January '56) Influenced by Rothko's painting in *Modern Art in the United States* at Tate Gallery, London. Studies at Royal Academy Schools, London; begins to draw seriously from the model and to paint figures. Interest in early Matisse, 'brown and white' pictures. Friendship with Paul Huxley, Basil Beattie, Keith Arnatt and Oliver Bradbury (who later becomes a poet)

1957
Paints land- and townscapes of Sheffield area, influenced by de Staël. Also painting still lifes that suggest growing interest in abstraction. Attends annual Summer School at Scarborough where Victor Pasmore, Harry Thubron and Tom Hudson teach colour, structure and form; here he experiments with colour. Visits south of France, painting landscapes between Marseilles and Toulon; also Italy – the Adriatic Coast, Milan, Arezzo, Florence and Assisi. Greatly affected by quality of life and light in Italy and France after greyness of Sheffield

1958
Joins William Turnbull's evening classes at Central School of Art, London; working mainly from still life but with expanded references, he explores the possibilities of abstracting from actual objects. Marries Airi Karkkainen; birth of son Jeremy

1960
Entire Diploma show of abstract paintings taken down by order of President of Royal Academy, Sir Charles Wheeler, but Diploma awarded on strength of earlier figurative work. Begins teaching part-time on basic design course at Hornsey College of Art under Maurice de Sausmarez; colleagues include Alan Green, Bridget Riley and Brian Fielding. Also at Oxford School of Art. First of several visits to wife's native Finland

1960–61
Exhibits large-scale paintings in the two *Situation* exhibitions at RBA Gallery, London, and Marlborough New London Gallery

1961–62
Teaching at Luton College of Art and Hornsey College of Art

1961–65
Studio at Primrose Hill

1962
Begins teaching at Croydon School of Art and Chelsea School of Art. Meets William Tucker, and sees Paul Huxley regularly (who introduces him to Bryan Robertson)

1963
Deeply impressed by Caro exhibition at Whitechapel Art Gallery. Meets Helen Frankenthaler

1964
Selected by Robertson for *New Generation* exhibition at Whitechapel Art Gallery. Travels to New York for first time on a Peter Stuyvesant Foundation Bursary; visits various artists' studios (Motherwell's, Newman's and Rothko's) and sees unexhibited canvases by Morris Louis. Meets Noland, Feeley and Olitski; also Clement Greenberg, who introduces him to Hans Hofmann via two small canvases at New York's Kootz Gallery. Builds studio in Kingston-upon-Thames

1965
Included by Robertson in *Private View*, book surveying British contemporary art scene; also selected for *The English Eye*, Robertson's personal anthology of modern British art for Marlborough-Gerson Gallery in New York. Principal Lecturer at Chelsea School of Art until 1969; occasional teaching visits to Royal Academy Schools. Contact with Philip King, Tim Scott, William Tucker and other *New Generation* sculptors

1967–69
(1967) One-man show, *Paintings 1960–67*, at Whitechapel Art Gallery. Makes first works in New York, in Peter Stroud's studio, and has first exhibition there at Robert Elkon Gallery. (Summer 1968) Works in studio of John Griefen. Spends time with Larry Poons and Ronnie Langfeldt

1968
Separates from wife, and subsequently divorces. Begins working for part of each week at a new studio (a disused chapel) in Market Lavington, Wiltshire

1969
Joins Waddington Galleries, London, and has first of several annual exhibitions at Andre Emmerich Gallery, New York. Travels to Brazil and the Caribbean with Anthony Caro; r epresents Great Britain, with Caro, at the São Paulo Biennale. In Trinidad meets American jazz singer, Eloise Laws, and shares apartment with her during regular working trips to New York (until 1973). Friendship with Hubert Laws, jazz flautist and composer, and Ronnie Laws, saxophonist and composer. Meets Dizzy Gillespie, Stan Getz and many leading jazz musicians of Motown (to whom Eloise was signed for a time); spends time in Detroit

1971
Frequent trips to New York. Continues to see Noland, Frankenthaler, Motherwell and Greenberg. Working in New York

1972
Charles A. Dana Professor of Fine Art at Colgate University, Hamilton, New York

1973
Travels to Provincetown with Robert Motherwell. Returns to live and work more or less permanently in London and Wiltshire

1974
Makes three lithographs with Ian Lawson and another series in Verona

1974–77
Visiting lecturer at St Martin's School of Art and the Royal Academy Schools

1974–89
Visiting lecturer at the Slade School of Art

1977
Selector and exhibitor, Royal Academy Silver Jubilee Exhibition, London

1978
Artist in Residence, Studio School, New York (summer); paints many small works on paper

1979–80
Full-scale retrospective at Serpentine Gallery, London. Artist in Residence, Melbourne University. Visits Bombay, Hong Kong and Thailand en route with Patrick Caulfield. Rome Scholarship Committee (printmaking) until 1989

1980
Selector and curator for the Hayward Annual. Moves to new studio in Charterhouse Square, London

1982
Working in Los Angeles

1983
Elected ARA (Associate of the Royal Academy). Makes prints and monotypes with Atelier Lacourière et Frélaut, France; screenprints monotypes with Advanced Graphics, London, and etched monotypes with Jack Shirreff at 107 Workshop, Wiltshire

1984–85
Makes ceramics in Todi, Umbria, Italy, invited by Piero Dorazio

1986
Set and costume designs for *Zanza* at Sadler's Wells and The Alhambra Theatre with Rambert Dance Company; choreography by Richard Alston, music by Nigel Osborne, lighting by Peter Mumford

1987
Travels to Trinidad, Antigua and Jamaica

1988
Travels in United States. Selects and curates Hans Hofmann exhibition at Tate Gallery. Sailing trip in eastern Mediterranean with Patrick Caulfield, Janet Nathan and Beverley Heath

1989
Visits Ken Draper and Jean Macalpine in Minorca with Beverley Heath; and Jamaica and Italy with Heath. Makes etchings in Milan with Giorgio Upiglio at Grafica Uno

1991
Elected Royal Academician

1992
Invited guest at Thupelo workshop, Johannesburg, South Africa; makes drawings of plants and roots. Visits Motherwell in Greenwich and New York

1993
Travels to the Caribbean, and to Sydney, Australia, visiting Bali, Indonesia, on return journey

1994
First visit to Murano, Venice; makes glass sculptures

1995
Joins Theo Waddington Gallery and shows Bali paintings

1997
Travels to Ocho Rios, Jamaica; Grand Cayman Island; Cozumel, Mexico; and Key West, Florida. Third visit to Bali

1998
Visits San Juan, Puerto Rico; Barbados, Antigua, St Martin, Martinique and Virgin Islands

1999
Appointed Professor of Painting at Royal Academy Schools. Retrospective at Royal Academy of Arts, London. Makes a second visit to Murano, Venice, to make glass sculptures. Visits Florence and Cuba

2001
Mural Design for Metro in Rome, Italy. Joins Beaux Arts, London

2003
Work included in *Formal Situations: Abstractions in Britain, 1960–70* at Tate Liverpool (April to November)

2004
Art in the 1960s, This was Tomorrow at Tate Britain (then touring to Birmingham, Australia and New Zealand)

2006
The Trajectory of a Fallen Angel, one-man exhibition at Tate St Ives

2008
Marries Beverley Heath

Selected One-Man Exhibitions

1964
Marlborough New London Gallery, London

1965
Chelsea School of Art, London

1967
Whitechapel Art Gallery, London
Galerie Heiner Friedrich, Munich
Robert Elkon Gallery, New York
Nicholas Wilder Gallery, Los Angeles
Waddington Galleries, London
Waddington Fine Art, Montreal

1968
Robert Elkon Gallery, New York
Waddington Fine Art, Montreal

1969
Andre Emmerich Gallery, New York
Waddington Galleries, London
Leslie Waddington Prints, London

1970
Waddington Galleries, London
Andre Emmerich Gallery, New York
Galleria dell' Ariete, Milan

1971
Waddington Galleries, London
Andre Emmerich Gallery, New York
Waddington Fine Art, Montreal

1972
Andre Emmerich Gallery, New York
Harcas Krakow Gallery, Boston
Picker Gallery, Colgate University, Hamilton, New York

1973
Waddington Galleries, London
Galleria l'Approdo, Turin

1974
Studio la Città, Verona
Waddington Galleries, London
Nicholas Wilder Gallery, Los Angeles

1975
Kingspitcher Contemporary Art Gallery, Pittsburgh
Galleria E. Bolzano, Italy
Rubiner Gallery, Detroit, Michigan
Waddington Galleries, London
Waddington Fine Art, Montreal

1976
Waddington Galleries, London (paintings 1966–68)
Galleria La Bertesca, Milan, Genoa and Turin
Studio la Città, Verona

1976–77
Galeria Modulo, Lisbon

1978
Waddington Galleries, Montreal
Waddington and Tooth Galleries, New York

1979
Andre Emmerich Gallery, New York
Waddington Fine Art, Toronto
Bernard Jacobson Gallery, New York (works on paper)
Art Contact, Coconut Grove, Florida

1979–80
Serpentine Gallery, London (Retrospective; touring to Birmingham and Sheffield)

1980
University Gallery, University of Melbourne (touring to Adelaide and Sydney)
Galerie von Braunbehrens, Munich
Galerie Krammer, Hamburg

1981
Gump's Gallery, San Francisco
Waddington Galleries, London

1982
Jacobson/Hochman Gallery, New York
Bernard Jacobson Gallery, Los Angeles
Compass Gallery, Glasgow

1983
Waddington Galleries, London
Waddington Graphics, London

1983–84
Hokin/Kaufman Gallery, Chicago

1984
Castlefield Gallery, Manchester

1985
Waddington Galleries, London

1986
Waddington & Shiell Galleries, Toronto (ceramics and paintings)

1987
Waddington Galleries, London
Oxford Gallery, Oxford
Lever/Meyerson Gallery, New York

1988
Erika Meyerovich Gallery, San Francisco
Edward Thorden Gallery, Gothenburg

1990
Austin/Desmond Fine Art, London (prints)
Waddington Galleries, London

1991
Eva Cohon Gallery, Chicago

1992
Galerie Josine Bokhoven, Amsterdam (drawings)
Graham Modern Gallery, New York

1994
Annendale Gallery, Sydney, Australia
CCA Gallery London, 'New Ceramics'

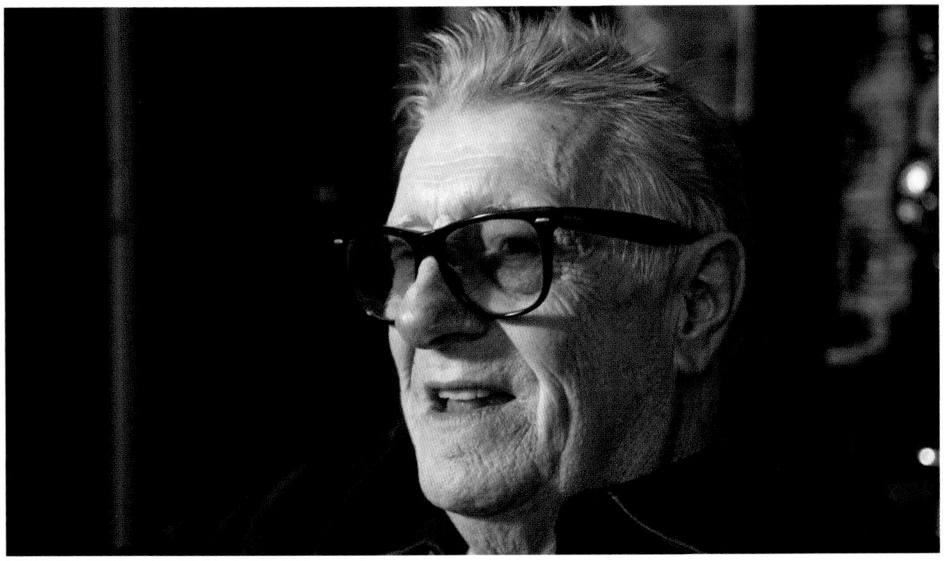

1995
Theo Waddington, London

1996
Carlow Arts Festival, Ireland

1999
Galerie Fine, London
Royal Academy of Arts, London (Retrospective)

2000
Galerie Josine Bokhoven, Amsterdam
University of Leathbridge, Alberta, Canada

2001
Graves Art Gallery, Sheffield (Retrospective)
Galleri Christian Dam, Oslo, Norway
Nevill Keating Pictures, London
Beaux Arts, London

2003
Beaux Arts, London

2005
Lemon Street Gallery, Truro, Cornwall

2006
Beaux Arts, London
Lemon Street Gallery, Truro, Cornwall
Tate St Ives
Michael Carr Gallery, Sydney, Australia

2007
Hillsboro Fine Art, Dublin, Ireland
Gallery Aalders, La Garde Freinet, France

2008
Beaux Arts, London
Lemon Street Gallery, Truro
Nevill Keating Pictures, London
Sarah Myerscough Fine Art, London

2009
Galerie White8, Vienna
Alan Wheatley Art, London
Beaux Arts, London

Selected Joint Exhibitions

1969
with Anthony Caro, X São Paulo Biennale, Brazil

1972
with Jules Olitski, Leslie Waddington Prints, London

1979
with Gordon House, Waddington Graphics, London

1980
with John Walker, Van Straaten Gallery, Chicago

1981
with Joe Tilson, Hokin Gallery, Miami

2007
with Andy Stewart, Sarah Myerscough Fine Art, London

Selected Group Shows

1959–60
Young Contemporaries, RBA Gallery, London

1960–61
Situation exhibitions, RBA Gallery, London, and Marlborough New London Gallery

1961
Nine Painters from England, Galleria Trastevere, Rome

1962–63
British Art Today, San Francisco Museum of Art (touring to Dallas Museum of Contemporary Art; Santa Barbara Museum of Art)

1963
7th Tokyo Biennial

1964
The New Generation: 1964, Whitechapel Art Gallery, London

1965
The English Eye, Marlborough-Gerson Gallery, New York

1966–67
Aspects of New British Art, Arts Council exhibition (touring to New Zealand, Queensland, New South Wales, Tasmania)

1970–71
British Painting and Sculpture 1960–1970, National Gallery of Art, Washington, D.C.

1974
Some Significant British Artists 1950–70, Rutland Gallery, London

1982
Aspects of British Art Today, Tokyo Metropolitan Art Museum (touring to Tochigi Prefectural Museum of Fine Arts, Utsunomiya; Hokkaido Museum of Modern Art, Sapporo)

1983
Recent Acquisitions in Contemporary Art, Part 1, Carnegie Institute, Pittsburgh

1991
Affinities in Paint, Crane Gallery, London

1992
Galerie zur alten Deutschen Schule, Switzerland
Peter Stuyvesant Foundation: Kunst Werkt Artworks (touring Holland, Spain and France)
Arts Council Collection, Royal Festival Hall (paintings from the 1960s; touring UK)
Redfern Gallery, London (with Robyn Denny and Guy Irvin)

1993
New Realities: Art from Post-war Europe 1945–1968 (The National Collection of Modern Art in the North of England), Tate Liverpool
The Sixties Art Scene in London, Royal Academy of Arts; Barbican Gallery, London

1994
John Hoyland and Anthony Caro, from the 60s to the 90s, Galerie Josine Bokhoven, Amsterdam, Holland
Here and Now, British Painters at the Serpentine Gallery from 1970 to the Present, Serpentine Gallery, London

1999
A Line in Painting, Gallery Fine, London

2003
Formal Situations: Abstractions in Britain, 1960–70, Tate Liverpool

2004–06
Art in the 1960s, This was Tomorrow at Tate Britain (touring to Birmingham Museum and Art Gallery; National Gallery of Victoria, Melbourne, Australia; Auckland Art Gallery, New Zealand)

2006 & 2007
Salon des Réalités Nouvelles, Paris

Selected Television and Radio

1976
British Art in Milan, BBC TV
The London Programme, London Weekend Television

1977
British Art 1952–77 (Royal Academy), BBC TV
Painting in the 50s and 60s, Open University (BBC Radio interview with Bryan Robertson)

1979
6 Days in September, Arena, BBC TV

1989
Signals, Channel 4

2003
John Hoyland – le chaos naturel, directed by Erik Levesque, produced by Univerne BEKA, Paris

2009
The Culture Show, BBC2, Royal Academy Summer Exhibition

Awards & Honours

Calouste Gulbenkian Foundation Purchase Award (1963)
International Young Artist Award, Tokyo (1964)
Prize winner at John Moores Liverpool Exhibition (1965)
Prize winner at Open Paintings Exhibition, Belfast (1966)
First Prize (with Robyn Denny), Edinburgh Open 100 Exhibition (1969)
First Prize, Chichester National Art Exhibition (1975)
Arts Council of Great Britain Purchase Award (1979)
First Prize at John Moores Liverpool Exhibition (with *Broken Bride*; 1982)
Joint First Prize, Korn Ferry International Award Exhibition (with William Scott; 1986)
First Prize, Athena Art Award (1987)
Elected Royal Academician (1991)
Wollaston Award, Royal Academy Summer Exhibition (1998)
Elected Foreign Painter Academician, Accademia Nationale di San Luca, Rome, Italy (2000)
Honorary Doctorate, Sheffield Hallam University (2003)
Honorary Member, Royal West of England Academy (2008)

Public Collections

Albright-Knox Art Gallery, Buffalo, New York, USA
Art Gallery of Ontario, Toronto, Canada
Art Gallery of South Australia, Adelaide, Australia
Arts Council of Great Britain
Art Museum of the Ateneum, Helsinki, Finland
Birmingham City Art Gallery, UK
British Council, London
Calouste Gulbenkian Foundation, London
Carnegie Institute, Pittsburgh, USA
City Art Gallery, Manchester, UK
Contemporary Art Society, London
Courtauld Art Society, London
Courtauld Institute, London
Frederick R Weisman Art Foundation Collection, Los Angeles, USA
Government Art Collection, London
Laing Art Gallery, Newcastle-upon-Tyne
Leicestershire Education Authority
Maclaurin Collection, Rozelle, Ayr
Manchester City Art Gallery
Melbourne University Art Gallery
Museum of Art, Rhode Island School of Design, Providence, R.I., USA
Museum of Modern Art, Rio de Janeiro, Brazil
National Museum, Finland
Neuberger Collection, University of Purchase, New York, USA
Perth Art Gallery, Australia
Peter Stuyvesant Foundation, London
Phoenix Museum, Arizona, USA
Picker Gallery, Colgate University, Hamilton, New York, USA
Power Gallery of Contemporary Art, University of Sydney, Australia
Royal Academy of Arts, London
Royal College of Physicians, London
Städtisches Museum, Leverkusen, Germany
Tate, London
Tehran Museum of Modern Art, Tehran, Iran
Toledo Museum of Art, Toledo, Ohio, USA
Ulster Museum, Belfast
Victoria & Albert Museum, London
Walker Art Gallery, Liverpool
Warwick University
Whitworth Art Gallery, Manchester

Author's Acknowledgements

My principal debt of gratitude is to John Hoyland, for his unfailing assistance and good humour during the research and production of this book. His wife, Beverley, has also been extremely helpful and resourceful in moments of crisis. Meanwhile the staff of Beaux Arts London – and particularly Emma Lilley – have provided the constant support and practical back-up that a project of this kind requires. My appreciative thanks go to Robert and Robyn Wilson, perfect hosts. Thanks, too, to Jill Hollis (Cameron & Hollis) and Susanna Fergusson (Nevill Keating Pictures) for their help with providing some of the images we were unable to source ourselves; to Andy Stewart for his brilliant organization of the main shoot; Colin Mills who took such care over the photos; and to Shantall Williams whose computer wizardry made our task so much easier. Finally, I should like to thank my wife for her good counsel and enthusiasm.

Sources of Illustrations

The majority of the photos of Hoyland's work (and some of the studio details) were taken by Colin Mills. For other sources, see below:

David Hills Photography p85; Ida Kar © National Portrait Gallery, London p17; © National Museums Liverpool p33; © Toby Madden p150; courtesy Private UK Collection/Nevill Keating Pictures p11; Arnold Newman/Arnold Newman Collection/Getty Images p28, p74; courtesy Prof. Paolo D'Orazio/Arte Metro Roma p95; © Royal Academy of Arts Picture Library, London p90; © Derrick Santini p80, p104, p115, p141, p156; courtesy Robyn and Robert Wilson p99.

Index

Bold page numbers refer to picture captions

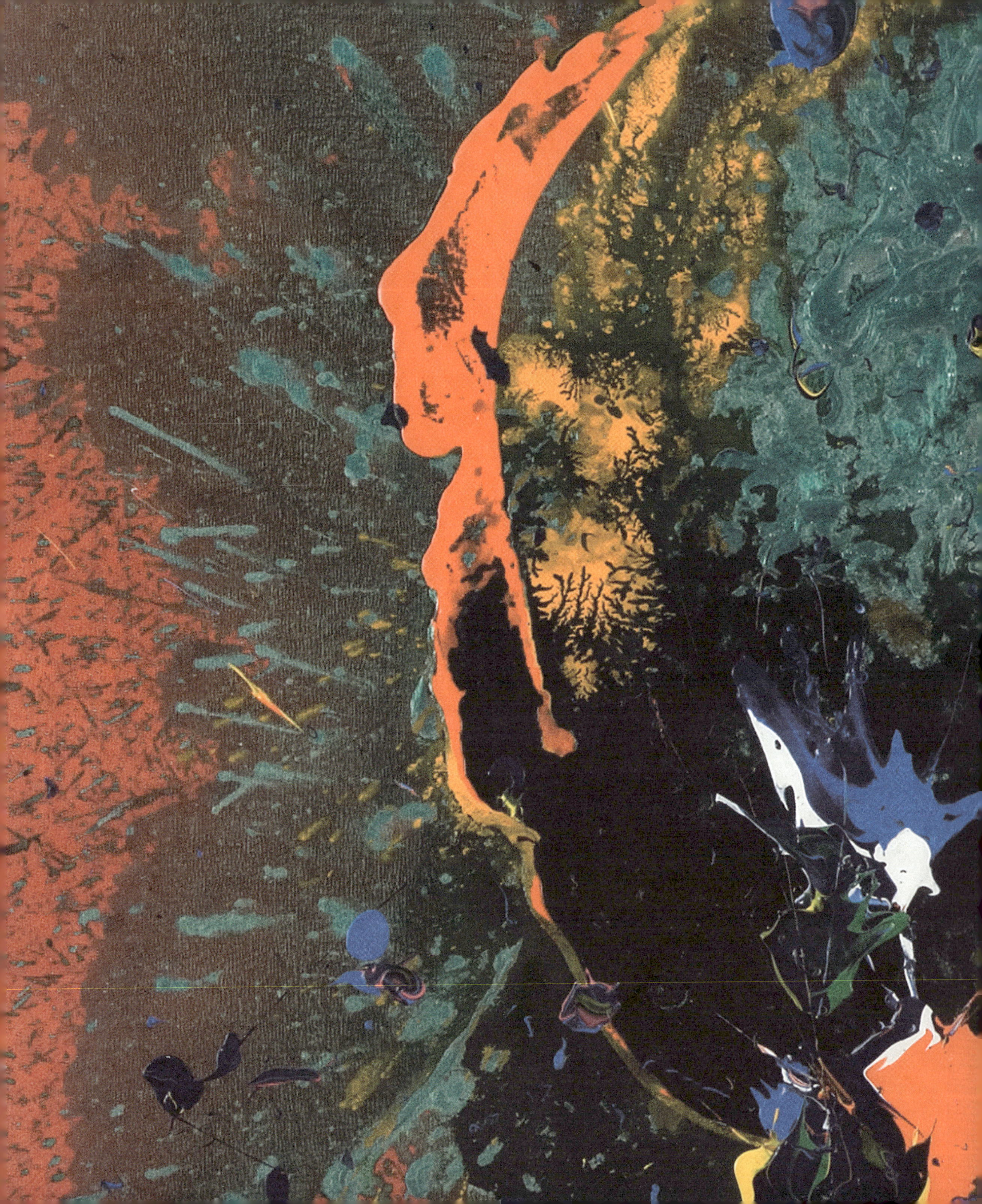